SO-ARF-655

The *Missouri* *Review*

Volume XVII Number 3   1994

University of Missouri-Columbia

EDITOR

Speer Morgan

MANAGING EDITOR

Greg Michalson

ASSOCIATE EDITORS

William Peden, Jo Sapp, Evelyn Somers

OFFICE MANAGER

Dedra Earl

SENIOR ADVISORS

Julie Gochenour, Brian Scroggs, Kris Somerville,
Kenneth Soucy, Jeff Thomson

ADVISORS

Susan Cummings, Pamela McClure

INTERNS

Mindy Berry, Mary Creger, Brett Foster, Matt Heidenry,
Dawn Klingensmith, Stefani Kronk, Betsey Lenz,
Tina Smith, Christopher Waltz

The Missouri Review is published by the College of Arts & Science of the University of Missouri-Columbia, with private contributions and assistance from the Missouri Arts Council and the National Endowment for the Arts.

Major new marketing initiatives have been made possible by the Lila Wallace-Reader's Digest Literary Publishers Marketing Development Program, funded through a grant to the Council of Literary Magazines and Presses.

Cartoons in this issue by Brad Veley.

Permission for the Jack Kerouac/Ed White correspondence by Ed White, Jr., John Sampas and the Estate of Jack and Stella Kerouac.

The King of the World in the Land of the Pygmies by Joan Mark, by permission of The University of Nebraska Press.

The editors invite submissions of poetry, fiction, and essays of a general literary interest with a distinctly contemporary orientation. Manuscripts will not be returned unless accompanied by a stamped, self-addressed envelope. Please address all correspondence to The Editors, *The Missouri Review*, 1507 Hillcrest Hall, University of Missouri, Columbia, Missouri 65211.

SUBSCRIPTIONS

1 year (3 issues), $15.00
2 years (6 issues), $27.00
3 years (9 issues), $36.00

Copyright © 1994 by The Curators of the University of Missouri
ISSN 0191 1961   **ISBN** 1-879758-12-1
Typesetting by HiTec Typeset   Printed by Thomson-Shore
Distributed by: Ingram Periodicals and B. DeBoer

The *Missouri* *Review*

1994

CONTENTS

**Bob encounters one of the bugs in the
Jean Paul Sartre word processing program...**

Foreword

This issue of *The Missouri Review* is about taking a chance, breaking the rules, living on the fringe.

Joan Mark's "King of the World in the Land of the Pygmies" describes the life of Patrick Putnam, one of those iconoclasts who was born to do great things, but who somehow never got around to it. In anthropology, his chosen profession, he was a failure, but one thing Patrick Putnam did manage was to live at the ends of the earth, among people about whom Westerners knew almost nothing, the Pygmies of the Belgian Congo. By this alone—putting himself out there and staying there—Putnam led a fascinating life.

The two twenty-something protagonists in David Borofka's beautiful little anatomy "Strays" do not put themselves out but are put out, or so they think. Rebels without a cause, they have reached that age when they are harvesting only what they sow.

Two of this issue's stories concern moments of risk, when people explore their own frontiers. Robert McBrearty's "A Night at the Y" points out the odd, comical connection between bravery and decency. Bill Roorbach's "Fredonia" is about a lesser act of bravery, a macho duel, that blossoms into a greater one, taking a chance with the heart.

In "The Byerson Test," E. S. Goldman describes a decorous coffeeshop friendship between two men that undergoes a big change when they try to find out about a mysterious holocaust memorial. Another story about the intervention of history in people's lives, Ranbir Sidhu's concise "The Order of Things," shows how political turmoil and extremism can draft even sons against their fathers.

Gary Fincke's poetry conjures a realm where asthma chokes the throat and angels count the worldly census of those who travel down bright tunnels of near-death experiences before returning to "the freeways of the chattering world." S. Ben-Tov's poems concern powerful moments of grief that take one to the limits of the self. Our Tom McAfee Discovery Feature poet, Ruth Ellen Kocher, offers us poetry that is reminiscent of chaos theory, where the smallest effect—a gesture or small accident—can swirl into massive disorder:

a moon hesitates on its orbit and veers into space, or a light wind in just the wrong place can be the start of a hurricane.

*

Jack Kerouac's second novel, *On the Road*, published in 1957, was quite recognizably set in mid-century America, yet for many readers its characters appeared to be from outer space. Wild and restless and defiantly uninterested in material security, they blasted back and forth across the country in an ongoing quest for intense experiences, for knowledge, and for philosophical meaning. Candid to a fault, imprudent, they threw themselves into the moment like runners on a broken field. In the conformist fifties, they were not just youthful adventurers but desperate types, criminals, people on the fringe.

The characters in *On the Road* really did have a desperate edge, as Kerouac repeatedly showed. What they wanted could only be found for brief moments. All four of the big journeys across the country urged by Dean Moriarty, the novel's impulsive protagonist, ended in exhaustion and collapse. Every élation was followed by a depression; friendships and love affairs vibrated apart from sheer intensity. Yet because so many readers identified with these characters, the book proved to be less like a novel than a minor religion, arousing both furious interest and antagonism. A lot of people read about Kerouac's fictionalized friends and tried to imitate them. *On the Road* became a phenomenon, a "generation-defining" book of conspicuous influence.

But what generation did it define? The novel was plainly set in the late 1940s yet not published until five years after it had been written and nearly a decade after the events that it relates began. Were these young people of the forties or the fifties? Or did *On the Road* and Kerouac's later novels really relate more to the 1960s and early seventies, when the ripple that the author had spotted initially became a cultural wave breaking across America? In some ways, the Beats were restless young Americans of just about any decade, rejecting the past, devising their own jargon, forging their own values, yearning, going wild, messing up, being miserable. Even in the nineties, young people have begun rediscovering Kerouac and the Beats, perhaps partly out of boredom with the cultural leavings of their parents' generation.

Yet when the first Beat literature began to be published in the fifties—*Go* by Kerouac's friend John Clellon Holmes, the poem

Howl by Allen Ginsberg and *On the Road* by Kerouac—the particular group of people who inspired it was small. Kerouac repeatedly fictionalized the same friends. He had gone to Columbia University as a scholarship football player in the early forties, before being injured, dropping out, and joining the Navy during the war. Kicked out of the Navy for psychological reasons, he joined the Merchant Marines. After the war he hung around Columbia, and this proved to be the early focal point for a widening circle of people later called the Beats. When recalling them, one can't help but wonder how characteristic they were of post-war New York, with their mix of veterans, nihilists, drug users, professionals in training, poets, intellectuals, and dabblers of all kinds. However representative they were, New York's post-war bohemia proved to be the original counterculture for the rest of the century.

Hal Chase of Denver was one of the crowd. Allen Temko, who in later life was an architectural historian and critic, described the brilliant and precocious Hal Chase and his New York friends as "into this Dostoevski scene. . . . It was just like *The Possessed*. Terribly destructive people. And they were the first people I knew who were seriously involved in drugs." Among the group was the somewhat older William Burroughs, Harvard graduate and disreputable scion of the St. Louis adding-machine fortune, along with the equally wealthy Lucien Carr, who was convicted of manslaughter. Temko said, "I found Burroughs fascinating. Very reptilian but brilliant. Carr . . . I found loathsome. I had no common ground with this spoiled and destructive boy." Kerouac's girlfriend, Edie Parker, introduced him to Lucien and Allen Ginsberg.

Hal Chase told Jack and the others about a young poolhall compatriot from Denver, Neal Cassady, who'd spent time in jail for car theft and had also read his way through the Denver Public Library. When he was in Denver, Hal told Neal Cassady and another friend, Ed White, about the wonderful poets he'd met in New York. Eventually, Cassady and White decided to come to New York.

Edie Parker's roommate Joan, who had a newborn, needed roommates in her apartment, and Hal Chase and Allen Ginsberg moved in. Jack, Ed White, and Ed Huncke—who was a criminal and junkie (author of *Guilty of Everything*)—also visited the apartment occasionally. Jack and Ginsberg matchmade between Joan and Burroughs, and he soon moved in. The six-room apartment was directly across the street from Columbia, where Ginsberg was still taking classes. It was the first clearly locatable center of the ongoing conversation between these people, and Ginsberg would later say that the conversation there was a lot more elegant than what he heard in the classes at Columbia. Among several relationships forged during this period was that of Jack and Ed White, who became lifelong friends.

Ten years later, near the time that *On the Road* was finally published, several in the Beat cast of characters had moved to the San Francisco area where they came to be linked with the newly emergent "San Francisco Poetry Renaissance." A poetry reading at the Six Gallery in San Francisco one night in November 1955 was a watershed event in American writing, bringing several new poets into the spotlight, including Michael McClure, Philip Lamantia, Gary Snyder, and Robert Duncan.

Gary Snyder later described San Francisco at that time as "a supersaturated solution" of poetic talent and energy, waiting for the single crystal that would solidify it. "Howl," by Allen Ginsberg, turned out to be that crystal.

While Kerouac sat near the front with a jug of wine cheering him on, Ginsberg started reading his poem:

I saw the best minds of my generation destroyed by madness,
    starving hysterical naked,
dragging themselves through the negro streets at dawn looking for
    an angry fix,
angelheaded hipsters burning for the ancient heavenly connection
    To the starry dynamo in the machinery of night

"Howl" was street poetry—personal, spontaneous, rhapsodic, and confessional—and, along with *On the Road* and Kerouac's soon-to-follow *Dharma Bums*, it marked a sea change in American literature.

The Beats hit the scene at a time when American writing was growing tired of the dominant influences of literary formalism and European existentialism. "Serious" literature was written and rewritten and refined to death. The author was supposed to be "invisible" to his work, sitting off to the side polishing his fingernails, while the flawless text hummed away with all of its balances and ironies like a perfect machine. John Clellon Holmes later called the High Modern fiction that he and most of his contemporaries were trying to write in the forties and early fifties "migraine headache" writing. *On the Road*, he said, was "not really contemporary in the fashionable sense of the term. It wasn't soured, anxious, existential or Europeanized [like] the bleakly allegorical novels that had previously dominated the landscape." Kerouac's novel and Ginsberg's poem were a blast of fresh air in the stale atmosphere of late modernism.

They were spontaneous, personal, revealing, and about as lacking in irony as they could be.

Although it wasn't obvious at the time, the poetry reading at the Six Gallery and the appearance of *On the Road* were a kind of Armory Show of twentieth-century literature. Within the next few years, the Beats began to influence writers of all sorts, including many who had little in common with them. The young New England poet Robert Lowell was a case in point. Under the spell of formalism, he had been writing tightly packed, oblique, "literary" poetry of a kind that was *de rigeur* in the forties. After reading "Howl," Lowell stepped down from the literary dais and broke open his own tangled heart in the highly personal poetry of *Life Studies*, published in 1959. The Beats rekindled openness, directness, and romantic excess in American writing, indigenous qualities that had been in hiding during the reign of late modernism.

They were a classic literary avant-garde: a small group engaged in an ongoing conversation about aesthetics and ideas, whose writings at first seemed too weird and threatening to publish. Eventually their work was published by means of random personal contacts in various corners of the publishing industry, including cheap paperback publishers (Ace books, publishers of grocery store paperbacks), *Playboy*-imitator *Cavalier* magazine, small literary journals like *Evergreen Review*, and startup ventures like City Lights Books in San Francisco. As Beat writing finally began to slip out of the shadows into the marketplace, it aroused controversy and influence far beyond its commercial significance.

From the time that Kerouac embarked on the adventures that were later immortalized in *On the Road*, until the year before his death, he and his friend from Denver, Ed White, kept up a steady and fairly unguarded correspondence. In a letter to him in 1947, Jack wrote, "I think we're trying to outdo each other with honesty." Ed and Jack's intimate friendship was based partly on the fact that they were both "insiders" in a crowd that neither of them fully identified with.

With the help of White and the Kerouac estate, *The Missouri Review* is happy to present fifteen of Kerouac's letters, spanning his career, from 1947, the wild years later written about in *On the Road*, through the first half of the fifties, when he wrote much of his important work despite rejection by the publishers, into the period of fame and decline to 1968, just a year before his death. In the last letter from this twenty-one-year span he relates to White the apparent death of Neal Cassady on a railroad track in Mexico, an event that Jack could not accept: Neal, the ur-Beat, the outlaw, would surely show up again.

"Look, we KNOW you're disappointed you're not on 'Oprah.' You've mentioned that several times. But the fact is, you ARE on MY show, your crummy book is on MY lap, and we have 8 minutes until a commercial. Why don't we talk about THAT for a while?"

FREDONIA / *Bill Roorbach*

G EORGE SKINNER DRIVES TO Michigan every six weeks for the store, and every six weeks he drives right past Fredonia, New York, where his sister lives with her husband Kevin. He doesn't stop. Every six weeks he thinks about brilliant Tracy Lynn, thinks about how he ought to stop this time, how he is going to stop this time, thinks about it from the toll booth at Nyack until just past the exit near Fredonia, and then he changes the subject in his mind, drives an hour more and finds a motel. He prefers not to drive straight through. He has her number in his wallet, on the emergency card, so if anything bad happens to him she'll be the first to hear. Twice he has gotten off at the exit and driven through Fredonia and looked at the SUNY campus and thought about her teaching there. Once he went so far as to park the truck at a pair of meters and walk around and ask where the Philosophy Department might be, and had dinner at a place she might go, a health food place, brown rice with some kind of sesame stuff, but she didn't turn up, and he drove on.

In Ann Arbor he stays at the Sheraton and eats well and drinks a little with Carl Gerhardt and they talk furniture—old furniture— the antiques Carl's collected in six weeks, or they talk people, the people Carl has bought from and bargained with and cheated, really, and swindled. George Skinner has begun to know a little bit about antiques thanks to Carl, who claims to be a world-class expert. They have never had a private conversation, yet this time George opens his mouth after two scotches in the hotel bar and says, "I'm going to stop and see my sister on the way back. She's in Fredonia, right off the highway, and you know, I've never stopped in."

And Carl says, "There's a barn back there, it's just above Fredonia, a delicious old place; well, it used to be a delicious place. New owner—the party, Georgie boy, is over—but at one time the old couple there would sell you an original Shaker table like it was a card table, something a bit plain but useful, just useful, you know. Morons. Look for it, it's a big old barn, used to be in poor repair—the new guy's got it painted. He's sharp. Too bad for us, it's right on the road, it's on 86, on the way down from Rochester. Yellow, I believe. It's not the same, but it's worth a look."

"I haven't even talked to her."

Carl looks a little surprised, raises his eyebrows. He is bald and the shining top of his head is always very white from wearing a beret, of all things, in the sun. He looks like some kind of duck hunter, red-and-white-checked woolen jacket, flannel shirt, like that, except for this beret, which makes him look exactly like someone who knows everything about every piece of furniture ever made or bought by a farmer in the history of the Midwest. "Who?" he says.

"My sister, Tracy Lynn. She's in Fredonia. I'm going to see her on the way back."

"They've gotten very smart back there. Well, smart everywhere. Now they want a thousand for some shop project a generation old. Morons."

"She's thirty-seven."

"Old enough to know better."

Carl and George are both forty.

"We'll get some college kids," Carl says. He means college kids to unload his truck and reload George's. "See you in the morning." And that's it; Carl picks up his beret and spins it on his finger twice, as always, and puts it on, looking humorlessly in the mirror behind the bottles. "Night." And he heads out of the bar. He's portly but manages a saunter, saunters out of the bar and stands in front of the elevator. In his beret. George wonders at the beret every time. It's the perfect affectation.

He orders another drink, unusual for him—it's eleven o'clock for christ's sake—and spends an hour thinking how he's going to call. Plans the call. He doesn't foresee a problem in calling. Hi, Tracy, he thinks, It's George. I'll be coming through Fredonia today and thought I'd stop and say hello. Or: I thought I'd stop and drop off a little something I got for you all. A wedding present finally! Or: Hi Tracy Lynn, it's George. Mom asked me to call. That would be a joke from the old days. His mother is in poor health and she does not ask him anything anymore when he goes to see her. She's nearer him than to Tracy Lynn, so the task of her has fallen to him. Or: Hi Trace, it's George. I thought you would like to drive down to New York with me. I've got a load of furniture and I'm alone anyway. Or: Hi Kevin! Long time. Tracy Lynn around? I'm on my way down from A-squared. I'd like to stop in for the night. It's too long a trip. Or: Hi Kevin! Tracy Lynn there? What do you mean, 'Who's this?' Who're you? That's the question, who the hell are you? Moron. *Professor.* Give me Tracy. I want to talk!

There are five or six other people in the bar but the happy young woman who is the bartender closes up anyway at midnight. George walks to the elevator and stands there. He thinks smiling of Carl in that ridiculous beret, puts his sister out of his mind, keeps waiting for the elevator. After a long five minutes the bartender walks by on her way to the kitchen with a tray full of glasses, including his. She seems friendly and soft-looking, like most people who don't live in New York, and smiles at him as he waits there, actually reaches out as she passes and pats him on the shoulder, an astonishing gesture.

"I'm all right," he says.

She just shrugs and smiles like a nurse and keeps walking to the kitchen with her clinking tray. George waits some more, patiently, then remembers to push the button.

George Skinner would be embarrassed to walk up to strangers, these college kids, and ask if they want to work. Carl is quite good at it. In the beret maybe he looks to them like some kind of history professor: "Hi, we need help moving some furniture. Fifty dollars for an afternoon's labor." Almost every kid stops and thinks about it, and it never takes more than twenty minutes to collect two, usually a pair of friends. Today it's a young man with long neat hair in a ponytail, a handsome boy, somewhat cocky, who has no trouble stopping whatever it was he was doing and standing with Carl and George, talking about furniture. His name is Eric. His mother has a dynasty table, his brother used to build furniture, his friend Arnold collects antique molding planes. George listens to Eric in small amazement. The kid is more comfortable than George. Carl has an aloof way with the boy, knows just the degree by which to ignore him. George feels like a dumb truck driver at the periphery of the boy's attention, keeps quiet, watches him.

Carl has never asked young women to help, but Eric, joining confidently in, asks everyone, and soon a large young woman is bargaining both Eric's and her own wage up to sixty dollars. She is athletic and confident, older than Eric, maybe a grad student, with freckles and a canny smile. No one is going to take advantage of her. She argues good-naturedly about getting paid in advance; Carl argues back, less good-naturedly, and wins.

She's wearing a skirt over some tight leggings or long underwear (George can't decide which), so she'd like to change her clothes before she starts. They arrange to meet her at the R.C. Quad—

which apparently Carl has heard of and can find—at noon. Her name is Tracy.

"That's my sister's name," George says, with more emotion than he'd like, sounding as if the young woman has stolen something valuable. It's a sweet spring day.

Carl mentions breakfast, and college-boy Eric wants to come along, which surprises George. At Eric's age George may or may not have said yes to a little work, but he knows and remembers clearly that he would never have stood around with two almost middle-aged guys and had anything to say, and knows further that he would have made any excuse to avoid sitting down to breakfast with them. But Eric comes along, even leads the way, talking and talking, as they walk to a diner Carl is fond of for pancakes. George finds something to like about Eric as the kid talks through the meal, though the same traits that are likeable—the confidence, the ready jokes, the desire to be admired—are also irritating. You might think the kid is a furniture major, the way he goes on. He actually knows something, more than George does. Carl wears his beret, corrects the kid from sentence to sentence. George remembers that Carl has two teenaged sons, back home in Nebraska.

At noon exactly they pull up in front of some old buildings on the campus. George fails to see anything to rightly call a quad, nothing square at all. When he mentions it, neither Carl nor the young man seem to understand his point, or that he is joking. Tracy, the college girl, is right there waiting, in bluejeans now, with careful new rips across the thighs. She has a big flannel shirt on. She is tall, and looks like she'll be able to move some furniture. Carl, surprisingly, hasn't made a single grumpy comment about her. She climbs in beside him in George's truck. Eric falls silent. He seems to have used up all his furniture lore. Carl has fallen silent too, leans forward out of the way of the two kids' wide shoulders, holds his chin, starting to fall into his bargaining funk, a mood that overtakes him at just this point at each of his and George's meetings. It's George's job to inspect the furniture Carl has collected, and Carl dislikes George for it, even though—probably because—it's not expert things George looks for, but bad flaws: missing legs, mismatched shelves, broken glass, rotten wood, worm damage, smashed glass, gouges, carvings, scratches, stains. Carl dislikes him for it because Carl is always trying to slip something by, and George generally catches it. Mr. Bergenstaedler, George's boss, understands Carl, somehow, treats Carl's dishonesty as a foible, the flaw of a genius. George doesn't see it this way at all, sees Carl as a creep, dislikes him a little more each time he finds something wrong, each time he points out a blown seat on a rocker described in Carl's bill of lading (mean, tiny handwriting) as perfect.

They're all quiet as George drives back through town to the hotel out next to the malls in destroyed farmland. They back up to Carl's truck, which is parked in the far reaches of a vast and empty parking lot. Carl says, "You folks go ahead and start," and trots across the lot and into the hotel. He'll come out just when his truck's been unloaded, and having established that he isn't needed for the moving, he'll stand for the reloading and supervise.

The unloading isn't a simple matter of running furniture from one truck to the other. Carl has the heavy pieces loaded at the far front of his box, and those pieces must go first into the big white Berganstaedtler truck. Tracy and Eric help George empty Carl's rented truck onto the blacktop of the parking lot, dig all the chairs out of the way, stand them up in the breeze, open the moving mats to have a look, checking each item off on Carl's list, noting the condition, noting whether Carl's description seems to match the piece. He's listed all the chairs as good, one or two excellent, none poor, and George accepts all of them as described. Next, as always, there are some small tables, then a couple of bedsteads, then some bookcases, then several large tables, then the really big stuff, which today is a desk and three bureaus. At the very back of the load there's a monster, all wrapped in quilted moving blankets. They begin to struggle with it just as Carl reappears.

"What's this thing?" Eric says.

"That's the prize," Carl says, "Let's move the oak piece first."

Tracy gets hold of the desk. George watches her down there in the darkness of the truck, amused, expects her to need to show how strong she is, maybe lift the one side of it, maybe be impatient as Eric has been. But she's only feeling its width, getting the heft. Eric when he gets there lifts his end up, acting like it's not heavy as hell, picks it up a few inches, moves it toward him, has to drop it boom! in the resounding box of the truck body.

"Careful!" Carl barks. He's standing out in the sun, just watching. "Let's back the trucks together. Stop and let's back the trucks. That's too heavy."

The kid, Eric, sighs. Tracy, though, immediately gets the picture, follows George out of the truck, stands in the parking lot just where he'll be able to see her and she can direct his short backing up. George climbs up into the cab of the Bergenstaedler truck, starts it, lets it run a moment, watching the girl in the mirror. He's startled, suddenly notices her sexiness, a small facet of her capability. He hasn't had a kiss or even a fond hug for something like six months, and she's a good-looking soul, strong and young and happy.

Admonishing himself, he backs the truck carefully up against Carl's, stops when Tracy signals he should, and pretty soon they're all climbing up into the gap between the two, moving into the dark, carrying the oak desk into the Bergenstaedler truck, putting it to one side, room to pass with the big piece that's left.

Back in Carl's truck, they stand around the monster, undraping it, looking for handholds. Carl sees there's no way he's not needed and joins them. "It's a delicious piece," he says, "It's a perfect piece. Go easy. It'll go for fifteen grand, at least. Wait till Bergle sees it!"

They horse it to the door of the truck and carefully, grunting with the effort, get it across the gap and into the back of Bergenstaedler's truck and rest a minute, making exclamations.

George says, "Let's uncover it so I can get a look."

"It's fine," Carl says testily.

"I want to see," Tracy says.

"It's perfect," Carl says. He puts his hands on it, ready to move it back into the darkness, but George isn't with him, and so the college kids aren't. Amazing how immediately, instinctively, they bank away from Carl's authority, side with George.

"Let's just have a look," George says. He's fighting a feeling of pointlessness. He knows from Carl's irritation that the piece has some major flaw, knows that the bill of lading is going to say *perfect*, knows that he and Carl will argue, knows that Bergenstaedler will admire the piece despite its horrible flaws, knows the old man won't listen or care. George pulls the first mat off the monster anyway.

The kid helps out, and soon the huge hutch-like thing is exposed. Immediately Eric starts spouting about its probable age, admiring it, but George isn't listening, focuses instead on the huge gash in its side.

He looks at Carl and says, "How did you list this?"

"It's a Turner breakfront," Carl says. "A delicious piece."

"Magnificent," Eric says, ready to adopt whatever personality is strongest around him.

"How do you list it?" George repeats.

Carl doesn't answer, the game has started. "Let's see the list."

"I've got it down as good," Carl answers, "And that's conservative as hell. It's a real piece."

"It's gorgeous," Tracy says. "But what's this big gouge? And all this here, I would call it a mess."

George is pleased to have an ally. Amazing how these kids can speak their minds. "I'd say fair," George says, though maybe "good" wouldn't be such an exaggeration. He knows that saying anything is going to get Carl going.

"Terrible gouge," Tracy says. "Did you drop it or something?" She acts like she knows what Carl is like, too.

"It's fine," Carl says. "Bergenstaedler's going to love it. So let's get it loaded so I can get out of here."

"Just a little refinishing," Eric says, sounding like a cocky, college-kid version of Carl.

Tracy picks up the printout, finds the hutch, "It's listed as perfect," she says.

"No way," George says.

"Oh, Christ," Carl says, pulling his beret down off his shining head, "just load the goddamn thing, will you George?"

George hesitates, scratches his cheek. "I don't think so, Carl." Something about the presence of the young woman has made George bolder than usual: "In fact, I think I'm going to refuse it."

"You can't refuse it."

"Consider it refused. If you can't write an honest report, then just consider it refused. And consider that walnut bookcase refused, too."

Carl slumps a little, smiles for probably the first time today, tries a good-guy approach: "You can't refuse this stuff, George."

"It's refused. Kids, let's put it back in Carl's truck."

Tracy is ready, seems excited by the argument, but Eric seems to have taken Carl's side, now.

Carl climbs down off the tailgate. George and Tracy are all grins, either out of fear or because Carl is so comical in his anger; George can't decide which. With Carl gone, Eric isn't sure what side to be on. Carl's truck starts and lurches, then he drives away, clear to the other end of the parking lot, hundreds of bleak yards of asphalt, where he leaps out and trots back over like someone about to get in a fight. He stands below George, says, "Should I call Bergie?"

"The piece is refused."

"It's in your truck, moron."

"It's going to get out of my truck." George leans into the piece, and with Tracy's help slides it till it's hanging over the tailgate at the balance point, dangerously close to falling.

"You fucking moron," Carl says.

And Eric makes his decision. He and Tracy get on the ground, tip the Turner breakfront toward them, and within seconds it's standing on the pavement of the parking lot.

"Refused," George says.

The college kids grin.

Glowering Carl says, "You *can't refuse it.*"

George picks up the bill of lading, writes *REFUSED* over the breakfront, shows it to Carl.

"I'm going to make a call," Carl says. "I'm going in the hotel to give Helmut Bergenstaedler a call."

George shrugs, and Tracy shrugs with him.

Carl is red right up to the edge of his beret, making an effort not to lose his temper. "Moron." He turns and marches to the grand entrance of the Sheraton, hundreds of yards the other way across the parking lot, disappears inside.

"Let's load the rest of this stuff," George says. And with the kids he pushes the biggest desk into place, then loads the bureaus, then the bookcases and tables, then all the chairs. Carl is gone a long time, and when he's back the Bergenstaedler truck is nearly full, the back of the load carefully tied so things won't fall. The Turner breakfront is alone on the pavement, just standing there. George and Tracy and Eric lean in the back of the truck in a space big enough for a breakfront. They watch Carl's progress toward them. He doesn't look as if he's calmed down any.

"You can't refuse it," Carl shouts before he's fifty feet away.

"I take it he wasn't there," George says.

"You can't refuse it, you moron," Carl says.

"Don't call him that," Tracy says. She's so game that George has to laugh.

Carl ignores her, stomps the pavement once in a childish gesture. "Put the fucking thing in your fucking truck, George!"

"Here you go." George hands Carl the bill of lading with the big *REFUSED* written on it, stuffs his own copy in his shirt pocket. Tracy jumps down from the tailgate, puts her hands about a mile deep in her pockets, the perfect gesture. Eric follows, then George jumps down, too, pulling the overhead door closed behind him. The breakfront stands naked on the pavement, forlorn.

"You can't refuse it," Carl says, trying to be nice again.

"I already have. Get your truck over here and we'll throw it in for you."

Carl says "moron," just that, two syllables powered with steam, then trots off across the parking lot and to his truck. He climbs in, starts it up, roars the engine a couple of times, backs up, starts forward, but instead of coming over for the breakfront he drives slowly to the parking lot entrance, waits for traffic, then pulls out into the street and drives away with an angry wave.

"Whoa," Eric laughs, impressed. "He'll be back," Tracy says.

"What about the Turner breakfront?" Eric says.

There's a long silence, really long, five minutes, the three of them just standing there staring off in the direction Carl drove. They're a little tired from the work.

Finally George says, "Let's go have a drink. If he doesn't come back in an hour, I guess we'll just load it."

All night George is sick with remorse. He knows he's overstepped his authority by about seven light-years, knows that he has to meet up with Carl again, work with him, work with Bergenstaedler.

Over drinks he tried to explain this to the young woman, Tracy (who as it turned out was working toward a Ph.D. in psychology, of all things), but all she could say was that he should quit if they expected him to act against his morals. He called her an idealist, and next thing he knew she was working on him, trying to ferret out the reasons for his life. She seemed surprised that he had a bachelor's degree from Columbia University, which struck her as a good school, worked this small discovery into her annoying analysis. Eric, the callow prig, just kept announcing how amazed he was, how you never knew, how it showed you shouldn't judge people or books by their covers: childish revelations that he seemed to find profound.

After a couple of drinks and an hour of the two college kids trying to allay their excitement over the tussle by deconstructing George, they all went out in the parking lot and stared at the breakfront. Then it was funny, just alone in the expanse of asphalt, the white Bergenstaedler truck standing safely away. George opened the rear door and the three of them loaded the breakfront in with much straining and groaning, much kidding around, much bold swearing.

Since Carl hadn't, George had to pay the kids, which he managed from his day money, which was Bergenstaedler's anyway. Then Eric left. But here was the thing: Tracy stayed around, just standing there in the parking lot, and the two of them talked another hour, hands in their pockets, losing the buzz from the drinks, and Tracy announced she was going to New York next week for spring break anyway, and asked if she could have a ride. Easy as that: Just blow off her classes and leave a week early.

Three in the morning and George still lies awake, thinking of the girl. He should have said no.

Tracy is there exactly at nine, exactly as planned, fed and ready, with a single small duffle bag that wouldn't hold enough socks for George. George is tired. He gets behind the wheel and Tracy sits way down the long seat from him, and he's sorry he likes her so well. They smile at one another and off they go, down the highway, slowly in front of the full load, a few laughs about the breakfront and Carl, some silence as the trip begins, then Tracy picks up on a single sentence George must have said in the bar, a sentence he has forgotten saying.

"Will we get to your sister's by tonight?"

George thinks awhile, says, "I guess we shouldn't stop."

They are quiet a good half hour then, listening to some talk on the radio.

By lunch they haven't said ten words, but the ride is companionable enough. George has the idea that Tracy likes him, too, and he's trying to decide what to do about it. In the bar she'd talked the way kids do about what age people said she looked, then said she thought George didn't look any older than she, if you thought about it. She was wrong, George thinks. I look exactly forty, and she looks exactly twenty-six, and that's exactly fourteen reasons why she and I are not going to get mixed up. Immediately he pictures his sister, realizes it's her voice saying all this, throwing all this doubt into the air. Why should a small age gap matter? Then again, who said Tracy wanted anything to do with him at all?

They eat lunch at a truckstop off the highway and George notices how the waitress assumes they're some kind of item. Back in the truck, Tracy seems to get off on the three cups of coffee she's drunk: "Why don't we stop at your sister's? You haven't seen her in how long?"

George remembers all he's told this voluble young woman, this strong, lovely woman who is suddenly his partner on the trip.

"Not that long, really."

"Do you guys talk on the phone?"

"Not that much. Some."

"Were you close when you were kids?"

"I think so."

"What kind of close?"

And George finds himself talking, talking at length, his childhood, his little sister, his struggles with girlfriends, his sister's brainy boyfriend, the death of his dad, his mother's way of being, which he'd never quite seen how strange it was—the kind of conversation you have with someone you want to see again, someone you want to date, someone you want to love.

"You were injured. That's what's wrong. That's exactly it. Your mother wounded you." Too earnestly.

"Oh, crap. Who said anything was wrong?"

"Yes, that's it exactly. You hate women, and you've set your sister up to take all the blame and you're lonely and guilty and the question is why?"

"I'm not sure I buy all this."

"You might not buy it, but you're leading a lonely life! Why?"

They were silent a long time, bouncing rhythmically on the joints in the pavement.

"Why would I hate women?"

"It's just an otherness thing."

"Oh, come on. That's gibberish. You've accused me of hating women—now you have to explain why."

"You tell me."

"I like women."

"All women?"

"No."

"Whom do you hate?"

"Don't you mean who?"

"It's whom. It's a whole direct object thing."

"I hate...."

"How do you get along with your mother now?"

"My mother is sick. She's eighty."

"So she was a pretty old mom, if you're forty."

"Well, yeah. She would have been my age when I was born."

"Did she pay attention to you?"

"I don't want to be psychoanalyzed, really."

"This isn't analysis, I just want to figure out why you're so afraid of your sister."

"All this 'how do you feel about that?' crap really bugs me. I do not hate my sister."

"I'm pissing you off. That's a good sign."

"I'm not pissed. You're the one that's pissed."

More silence, more bouncing down the road. A farmhouse, a bigger truck passing, grand clouds ahead and to all sides.

Tracy says, "So let's stop and see her."

More serious than he wants to sound, George says, "Maybe we should."

"Be fun!"

"How am I going to explain you?"

"We'll say I'm your therapist." Tracy holds a straight face for a second, then laughs.

"Crap," George says. He likes her laugh, laughs too.

"We'll say I'm your helper, all right?"

George just shakes his head mildly, drives in silence.

"Which is what I am."

A long silence, twenty minutes, just the road coming, the truck bouncing.

"You are a very beautiful girl," George says, finally. "I don't mean in the physical sense. I mean, you are a good soul. But I think you're beautiful too. A very beautiful girl."

"That's a pretty aggressive thing to say," Tracy says, looking at him. She seems to be kidding.

"Crap." This comes out lightly, humorous as George intends.

"Anyway, if I'm beautiful I'm a beautiful woman, George."

"Oh double crap."

"Have you ever had a girlfriend?"

"No, just women friends."

"Any of them romantic friendships?"

"Of course."

"Ever been married?"

"No, I hate women too much."

"Ever had a gay lover?"

"Dozens."

Tracy laughs, "Come on. Truth or dare."

"If I say no—which is the truth—you're going to say I hate men."

Bill Roorbach

"It's yourself you don't like."

"Let's talk about your problems for a change. Did you ever have a boyfriend? or do you talk too much?"

"You are so aggressive."

"Sorry. No really. Did you ever have a boyfriend?"

"Of course."

"See how silly the question is?"

"I've gone out with three guys, long term, and all three were assholes. Blunderbusses. Numchucks."

"I get it. You go out with blunderbusses, so now I have to hate women."

Silence. Then: "Geez, that was pretty right-on."

"Thank you."

"But you're still a pretty pissed-off guy under that laid-back surface thing."

"Bullshit."

"Aggressive response."

"Aggressive question."

"So how come you avoid your sister?"

George smiles wearily, gazes out the window at nothing. "Can we just listen to the radio?"

"Take all the time you wish, but at some point you'll have to just forget about her. Say, 'So be it.' Send her a Christmas card and don't feel guilty."

"Let's put the radio on."

Tracy switches on the radio and searches interminably for a song she likes on the crowded bands. Finally she settles on some woman singing about how she's not aware of too many things, and calls it an oldie, though George has never heard it at all. They listen to the music, but the tension in the truck is pretty high. George wishes he hadn't called her beautiful, though it's true, he thinks, looking at her. She's started to seem the most beautiful girl he's ever talked to, and this revelation makes him self-conscious in a way he hasn't been for years.

Tracy can't contain herself, turns the radio down, almost off. "Funny that she's a college prof and you're a truck driver. I mean, okay, I know you're more than that, and I know you're going to do a lot of cool things in life. It's like you're just waiting to clear the air with this family stuff. It's hard to grow past all that. I have this student in my Intro section who just started *college* at thirty-six. She had to work out this major fear that she couldn't *do* college. That she just wasn't smart enough, you know? And it turns out she'd been more or less told this her whole life by her parents—they didn't mean it I bet—but they told her in a million ways that she wasn't as good as her stupid gorgeous Harvard sister and her football hero loser brother, I mean, I *know* these people. She's the excellent one. She had to dump the whole tribe. She dumped 'em. Said goodbye. Resurfaced a year later as her new self. Spectacular. She's the smartest person I've ever had in class. The best."

George drives a long time quietly. Finally he says, "That's a nice story."

And Tracy's quiet a long time too before she says, "And I think you're the sweetest guy I've talked to in about ten years."

It's the right address, and George and Tracy are standing beside the truck, which takes up the whole curb in front of George's sister's house.

"Let's just forget it," George says.

"We'll tell her I'm your helper. Come on."

They walk up the neat flagstone walk, go side by side to the door. The place seems so nice, so tidy, so Tracy Lynn, somehow, that George wants to just walk away. He's unpleasantly full from the diner dinner he and his new helper just ate. He's got clouds in his head, the fragments of several hundred planned and replanned opening speeches. It's absurd, she's only his sister.

Tracy rings the doorbell, and in one second the door flies open and there's an Asian woman standing there, looking slightly annoyed.

George seems to find himself, says, "I'm looking for Tracy Lynn Skinner-Peabody. Professor Skinner-Peabody. Or Kevin. Are they here?"

"Oh, dear," the Asian woman says, her face opening at the familiar names. She's about fifty years old, George thinks. Just the kind of friend Tracy Lynn would have.

"I'm her brother," George says, to move things along.

"You look like her. But, you must know she on sabbatical this year. She and Kevin in Argentina. You know this."

"Ah, yes. Of course."

"We just have something for her," Tracy says, professional tone, delivery person. "We have a piece of furniture George would like to drop off."

George smiles, then starts to laugh, turns and walks into his laughter, trips back up the flagstones, leaving Tracy to chat with the woman. In a minute his helper is back, opening the rear truck door, and it's all the two of them can do to tip the ungainly piece off the tailgate and through their laughter onto the dolly. They roll it competently into the garage together, supervised by the Asian lady, who is really pretty nice about their silliness, who smiles and nods her head—the antics of brothers!—as they push the $15,000 Turner breakfront up against the absolutely spotless sheetrock wall at the back of the absolutely spotless garage.

The Asian lady wants to get George a piece of paper for a note, since he's refused tea, refused even to come inside, and though George has said, "Please don't bother," Tracy has said, "Thanks, some paper would be nice," and George finds himself alone in the garage with a piece of notepaper, scarcely believing he's about to steal the breakfront.

Tracy Lynn hello, it's George. This is a little wedding present from us to both of you. Thanks for being patient. Welcome back from Argentina. Sometime I'll stop by to fix the gouge on the side of this thing. Really, though, it's a delicious piece. Come see us in New York.

The *us* just sounds right, maybe means Bergenstaedler, maybe Carl.

In the truck Tracy and George giggle uncontrollably clear to the highway and for several miles thereon. "I've stolen it," George says, suddenly depressed, "I've stolen a perfect Turner breakfront and I'm screwed."

"Stolen it? You didn't steal anything. You refused a defective piece and Carl the Blue Beret abandoned it in the hotel parking lot!"

They laugh, but not with quite the same silliness and abandon. They roll through many miles in silence. It's getting late, and there's the issue of the night, of where to stay. George is sleepy now, driving. It's near eleven o'clock and Tracy says she can't drive the heavy clutch of the twelve-wheeler.

So she puts the radio on and sings softly to several unfamiliar songs, sings nicely, looking at George, sings in that kind of serious singing voice that young women have sometimes, good enough to perform, if only they could do their singing a little more loudly or in front of more than a couple of friends.

Somewhere near Syracuse, Tracy slides over on the seat and puts a hand on George's knee as he drives, puts her hand on George's knee and sings as the big truck bounces merrily, lullingly down the road.

"Let's stop awhile," she says in his ear, and immediately, almost like magic, there's a rest area, so George pulls in to comply.

Bill Roorbach is the author of *Summer with Juliet*, a memoir.

STRAYS / *David Borofka*

AFTER SCOT IS KILLED, Frank takes Connie, Scot's girlfriend, to the funeral, thinking it might be a way to score points. He hoses down his old mustard-colored Corolla, dumps the ashtrays, even repairs the four rips in the passenger seat. The morning of the funeral he gets a haircut, then buys a new shirt and tie in solid, dark colors. Scot had been a good friend, his best friend since grade school, but after all, dead is dead.

For her part, Connie has been acting a little glazed about the whole situation. She and Scot had never been real serious, but now that Scot's dead, she's been elevated: everyone expects her to act like the mourning widow in weeds, and life is supposed to come to some screeching, smoking-rubber halt, and that might be even more intimidating than the fact that Scot is indeed now dead and not just off somewhere on some fool backpacking trip. Which is the sort of thing Scot could do—like the evening he announced that he was going to walk to Mount Hood then hitchhike back, and that he was going to accomplish all this in the space of twenty-four hours. Fifty miles walking and fifty of thumbing rides. Jerry and Frank just laughed and said they'd talk to him later, like when he got to Sandy and tired of the whole thing. But they didn't hear anything and then there he was, pulling up to the curb in the back of some farmer's pickup truck, asleep. The farmer went to the back, woke him up, then helped him down to the ground. His boots were off and his feet were bleeding, but he'd gone to the mountain and back, and he'd done it in a day.

But that doesn't mean Frank can't take Connie to the funeral. They both have to go, anyway, the Girlfriend and the Roommate.

At the mortuary, the undertaker motions them to the waiting room. Connie looks right at home. She's practically been living here for the last three days, ever since the accident, and Frank imagines she knows every bit of the funeral business by this time; she could give guided tours of the place.

Scot's parents are already there and waiting, and they're ready to pounce.

"Connie," Scot's dad says, "Connie."

"Frank," Scot's mom says, "dear Frank."

They shake hands, they hug, they say each other's names about a dozen times, then they stand looking at each other and shifting their weight from one foot to the next.

"Glad you could make it, kids," Sam Coldine says. He tries to make himself sound like the Good Dad, complete with barbecue apron and beers in the reefer—no matter how indifferent he is toward Connie and Frank; their respective parents are mediocre nonentities, their prospects are even less promising, they're just two strays that Scot picked up.

"Wouldn't have missed it," Frank says. For that he gets a nudge in the ribs from Connie, a gesture he doesn't mind in the slightest.

Scot's old man is the hale and hearty type—white shoes, white belt, and curling gray sideburns. He's big enough that when he wears a tie there's no proof of his ever having had a neck. He has a glad hand and a booming—"ain't we having fun, yet?" voice; he looks like the stereotype of a used-car salesman and acts the part, when, in fact, he's the largest manufacturer of optical lenses west of the Mississippi. A success. Someone who knows. Frank has never figured things out; he once went camping with Scot and Sam at Scot's request, and while the three of them were drinking from a bottle of Jack Daniels, quietly getting drunk together, he could almost believe that he was on a level, equal, connected with Scot's assumption that the world was orchestrated for one's consumption and enjoyment. In the daylight, however, the connection was broken, he was again just a satellite orbiting around the Coldine planet of energetic enthusiasms, forbidden by the law of social gravity ever to land.

He would like to think that he was too smart to get greedy, to let himself hope for some sort of sign that he was regarded as something other than a parasite, but he knows now that he has always carried this buried wish: that Scot's dad would put his arm around his shoulders, tell him that he, Frank, was indeed one of the good guys. He also knows that he has failed somehow, in some desperate too-eager way, that with Scot gone, he can forget about the Coldine door swinging open ever again. The thought makes him want to slash Sam's tires.

Scot's mom on the other hand is one of those timid types, a mouse with dead brown hair who has been folding her husband's underwear for the last thirty years and still pretends he's some kind of demigod. She's Mrs. Loman with a lucky husband and never a doubt to test her loyalty. So Frank is not a little surprised when she puts her hand on his arm and says, "I blame him, you know."

By this time there are plenty of other prostrate mourners in the room and Sam can spread himself out, deflect his own grief by treating his son's funeral as a summer cocktail party, mingling, playing the room, acting the good host. "No," Frank says, "I didn't know."

"Him and his motorcycles."

"It wasn't anybody's fault, Mrs. Coldine, except the drunk in the truck. If he'd been driving Sam's Caddy, it wouldn't have made a damn bit of difference."

When you are coming up the on-ramp to the Interstate and get hit by a cement truck which is coming down in violation of all the driving laws known to man, a Sherman tank is maybe your only possible protection. What does it matter what you're driving when afterwards the only question is how much twisted metal they'll have to pull apart in order to find what's left?

"If you want me to go after that son-of-a-bitch cement-head, just let me know."

"Frankie, Frankie," she says. She makes his name sound like tsk-tsk, as if she is speaking to her other, more troublesome son.

"He just had a light about him, don't you think?"

"You just let me know. I'd kill him." He is only jabbering, of course, killing the direction of Scot's mother's thoughts, unwilling as he is to start debating Scot's luminosity. But the words seem to be sufficient. He would like to be able to say something like, "I'm sure Sam's going to miss him in the office," something of the sort of thing that Jerry—Eddie Haskel in another life—knows how to get away with because he can say it with all sincerity while not believing a word of it. It's just not in Frank's vocabulary. If he tries, it will come out an insult, so he sticks with threats of violence which seem like safer social territory. As it is, Mrs. Coldine pats him on the arm, then moves away to greet others of her family—more timid, sad-eyed mice.

The room is filling now, knots and clusters of sober-suited men and women, friends of Mr. and Mrs. Coldine's, all of them glancing at their watches and darting quick looks at the door, wondering when the whole shebang is going to get under way. At the fringe of one of these groups, Connie sits in a metal folding chair, her knees together, her feet apart. She seems to be studying the heel of one shoe.

Frank grabs her hand. "Come on."

"I can't." She waves her free hand to indicate the room. "I should stay."

"They don't care. All they want is out of here. Besides we can find out what chapel we'll be in."

She rises reluctantly, a tall girl in a borrowed, too-short black dress who collects stares and ready-made disapproval from the dress-for-success-ers.

The mortician is nowhere to be found, so they stand on the front steps, watching more of Sam's business acquaintances go trooping inside.

Outside, the air is golden and hot, perfect weather for a picnic or a softball game, a trip to the beach or a bike ride, a mockery of their purpose. Frank and Connie hold hands and create a picture of the Two Friends comforting each other in their time of grief.

"It's such a sad and sorrowful day," she says in a voice she must have borrowed from the sixth grade, a voice used when confronting adults.

"It won't take long. Then it'll be over," Frank says.

He watches as the sides of her nose begin to quiver, and she combs her fingers back through her hair. "Shit," she says. "I'm not going to cry."

He puts his arm around her shoulders, but she pushes him away.

"I'm okay. I don't want to cry. It's just when you say something stupid like that, stupid and mean, then I feel like I ought to cry, to make up for what you said."

"I can't help thinking that once Scot's in the ground, it's over. All these dickheads will go back to their offices and wish they hadn't wasted the morning."

"Don't." She sits down on the steps, folding herself into a jackknife of beaten reserve. "You want to see me cry, don't you?"

"Yes." All of a sudden he wants to see her face collapse in a flood. That "sad and sorrowful day" business has gotten to him. The feeling that this entire business has been scripted for them without consultation. He hasn't felt anything about Scot's death except guilt. He doesn't feel even the quiver of a tear. My best friend is dead. It doesn't work. He feels pissed off and horny when he looks at Connie. But Scot? Nothing. He finds himself humming some meaningless fragment and wondering when the rush will come. In the meantime there's Connie who's got all the symptoms, and he wishes suddenly that he'd never seen this girl before. "Cry till your eyes fall out."

"You're such a shit." She starts to get up and he can visualize quite a scene starting—the Grieving Girl Widow running to the ladies' room in the funeral home, her mascara streaked into stars around her eyes, the Shithead Roommate getting a closed powder room door in the puss.

But before things can get too out of hand, Jerry and Tabitha arrive, Jerry pulling his father's Corvette into the space reserved for the hearse. "Is this the party?" Jerry says.

"You got it," Frank says. "This is it."

"Scot's dead, you know." Connie's lower lip is trembling, and her fingers are again raking her hair. "Scot's dead and all you dumb fucks can say is, 'Where's the party?'"

Jerry slaps her face lightly, a glancing, almost caressing type of slap. Just a touch. But Connie's face goes slack all the same, all the little muscles around her cheeks turning rubbery and soft.

"Don't try to hog it all, Connie," Frank says as softly as he can. You can push them and push them, and then, just when they can't take anymore, if you're nice, they'll fall all over themselves with gratitude. It's cold, but that's how it is: Scot dies, Frank starts campaigning for Connie.

Besides, he has seen her face turn to mush and he can't be angry at her for his own failing. He can't feel a goddam thing. And he's tried. "You're not the only one who's trying to figure it out."

Connie crumples on the steps, her head between her knees. "I hate him," she says. And now . . . now it hits him like a slap to his own face, but it is a different blow from the one he's been expecting. He remembers Scot, the morning after he first brought Connie to the duplex, he remembers him sitting at the kitchen table, his face smudged and blurred by his night's exertion, laughing about the little slut who was still sleeping in his bed, snoring like a truck. Frank remembers the Scot who could say the word "slut" and make it a term of near-endearment. He remembers thinking that Scot needed him, needed Frank, if for no other reason than that he needed the audience, that Scot needed Frank and the girl in the other room who turned out to be Connie. He needed someone to whom he could condescend.

Now, Connie has continued to say, "I hate him, I hate him, I hate him," but whether she means Jerry or Frank or Scot, it is impossible to say.

Ultimately, Frank has to admit that Connie holds her end up well. After that little episode outside on the steps, she pulls the strings of her composure together and no one hears any more high notes of manufactured grief. She holds his arm, going in and out of the church. After the funeral, they drive to the cemetery, and at the gravesite, she rests her head on his shoulder and closes her eyes. They listen to more mumbo-jumbo, then wait to see the coffin go down. But, evidently, they don't do that anymore. Frank thinks it would be nice to throw a clump of dirt on top of Scot, it would put a little finality on the day. As it is, they leave with the casket still resting in the shade of the awning, as if everyone has left before the party is over.

Frank half expects Connie to face backwards in the car so she can watch the gravesite as they drive away, turn herself into self-righteous salt. But she does no such thing, there's nothing to see anyway, just the casket and the awning and the community of tombstones, and who knows what happens after dark? Even so, it doesn't stop him, as much as he tries not to, from looking in the rearview mirror. It doesn't stop him from waiting for some sort of *National Enquirer*–style miracle—"Best Friend Rises from Dead to Mock the Ravishment of Girlfriend"—something so out of this world that all of his doubts about the value of his own life are confirmed. As if by fucking Connie, Scot has now raised the ante beyond his reach. Nor does it stop Frank from whispering to himself, so low that Connie can't hear: Ass. You're such an ass.

Because his best friend in all the world has just died doesn't mean Frank gets to take a day off from work. He would like to go off somewhere and get drunk or try his luck with Connie, but no way. He works at Widmer's in the mall next to the freeway, and although he broached the subject of time off to his crew chief, he knew it was a lost cause right from the start. He goes in at six in the evening, three hours before closing, and along with the rest of the janitors begins cleaning the executive offices up on the second floor. Then at nine o'clock when the customers have been chased out, they move out onto the floor and try to repair the damage that another day of consumerism hath wrought. At two o'clock in the morning, the doors are unlocked, the alarms momentarily turned off, and they are free to go, but there is always a security guard standing by the door, checking for suspicious bulges. It is not a place to inspire trust.

Tonight, Frank is in no mood for it. He sits in the executive can and smokes sixteen cigarettes down to the filters while he is supposed to be cleaning the office suite belonging to Mr. Donatelli,

Jerry's old man, who happens to be the vice-president of Marketing, and who also happens to be the one responsible for getting Frank this shitty job. Jerry also has an office upstairs, and Frank has been meditating for the last forty-five minutes on the sabotage which will occur tonight in honor of Scot. In his lunch bucket he has included, besides the usual bologna and cheese, potato chips and forbidden bottle of beer, a nice, gray piece of three-day-old, unrefrigerated bass. The offices all have floor vents for the air conditioning, and Jerry's office has a vent right underneath his desk. It is a perfect coup, made even more so by the knowledge that Jerry would never rat, not even with dead fish breath permeating his office air. It's a small rebellion, but better than none at all.

Five minutes later he's replacing the vent cover when Lou Chabala, the crew chief, orders him down to the basement to break up cardboard in the compactor. Lou sniffs the air tentatively, but Frank is as bland and unfathomable as an angel.

Downstairs, Frank finds that Lou has teamed him up with Headcase Harry. Harry is a fifty-eight-year-old fruitcake from the VA, on a life experience furlough. It is the sort of program that looks good for Widmer's even though the VA pays them to babysit Harry for eight hours a day, and Widmer's gets a little work out of him besides. Harry is carefully slicing up cardboard boxes with a razor, then just as carefully placing them in the open jaw of the compactor. When the bin is full, he punches the red start button and waits outside the compactor room until the noise has subsided. Frank bides his time. When he sees that Harry has wandered over to the Coke machine, Frank slips into the compactor room, locks the start button into place, and, when the jaw opens wide, slips a full box of fluorescent tubes into the open maw. Frank slips out, Harry wanders back inside. Suddenly, hellzapoppin in the compactor: sparks, lights, sizzles, dying electrical gasps. It sounds a little like gunfire from a distance. Harry comes tearing out, screaming, arms clawing the air, his face ashen, his eyes bulging. Frank begins to laugh, but the humor cuts itself off before the ha-ha can make the freeway interchange between his throat and mouth. A dead fish in Jerry's office is one thing. This only has the makings of depression. Part of adulthood, Frank decides, is knowing the appropriate targets for revenge.

He makes it home, whipping his poor, gasping Corolla into the driveway at 2:30 in the morning. The August heat has settled like a buzzard in the trees, and even the air pouring through the car windows does not come close to alleviating the rank smell of vegetable summer. It is hard to picture Scot as now part of the soil's corruption and decay. Despite the late hour, lights are still on in the back half of the duplex, his own habitation. The front half, occupied by a retired couple named Cloud, is as dark as a tomb. Cars are double-parked up and down the street. Before he can get his key into the lock, the door flies open and Jerry pulls him into a party.

Even though Jerry is educated, college and culture and all that crap, he still lives with his parents and uses Frank's place whenever he wants to party or quick-bang Tabitha. Scot gave him a key. Now, there must be thirty people in the twelve-by-fourteen living room and eight-by-ten kitchen. Connie is not among them. Before he can say, Whoa, Frank finds a beer in his hand. And while he wants to ask, What's going on? there is no silence in which to place the words. Instead he squeezes through the sweating throng, down the hallway, and slips through the thinnest dark crack of the doorway, into Scot's room. The window is shut tight, and the air in Frank's nose smells like the second-floor fish. Connie is stretched out on the bed, face down. She is still wearing Tabitha's black dress, and the skirt has worked its way up to her hips. The reverberations from the outer rooms drum through the shut door. This figure on the bed is the epitome of absolute wretchedness. Unconscious, she can break his heart; a photograph of her now, in this position, could drive him to suicide. He is about to touch her when Connie rolls over, pushing her hair away. "I took Valiums, Frankie," she says, "and I feel ever so much better. I feel like I've been gift-boxed in cotton."

"Good. That's good."

"I never knew."

"What?"

"I never knew it felt so good." She sits up, hugs him around the legs. "I don't do drugs," she says in all seriousness, "you can't high when you're fly."

"That's right."

He pulls her arms from his legs then settles her head back among the pillows. Like an idiot, orphaned child, she plays with her fingers in front of her face.

"Frankie?"

"What?"

"Scot. He didn't like me all that much."

Frank fights back the smile that is spreading across his face and the wave of gratitude he feels washing in from his stomach.

"Sure he liked you."

"No," she sighs, "It's a lot more complicated than that."

"Go to sleep," he says.

Just then, Tabitha bursts into the room, crying, "What's going on in here, you two?" Then, waggling one finger: "Ah, ah, ah!"

She is a silly girl, and Frank has, on more than one occasion, wished he could break her neck. What Jerry finds in her, other than a humping partner, he can't understand. Tonight, her hair is the color of bricks. She speaks in whispers and shrieks and lisps. A little-girl pout hangs like a cigarette from her lower lip.

"Get out," Frank says. "Now."

"Touchy, touchy."

He pushes her toward the door.

"Hey," Tabitha says, "what's the big idea?"

"Out."

"We're all friends here, right?"

"Out."

Frank grabs her around the waist and throws her across his hip, as he would a particularly obnoxious child.

"Out," he yells to the crowded living room while the babbling Tabitha says, "He means it, I think he really means it."

Jerry—red-faced, angry at being interrupted in his pursuit of a seventeen-year-old brunette with cantaloupes for tits who is already halfway out of her sweater—Jerry begins to go British, speaking in an accent full of starch and offended propriety, "What is the meaning of this?" I say, Frank thinks, and after setting Tabitha into the trash can filled with ice and beer, he rips the needle across one full side of Jesus and the Mary Chain, and the noise quacks and dies.

"Really," Jerry says, "that's really quite unnecessary."

"Party's over," Frank says.

Later, Frank watches Connie. In her drugged slumber, she snores like a storm drain, her mouth sagging open, a glob of spit zigzagging its way down her chin.

When he sits on the side of the bed, his weight sends the headboard thudding into the wall, the sound and movement promoting its own idea. "I'm sorry, really," he tells the unconscious girl, uncomfortably aware as he does so of how tarnished his chivalry is. "I'm sorry. What can I say?"

"You didn't get a helluva lot of sleep, did you?"

"I'm sorry," Frank says. "I got them out as soon as I could."

"I'm not talking about the party."

It is seven o'clock the next morning, and Joe Cloud is lying on his back underneath his '67 Rambler Cross Country station wagon. Frank can only see Joe's black dress shoes, his white socks that look like remnants from a Goodwill sale, and the bottoms of green khaki uniform pants. Just because he has emphysema and he can barely breathe, the Transit Company has forced Joe to retire from his position as a driver. So now, the Rambler gets its oil changed every four hundred and fifty miles while Joe and the Mrs. try to live on disability. The last few times Frank has been inside their half of the duplex he has found Amway brochures littering the coffee table and the sofa.

"They're fuck-ups," Joe says. Looking up: "You too," then after another moment's consideration, "maybe just half a fuck-up."

"Well, I don't think they'll be back for awhile. And I'm sorry about the other."

"Connie's okay."

"Yeah."

"But those others," Joe lights a cigarette and struggles to a sitting position on the rollaway. "Those others are fuck-ups. Scot too. The last conversation I had with Scot was about his goddam bed and his goddam headboard. 'Put it in the middle of the goddam room,' I told him. Fuck-ups."

"I know it, but I've known them for as long as I can remember."

He can't remember not knowing them, nor can he remember not being envious. Because even if they are fuck-ups, their asses are always covered, and their feathers are always dry. From their money and their education, they know all the secrets, they know the way to the offices, all the things that Frank is afraid he'll never know. He'll always be a janitor in some store with lousy stuff. Fuck it. Fuck them. Year after year, hoping that something, some secret, would rub off. How did he get so stuck?

Joe leans his head back against the ice-blue skin of the Rambler. "When you gonna trade me cars?" he asks, the opener to a conversation they've had about a million times.

"I'd be stealing from you."

Joe wants to trade his mint-condition, impeccably maintained Rambler for Frank's mustard-colored ruin. Joe is bored by retirement.

David Borofka

"You'd be getting a sweet deal."

"I know it. That's why I can't figure it."

"Straight six engine with overdrive never gets above twenty-eight hundred R.P.M. You baby it on the freeway, she gets twenty-five miles to the gallon. New tires last month."

"I'll think about it."

"I'm just changing the oil now."

It's a process as mysterious to Frank as inherited income. Joe once tried to show him on the Corolla. Frank drained the oil, replaced the filter, funnelled in the new four quarts of oil. The one thing he forgot to do was replace the drain plug. Joe came out of the front half of the duplex just in time to see the spreading brown puddle underneath the mustard-colored car, said, "Hirohito's Revenge," and turned on one black dress-shoe heel. Since that time, Frank has not once changed the oil, checked the tires, or opened the radiator; he has taken a vow never to touch the innards of any automobile ever again, and he is waiting for the moment when the engine seizes, so he can kiss this testimony of his gross incompetence goodbye. Goodbye forever with dignity. Although by all rights he belongs on the fuck-up list as well, Frank understands that, in the strangest sort of way, his disintegrating car and his conscious refusal to do anything about it may be the two reasons Joe has for respecting him.

Three weeks later: Frank wakes, encrusted from the waist down in the dried sea rime of sex. Connie is lying on her side, breathing through her mouth, snoring with pharmacological abandon. She has discovered that she really and truly likes the Valiums, and he can no longer tell if her nightly dose is medicinal or recreational or simply, given all circumstances—Scot's death, his own need—the last best escape. Frank can't sleep because of the heat: the windows are open but not a lick of air breathes through the screens. He also can't sleep because of Connie, who, besides making her shitfaced racket, takes up more than her fair share of the bed. She's slept here for the past two-and-a-half weeks, and Frank wonders if, between the novelty of unaccustomed sex and Connie's vibrating palate, he will ever sleep undisturbed again. Scot's folks came three days after the funeral and hauled his furniture away—the bed, the headboard, the dresser, the kitchen table, the sofas, the TV, all the pots and pans, and the vacuum cleaner which Frank wasn't about to use anyway.

They even took all the clothes hangers. They asked him if he wanted to buy anything before they set up the yard sale. They'd make Frank a special deal, they said. It made no sense, neither as purge nor greed; they are crazy, he can see that now, their grief manifesting itself in this war between their obsessive thrift and their insatiable appetite for the comforts of money. He will probably never figure out why Scot lived here, lived in this junky hole. Other than slumming, he can't figure it. To believe that his own personality could be so compelling would be dreaming.

Sam couldn't take the closet, so Connie's jeans and her t-shirts and her shoes lie in a heap in one corner of the closet in Scot's empty room while she sleeps in Frank's room on top of Frank. He would like to think that they are sleeping together for reasons of passion, but the absence of available beds is probably closer to the truth. He has a mattress, but not much else; when he gets up now, he's walking through the litter and leftovers of the Coldine Transfer and Resale Company, out the screen door to the patio, there to watch the hot stars.

Actually there is a third, simpler reason for his failure to sleep—time. It is only twelve-thirty. Tonight is the third week of cohabitation, but only the second week of sleep at such an early hour. In other words, this is the fourteenth day since he's been fired, and his body is still having a hard time getting used to the idea. Two weeks ago, he mounted the back stairs at Widmer's— the servants' entrance—in the presence of a familiar aroma. He opened his locker to find his fish, his aging friend going grayer and greener by the minute. In its mouth was a folded, spindled and mutilated payroll check marked "Final Compensation," a door key, and a note from Jerry containing suggestions for the demise of said bass. The suggestions were neither pretty nor possible, nor, given his long-standing acquaintance with Jerry, predictable. The unpredictable is sucking him down a drain that he is not at all happy about.

And maybe a fourth cause of sleeplessness is also rearing its ugly head: Connie. The idea of Connie. Be careful what you wish for, he thinks. She's turning herself into a zombie, walling off her pain behind a dam of Valium, even as he struggles to feel anything. A great match. Maybe Mr. Coldine had it right:

"You two kids look good together," he said as he left with the last of Scot's stuff. "Everything will work out, you'll see."

Frank sees both sides of his meaning. Charity might say that Frank and Connie can be good for one another, that even in the midst of tragedy, there is an order and orchestration in the events. His own sense of what Sam means is this: he and Connie are just more of Scot's leftovers, more Coldine junk, not the sort of people for whom Providence exists . . . they don't have either the money or the position, and if his own son had to die in order to dump them, so be it. He can see it, too, in the indifferent stars that stare down at his patio night after night—stars which, in the eyes of Jerry and Scot and their kind—fuck-ups or not— form constellations and relationships and connections, but which in his eye hang separately, hundreds of thousands of cold miles away from one another. Orion, the Dipper—nothing but dot-to-dot pictures for adult children wishing to find order where there is, in fact, none. No connections. That's the thing with Connie and him. They're both strays. Both of them. And when you get right down to it, down to the bottom line and the fine print, where the rubber meets the road and the cement truck meets the bike, Scot and one bed and this one refuge for the abandoned are the only attachments they've got.

David Borofka has published in a number of literary magazines and was the winner of the *Missouri Review* Editors' Prize for 1992.

COUGHING THROUGH THE BRAMBLES
/ Gary Fincke

Some days the asthma wakes me early,
Makes me walk through the underwater dark
And trust my footing to prescriptions
While I find the shallow end of wheezing.
So quiet, this illness, so unlike
The bark of the common cold, the great whoops
Of the cough more serious which killed
One classmate the winter the whooping crane
Stood extinct, almost, on the front page
Of our *Weekly Readers*. We watched slides
Of condors and grizzlies and pale fish
We were supposed to care for, and even now
I watch for Harvey Walker, the sun
An hour away, because his spirit
Might choose to retrace itself, search for
An arrangement of houses and yards
And debris which calls up our childhood,
The dwarf shape of fear whose messages
Stay simple as those folded inside mittens.
For asthma, once, you swallowed spider webs;
For whooping cough, some parents would push
Their children through blackberry brambles,
Those stems which arced to thrust themselves
Back into the ground like living hoops,
Listening to the terrible thrusts
Of air through the constricted hoops of throats.
It was like the laying on of hands
For tumors and tuberculosis;
It was the faith and prayer of my parents
Who passed me through the brambles of eternal
Damnation, expecting answers the way
Some men listen for responses to
Radio waves they transmit to outer space.
The year Harvey Walker died, I read
A story about the first broadcasts
Reflecting off the edge of the universe

And returning for rebroadcasting.
"O, Holy Night," the radios played,
By Professor Fessenden, 1906,
And then Bible verses from St. Luke,
Stutters of stations working toward
The cacophony of perpetual
Retransmission of a billion broadcasts.
And I might pass all of the past's coughing
Through the brambles which run the border
Of the lot I live on, three times each,
One thrust exactly like the others
In distance and direction until
The heavenly white magic takes hold.
And I might lay my healer's hands
On the vulnerable spots of those
I love, trusting the medicinal
Power of faith, but I've weaned myself
From the vanity of prayer, believing
Enough voices are rocketing toward
The imagined edge of the universe,
So many supplications seeking
The thin, improbable antenna,
The unlikely decoding, and then,
So far to return, so many requests,
The everlasting shower of granted
Wishes soaking the astonished
Descendants of the faithful and
The faithless, flooding both with bitterness
And joy, and drowning the need to believe.

THE NEAR-DEATH FERVOR / *Gary Fincke*

In Egypt, thousands of years before Christ,
Some pharaohs settled into wax-sealed casks,
Buried alive and watched over by priests
Who kept time and the hypoxia score,
Counting and guessing and welcoming back
New god-kings to the living. Those pharaohs
Who lived saw the bright lights where souls travel,
Glimpsed the spirit world and returned with news
We hear, these days, from the resuscitated
Who emerge from the cask of the quiet heart.
Near Pittsburgh are miners who, when rescued,
Tell stories of descending shafts of light;
All summer I follow the forklifts which
Enter the tunnels of boxed beans, tinned soup
In crates; listen to their beeped monotones
Of reverse seep toward the light while I work
With a partner who knows how deep we are
In canned goods by giddiness, by darkness,
The air close as judgment where we restack
Shifted pallets while he repeats near-death
Stories, the luminous peace as the brain
Breaks down. The angels are those who love you,
He murmurs, laying one hand, suddenly
Ungloved, on my shadowed shoulder. Those crates,
Reloaded, separate us from the world.
So little air, he says, we wouldn't burn,
And I back into the light where trucks come
And go in silhouettes and the silence
Of drivers with deadlines who smoke and back
Into the brilliance of River Street,
Its choice of bridges which sweep them into
Or away from the sun, redescending
To the freeways of the chattering world.

THE ONE BIRDS / *Gary Fincke*

Within the worst winter of the century,
I've started to foresee the sites for each set
Of drifts, the possibilities of sheer ice
On asphalt. I've had time, snowed in, to locate
The early signs of a dozen diseases
Which prove fatal, time to consider further
Examination and the self-serving prayer,
Both as likely as the drifts turning to waves
Which would crest and crash and wash away despair.

Twenty below, a black settling of feathers
On the mailbox, surely the obvious bad
Judgment of this morning, and I remember
The poorwill is the one bird that hibernates,
Sleeping in the cracks and crevices of rock.
I rouse myself with lift and throw, lift and throw,
And fine spray into my unprotected eyes
When the wind shifts, that unlikely bird sitting
Quiet as a vulture until I recall
The pale chanting goshawk, the one bird of prey
Which sings, celebrations possible for acts
We think would mute us, forcing apologies
From the faithless tongue: I'm sorry for the weeks
I've wasted, the years I've badly used. I'm loud
With remorse, and the bird, whatever its name,
Squawks and lifts large and heavy with survival
When I spike the plowed ice near the roadway, lift
A full load like someone who sees shoveling
As a way to heal the fatted heart, who is
Astonished, again and again, by bright sun
Which warms nothing, and by each of the one birds,
Like the mallee fowl, which at birth, takes flight,
And is not surprised by its singular might.

THE WONDERFUL RESOLVE TO BREATHE
/ Gary Fincke

Hush, she said, headaches are pimples.
Don't pick and they go away, but
In emergencies (Don't ask again)
I could shake two full-strength aspirin
From the bottle uncapped, then locked.

Your mother never had migraines,
My wife told me, the first morning
She lay in the dark, describing
Blind spots as holes in my face, slurring
Her child's description. Parts of you

Have disappeared, she said, gouging
My cheeks with fingertips gone numb.
Go to sleep, forget about it,
I said to myself. Put scissors
Under your pillow, something to try

When the aspirin is hidden,
And aloud, how my mother offered
The cure of the hangman's rope, the skull
Bound in the used noose for relief,
How I believed she would slip it

Around my throat for another kind
Of test, listen to my breathing
For the first hushed sign of failure
And wait for my headache to leave
In shame. Now, I think, I might tighten

That cord until the blood suffused
My face and I heard the sweet singing
In my ears, dog-whistle alarm
For the robbery of myself.
Some sufferers, once, submitted

To trepanning, holes bored right into
The skull to give headaches or what
Drove them crazy a route to leave.
Flint drills in caves. The aspirin
Of the Stone Age. But some patients lived,

Returning for further treatments,
One museum skull showing five borings
Survived, migraines or lunacy
Or acquiescence to whitehead pain.
At intervals, now, my wife drinks

Coffee to subdue her headaches,
Swallowing the caffeine which lies
At the base of the medicine
I regularly take to prevent
My lungs from closing, though I've woken

To lost airways and discovered,
In panic, the wonderful resolve
To breathe, submitting to ambulance
And oxygen, trying to drill
Something through my thick skull about

The insanity of swallowing
Red wine, champagne, or heavy cream,
Three things which have slipped a noose
Around my throat while I've teetered
On asthma's unsteady ladder,

Looking clearly into the blind spots
Where the dark gives up its pinwheeled light.

THE ETYMOLOGY OF ANGELS / *Gary Fincke*

In Beloit, Wisconsin, a woman answers
The door in wings and halo, silver dress,
Welcomes me to her ten thousand angels
With "take your time and enjoy," fluttering
Like the authors of books who promise
Winged guardians are keeping us from harm.
The angel of the good deed, the angel
Of the safety net—half who answer polls
Believe, anxious as hospice visitors
Who avoid the terrible use of next.
Here is the theory of the angels who
Started a pilot program to transform
The world, two hundred fifty years renewed
Like a government grant. Here is the woman
Who encourages us to relax into
Our "sacred space" and wait for personal
Messages from heaven. Here is the handbook
For aspiring angels, how to provide,
How to facilitate, how to answer
The phone for the great CEO and transmit
The celestial e-mail to the faithful.
In the etymology of angels,
Diminishment sticks like a persistent gene
Until they sparkle like ten thousand pieces
Of kitsch, a woman's dress, the eyes of Azrail
Staring from the upstairs window as I leave,
One of his six billion eyes fixed on me.
And all along the rainswept interstate,
From the passenger side of each car which
Hisses by, Azrail mouthing the census
With one of his six billion tongues, adding
And subtracting while I form six billion
Questions of my own for the earnest angel
Who folds her pale hands, leans forward with knees
Together. This interview starts with *Where*
And *When* and *Why*, and this personal angel,
So professional, asks me to answer these

Myself because she's been employed and trained
By the great deflector, or because that's what
Matters or else nothing matters at all.

Gary Fincke's most recent collection of poetry is *Inventing Angels*.

"Those are pretty big numbers, Frank. I hope you're
prepared to back them up with some solid,
well-researched rhetoric!"

THE KING OF THE WORLD IN THE
LAND OF THE PYGMIES / *Joan Mark*

Introduction

"...on the whole, I think I am glad that I have remained a dilettante," wrote Patrick Tracy Lowell Putnam shortly after World War II. On the surface it seems like an odd statement for a Harvard-trained anthropologist, who at the time was the world's greatest authority on African pygmies. But Putnam was only being truthful. He *was* a dilettante, who had chosen to dabble in anthropology because it allowed him to flee America and live by his own rules in Africa. While he learned volumes about the pygmies, it was the kind of knowledge that comes from life, not scholarship. He recorded data sporadically, and was careless with the notes he did take. A charismatic individual, who inspired others to write about the pygmies, he lacked the discipline to do it himself. His twenty-four years in Africa were to yield just one published essay.

Putnam was a failure by academic standards, yet his life was anything but unproductive, as Joan Mark shows in the following excerpt from her biography, *The King of the World in the Land of the Pygmies* (forthcoming from the University of Nebraska Press in March 1995). The numerous accounts of Putnam describe a magnetic personality, energetic, intensely interested in everyone and everything. Temperamentally he was too restless to be an academic. Instead he became what Mark calls "a middleman in the production and distribution of anthropological knowledge."

It was chance that took Putnam to the Ituri Forest in the Belgian Congo (now Zaire), and determination to live as he wanted, outside the constraints of white society, that kept him there. A descendant of the Massachusetts Lowells, he entered Harvard as a chemistry major in 1921, and switched to anthropology the following year. Of the three professors in his department, the best known was Earnest Hooton, an exponent of eugenics. When Hooton sent an expedition to Africa to take physical measurements of the natives, he chose Putnam, by then a Harvard graduate, as one of its three members. The group set out in 1927 for French West Africa and the Niger River, but an outbreak of yellow fever caused them to change their route and study an alternate group of tribes, among them the pygmies (Mbuti), of the Ituri Forest. The hunting and gathering pygmies intrigued Putnam because of their unique cooperative relationship with the village-dwelling tribes in the vicinity. He returned to Harvard without the pygmy blood samples and physical measurements he was supposed to obtain, but with the conviction that their culture should be studied before it was wiped out by colonialism.

In practical terms, Putnam had done nothing but waste grant money. He had gathered no publishable data; he could hardly expect Harvard to sponsor him again. Finding a way back to the Congo looked difficult, until he hit on the idea of becoming an *agent sanitaire* for the Congo Red Cross. He returned to Africa in 1930, married a Mboli chief's daughter, Abanzima, with whom he had fallen in love on his first trip, and ran a hospital, until he was fired, partly for neglecting his census-taking duties, and partly for polygamy (along with Abanzima he had taken several more African wives). He had no intention of leaving Africa, though. He'd gotten the notion of starting a tourist hotel, a sort of African dude ranch, in the Ituri Forest, near Stanleyville, on the Epulu River. With the income from paying guests—scientists and big-game hunters—he could support his own continuing studies in anthropology and natural history.

In 1933 he married the American landscape architect, Mary Linder, and with her help he established Camp Putnam, on the Epulu. Staffed by twenty to forty Africans, it became famous for its "pygmy shows" and its okapis—shy forest giraffes. Putnam lived there for the rest of his life, with a series of three American wives, and various native ones whom he maintained concurrently. He died in 1953, at age forty-nine, following a prolonged struggle with emphysema, and intermittent bouts of madness.

The excerpt published here covers the period from 1945 to 1951, and describes the genesis of Putnam's single publication on the pygmies and the second flowering of Camp Putnam after World War II. Mary Putnam had died in 1937, and Putnam's second marriage had resulted in separation. During the war, his tourist hotel project was dormant while he supervised stepped-up rubber production in the Congo. When his father underwent surgery in 1944, he returned to America, and in the summer of 1945, as he waited for Dr. Putnam to recover, he finalized his divorce, hosted a lively house party at the family farm on Martha's Vineyard, and met and captivated Anne Eisner, the New York painter who would become his third wife. One member of the house party was Carleton Coon, the renowned anthropologist. Coon had studied with Putnam at Harvard, under Hooton, and like Hooton he was a believer in eugenics. Reluctantly Putnam allowed Coon to tap his knowledge about the pygmies. It was thanks to Coon that he published "The Pigmies of the Ituri Forest." Afterwards he felt that the collaborative essay misrepresented his ideas about the pygmies' culture and denigrated their intelligence.

Putnam returned to Epulu with Anne Eisner in 1946, to the delight of the Africans there. Alimony payments to his second wife and decreased support from his father had sharply reduced his personal income, and he had to look for new sources of money. His rift with Anne when she learned that he already had an African wife and his own failing health were additional obstacles that confronted him. Despite these problems, Camp Putnam thrived again for a few years, until Putnam's worsening already confined to a chair, and had to be carried, by the time Colin Turnbull, a young Scotsman, visited the camp in 1951. Turnbull was en route from India, where he had been studying music and philosophy. He was very taken with Putnam, and so fascinated with the pygmies, especially their music, that he went on to obtain a degree in anthropology.

Putnam's legacy to Anne Eisner Putnam and Colin Turnbull was the introduction he gave them to pygmy culture. Both drew on their experiences at Camp Putnam to write books after his death. In 1954 Anne published *Madami: My Eight Years of Adventure With the Congo Pygmies*. And in 1961, after returning to the forest several times to gather additional data, Turnbull published a best-selling classic about them, *The Forest People*.

What follows takes up Putnam's story from the time of his first collaborative efforts with Carleton Coon in the summer of 1945.

———

Carleton Coon, recognizing that Patrick Putnam was wooing Anne Eisner and was going to tell her about the pygmies, decided to make use of the situation. He suggested that he and Putnam collaborate on a work about pygmies as one way to get some of what Patrick Putnam knew into print. Putnam agreed enthusiastically. Coon gave him a list of ethnographic topics, and for several days Putnam talked and energetically acted out events in pygmy culture. Coon took all this down in longhand and typed it. Then he cut it up into topics, added information from Paul Schebesta (an acknowledged expert on the pygmies of the Ituri Forest), and wrote some interlinking commentary. The result was a 130-page manuscript that he titled "Pygmies of Africa" and bylined "Carleton S. Coon and Patrick Putnam." Coon sent it off to Patrick for approval.[1]

Putnam did not like it. He thought it hastily and sloppily done; he feared that its publication would preempt a book of his own, which he still intended to write; and he did not want his work merged with Schebesta's. He sent Coon a detailed criticism of a single chapter, "The Use of Drugs," going through it sentence by sentence, objecting to generalizations and amplifying them with long paragraphs of additional details. Then he wrote:

---

[1] The first draft of this manuscript (in Coon's papers in the NAA) has the typed transcript of what Putnam told Coon pasted on sheets to which Coon has added his own comments and information from Schebesta's published accounts of 1933 and 1937. From this first draft it is possible to see almost exactly what Putnam told him. It is this that Coon eventually published, with a few changes, in his General Reader, 1948.

Well, Carl, I hope I have made my point clear. It would take some time to get through your 53 chapter headings with such a fine-toothed and critical comb. What about it. We could:
1. Give the whole thing up.
2. Go through it chapter by chapter in this way and have it ready months from now.
3. Publish it without my name as collaborator, and citing me only for specific sentences, which sentences I could mark for you and get back to you in a couple of weeks.
Think it over, and let me know your decision.[2]

Coon immediately chose Option 3. He offered to publish under his own name a carefully edited version in which "facts stated and endorsed by Putnam," "statements quoted from Schebesta," and "connective material and deductions made by Coon" would each be clearly indicated.[3]

But Putnam could not agree to having his material published in a book written by a friend. The result was a stalemate, with Coon wanting to publish the manuscript and Putnam not answering his letters. "Shall I say, 'Published over the dead body of Patrick Putnam' or 'Published with Putnam's begrudging consent' or what is the least repulsive thing I can say that satisfies your scruples? PLEASE GIVE ME AN ANSWER," Coon wrote him in February 1946.[4] Putnam did not reply.

Nearly a year went by, and Coon tried again. He was editing a new source-book of anthropology for colleges, to be published by Henry Holt, and he begged to be allowed to use the pygmy manuscript. Coon promised to remove anything that Putnam considered controversial and to make it clear that this was only a sample of a large monograph to follow.[5]

Putnam, en route back to the Congo, finally agreed: . . . "my first tendency is to shout 'No.' But I am really getting slightly wiser as I get rapidly older (and may be wise enough to write by the time I'm sixty), and so I say 'Go ahead,'-give you carte blanche, in fact, and add only that if you think wise you might say 'by C.S. Coon, based on conversations with Patrick Putnam, who many years ago had anthropological training at Harvard and who has spent most of

[2] Putnam to Coon, Dec. 21, 1945, Coon Papers, National Anthropological Archives, Smithsonian Institution.

[3] Coon to Putnam, Dec. 24, 1945, Putnam Papers.

[4] Coon to Putnam, Feb. 14, 1946, Putnam Papers.

[5] Coon to Putnam, Jan. 14, 1947, Coon Papers.

the last 20 years at his place at Epulu in the Stanleyville Province of the Belgian Congo-that is to say, in almost daily contact with the teeming pigmy population of the Ituri Forest.' But if you don't like this, omit it, and, as I say, go ahead in any way you think best."[6]

With this grudging carte blanche in hand, Coon in turn was magnanimous. He removed most—but not all—of what he had added to his original transcriptions of what Putnam had told him on Martha's Vineyard and published the remainder as "The Pigmies of the Ituri Forest" with Patrick Putnam named as the sole author, and this disclaimer in a footnote: Putnam has been living with the people of whom he spoke for nearly two decades. He dictated to me a somewhat longer story of pygmy life, which I have condensed to its present compass. He went over the copy carefully and made corrections. He is not satisfied with it, and has gone back to learn more. Meanwhile he is willing to let you read what follows. This material has never before been published.[7]

Thus Carleton Coon had dragged Patrick Putnam willy-nilly into print. "The Pygmies of the Ituri Forest" was to be Putnam's only publication on the pygmies. He never liked it, for reasons that are understandable if one compares it with the original typescript. The twenty-page unpublished essay was a matter-of-fact, nonromantic, but rather charming and appreciative account of a rigorous way of life. It described how pygmy men climb a hundred feet up trees to get honey and to gather bark for cloth. Falling from high trees and being hit by falling tree trunks in a storm were among the major causes of death among pygmies, Putnam said, along with diseases such as pneumonia and dysentery. Unlike the villagers, who bathed often, pygmies disliked water and were usually dirty and full of lice. They were fond of smoking hashish, and some were addicted to it. They were skilled at stalking game in the forest but not good marksmen, at least the net hunters were not. According to Putnam, pygmy camps usually consisted of about twenty-five people and were governed by two factors: respect for older people, and the right of every man in the camp to state his views on any subject, with the "pungent remarks" of the women also having considerable influence.[8]

---

[6] Putnam to Coon, Kano, Feb. 7, 1949, Coon Papers.

[7] C.S. Coon, A Reader in General Anthropology. New York, Henry Holt and Co., 1948, p. 322. Coon continued to like his own twice-as-long version and gave a manuscript copy of it to the Peabody Museum Library in 1957.

[8] Ibid., p. 334.

Putnam suggested that it was unlikely that the pygmies had ever lived alone in the forest. He doubted that they could survive there without the iron-tipped arrows and hunting nets, as well as the plantains and other vegetable food, that they got from the villagers, although they did eat many products of the forest, including ibambi fruits and baselli nuts, wild vegetable foods, mushrooms, and "slow game"-small animals that do not move rapidly and can be caught by a woman or child, tossed in a back basket, and carried home. Putnam asserted that the traditional role of the pygmies had been to serve the villagers as scouts, intelligence agents, and soldiers in the forest; in return the villagers provided them with plantains, their major food, and with manufactured goods. The relationship was an ethnic caste system; the pygmies were "a genetically and occupationally segregated segment of a larger economic entity."[9] Since the Belgians had brought peace to the forest, the pygmies had only part of their bargain left to fulfill, the bringing of meat and honey from the forest, while the villagers continued to carry out all their traditional obligations. Thus Putnam thought that what looked like a bad bargain for the villagers was the result of a changed historical situation.

Coon kept in the published piece the historical changes in elephant hunting noted by Putnam: that it was incidental in the Ituri Forest until the traders began demanding ivory at the turn of the century, at which time some pygmy hunters developed elephant hunting as a specialty in order to please their village masters. But Coon omitted the more recent historical changes in the forest that Putnam had noted. Coon's version gave a timeless quality to the life of contemporary pygmies, instead of the ever-changing historical situation Putnam had described.

Even more serious than his omissions were Coon's added summary statements and irrelevant editorial comments. The effect *of many of these* interpolations was to denigrate the pygmies' intelligence, even to make them seem less than human, which was obviously contrary to Putnam's beliefs and intent. These sentences would later be singled out by Putnam's critics.[10]

Putnam's eagerness to be recognized as an expert on the pygmies had led him to cooperate with Carleton Coon. He knew that alone he would not write the great book he envisioned. Perhaps he knew

---

[9] Ibid., p. 328.

[10] See for example Jean-Pierre Hallet and Alex Pelle, Pygmy Kitabu. New York, Random House, 1973, p. 62.

---

that alone he could not do it. He was floundering in data and was so far removed from the academic world that he no longer knew, if he had ever known, what questions he should ask. But he had grown increasingly dubious about the collaboration with Coon and displeased with the result.

Around this time Putnam did write a ten-page personal manifesto to defend himself as a dilettante. Describing his personal philosophy as "veritas, and away with hypocritical camouflage," he continued:

Many years ago, when I went out to Central Africa as a young assistant on an anthropological expedition, I found the country pleasant and decided to stay there. I do not choose to speculate on the type of neurosis which made Central Africa seem to me pleasanter than the country where I was born and brought up. Once settled there, I have never stopped examining my environment. I have learned to speak one of the many native languages well; I have conversed with my native employees; I have had various native women as acting wives, relationships which have sometimes engendered considerable mutual affection. I have struck up friendships with Europeans of the most diverse occupations, doctors, Belgian district commissioners, Greek retail traders, German Catholic missionaries, Scottish Protestant missionaries, and many other varieties of resident white-men. With my late wife, Mary Linder, I built and operated a tourist camp, on one of the main automobile roads but fifty miles from the nearest white-man's residence, and there as paying guests have had Belgian financiers, globe trotting retired American whiskey manufacturers, German spies disguised as movie crews, an ex-English governor of the Punjab, etc. etc.

In the United States, each time I have revisited it I have spent considerable time in looking up the complementary knowledge which can be found in books, whether on early Portuguese, exploration of the Guinea Coast or on the interlocking directorates of huge diamond and palm-oil concerns which, between them, are the masters of the whole mid-continent.

After fifteen years I have learned how little I know, and wonder if my personal satisfaction would have been greater if I had become a world-recognized authority on some reasonably limited subject such as the subjunctive infixes in Bantu languages.

However, on the whole, I think I am glad that I have remained a dilettante. . . . [11]

---

[11] Putnam, draft of letter to unidentified correspondent, who had apparently inquired about Elisabethville, n.d., but c. 1946, Putnam Papers.

Patrick Putnam's renewed contact with his anthropological friends and former professor, after the wartime years of isolation in Africa, had not been easy. He found himself having to scale down his dreams and his self-image. The manifesto he wrote set forth the new persona he was trying to develop and be content with: the dilettante who was an all-around practical Africa expert.

In May of 1946, on the literal eve of his planned departure for Africa with his new companion, Anne Eisner, Patrick Putnam became ill with pneumonia. He recovered, and they sailed ten weeks later, but in the interim he had been diagnosed with emphysema, the disease that would confine him to a chair in just a few years, and eventually kill him. With failing health and a thin wallet, Putnam set out with Anne from New York. He knew that for the first time in his life he was going to have to use whatever resources he had, of knowledge or influence, for his own benefit. He decided to try to become an exporter of African raw materials and curios. While still in New York he contacted various importers and planned a route back to Epulu "hell bent on trade," as he wrote Carleton Coon.[12] He would look for derris root, an ingredient in insecticide; for piassava, a palm fiber used in making brooms; for rattan; for gangi, a substitute for chicle in chewing gum; for copal, an ingredient in varnishes and assorted leather goods; for snake skins, crocodile skins, and leopard hides; for arabica and robusta coffee.[13] He wanted to buy masks, for he intended to open a museum and a shop with masks and curios at Camp Putnam and also sell his best masks through the Knoedler Gallery in New York. He thought he might try again to write travel accounts for the popular press, and he asked Carl Coon if he would peddle them in New York.[14]

If he were to continue living in Africa, he would have to exploit it in some way. He could no longer choose to be above the fray, neither taking nor giving orders, as he had once expressed it. Patrick Putnam returned to the Congo in 1947 knowing sin, recognizing that with his white skin and European connections, he was among the powerful in Africa, and that by his very presence

[12] Putnam to Coon, Feb. 7, 1947, Coon Papers.

[13] Putnam to Wessel Duval and Co., 67 Broad Street, N.Y., July 21, 1948, Putnam Papers; Helen Gould ms, Anne Eisner Putnam Papers.

[14] Putnam to Coon, June 16, 1947, Putnam Papers.

there he was a beneficiary of colonialism. He had lost his innocence. He no longer thought he could live outside of history.

He saw the colonial situation ever more clearly as he became increasingly disillusioned with the United States and its Western allies. In Washington and elsewhere in the United States in 1945-46, Putnam was appalled at the discrimination directed against blacks and Jews. In lecture notes he prepared around this time, he wrote, "In all these years in Central Africa, two things have been most distasteful to me, one is Forced labor. *The other is* the Colour Bar." Forced labor he called "a subject with which I've had only too much contact during my African years," and on the color bar, "Social discrimination seems to me to be a worse thing for the happiness of the world's people than political..." His notes go on to say that he "went out there long ago with the feeling that natives are natives and in all these years have learned one big thing and that is that they are people differently brought up from us, to be sure, but nevertheless people.... Africa is a wonderful place for thinking objec*tively* and for seeing soc. ineq. and miserable bitterness it eng*enders*."[15] The "miserable bitterness" he had observed in Africa was a product of the same social prejudice he had found in the United States.

The arrangement that Patrick Putnam had made with Anne Eisner was carefully casual. She was to travel to the Congo with him in order to make more paintings of the Ituri Forest and to see whether she liked living in Africa. Anne paid for her passage by offering sales in advance of the paintings she would do there, mostly to family and friends.

They left New York on July 28, 1946, aboard the tramp steamer, M.V Freetown, with different expectations. Anne was following the man she loved; she would have gone anywhere with him. That it was the Ituri Forest toward which they were heading was irrelevant. She had been promised a marvelous sightseeing trip across Africa along the way, and to her it was almost a honeymoon. With a last-minute gift from her parents of $1,000, they planned to buy African art en route.

Patrick, on the other hand, was heading back to Camp Putnam, which he knew he could no longer afford to support and where, unknown to Anne, he had an African wife (Mada) waiting for him. For him the trip across Africa was not just a sightseeing and art-buying sojourn but also a business trip on which he hoped

---

[15] Putnam, scraps of lecture notes, c. 1945, Putnam Papers.

to establish trade relations with producers of agricultural products and manufacturers of African goods. Anne was a timid traveler and disliked being left alone even for an hour or two. When Patrick returned from an appointment, distracted with business worries that he did not particularly want to share, she would chide him for being moody. To add to their difficulties, they were both frequently ill, Anne experiencing her first African infections, and Patrick having recurrences of old and serious illnesses. Their six-month journey across Africa stretched into a year. At every stop Patrick gathered information on importing and exporting.

They moved through several worlds, from the court of an African Muslim ruler, to villagers dancing in the bush, to English and Scottish colonels drinking gin on a hotel terrace. Patrick had little patience with the pomp and protocol of local rulers, and in an audience before the Oba in Benin he did all the talking (the obverse of the usual procedure) and declined brusquely an offer to be shown the shrine to the Oba's ancestors, saying he did not have time.[16] His disdain for authority included black rulers as well as white.

In February, on the border of the Belgian Congo, they discovered that Patrick's passport had expired and were forced to wait in Libenge for months until a new one arrived. To pass the time they made frequent visits to a nearby pygmy village, and they were there during a three-minute eclipse of the sun. Putnam had told the pygmies that the sun was going to be sick, hinting that it was because they were not bringing him enough meat. The pygmies watched disbelieving as it got dark. As it began to get light again, Putnam stood up and walked away in triumph. It was the sort of dramatic performance he loved, where he could pretend to be an all-knowing and all-powerful person, Patrick Putnam, King of the World, as he had written long ago in his geography text on Martha's Vineyard.[17] It did not matter that his kingdom was only one small pygmy village and one admiring American woman.

Their two-car caravan drove into Epulu on the evening of August 23, 1947. Patrick had been away from Camp Putnam for almost three years, since December 1944, when he had been called home by his father's illness.

He wanted Anne to see the local pygmies immediately, for

---

[16] Anne Eisner, "Benin Page" *also* "Thanksgiving", loose sheet, Anne Eisner Putnam Papers.

[17] Anne to Colin, April 15, 1957; Anne, notebook, journey to Epulu; Anne to Denis, Sept. 22, 1947, all in Anne Eisner Putnam Papers.

it was his friendship with them that had made him famous. The first morning at Camp Putnam they had themselves carried out to the pygmy village in tepoys decorated with leaf fans and hibiscus flowers and in a procession with drums and rattles beating time as the bearers sang. The African workers and tepoy bearers had replaced their assorted Western clothes with brightly colored lengths of cloth tied around their loins, and they wore basketlike caps decorated with feathers. "Putunami" was back. It seemed to Anne that everyone—villagers and pygmies alike—adored him.[18] In typical Putnam fashion he turned his homecoming into a gala performance and a party for all. But the procession of tepoys had a darker side. It masked the fact that his health had worsened and that it was difficult for him to walk even the few kilometers to the pygmy village. In earlier days he would have scorned to be carried.

They settled in at Camp Putnam. Anne wrote to one friend, "The place is just magnificent, my idea of Paradise, except for the biting ants."[19] To another friend she complained, "This place is magnificent and Pat is in his element bossing fifty people around. He's also so busy I hardly ever see him, in fact I miss him, after being with him almost every minute for the last two years."[20]

Then the reason for some of his absences appeared: his African wife. There was turmoil at Camp Putnam as Mada Gobaneka returned to live there, and Patrick began publicly to show his affection for her. Mada was thirty-two years old. She had joined Patrick Putnam's household when she was fifteen, while he was still at Panga.[21] Patrick was back in his African world, his African kingdom, where he was virtually chief of an African village and had an African wife. Anne found herself being treated as a casual acquaintance, a European guest at Camp Putnam.

She was torn apart in anger, indignation, and embarrassment and was no longer sure she was even welcome at Epulu. Was she just a summer romance who had hung on too long and was now spoiling his life? But she had not come all this way simply to turn around and leave. What ought she to do? Should she travel

---

[18] Anne Eisner Putnam, notebook, criticisms of Allen Keller's MS, p. 28, 1953, Anne Eisner Putnam Papers.

[19] Anne to "Charlotte" [Klonis], Nov. 8, 1947, Anne Eisner Putnam Papers.

[20] Anne to "Via" [Wood], n.d. but 1947, Anne Eisner Putnam Papers.

[21] Mada's year of birth, 1915, from a medical report sheet for her, diagnosing bronchitis, etc., date 3-10-50, signed P. Putnam, Agent Sanitaire, in Putnam Papers. Putnam's notes on a visit to the caves in 1931 show that Mada was a member of his household.

on through Africa, perhaps to Ruanda, by herself? Should she head back home? Or should she stay? Too embarrassed to return immediately to New York but too timid to travel on by herself, Anne decided to stay for a few months and do the paintings she had been commissioned to do. But she could not continue to live at Camp Putnam. Never one to hide her feelings, she directed acid barbs at Pat and at Mada. Camp Putnam, which had seemed Paradise, became the scene of constant unhappiness and tension. She had no friends among the colonials to whom she could turn— they were all Pat's friends. But she could go into the forest—with the pygmies, and that is what she did.

In January 1948, Anne Eisner headed off into the forest with the official Camp Putnam band of pygmies. In a clearing they built her a hut of leaves that was slightly larger than the huts they built for themselves. The group was led by Faizi, a quietly authoritative man about thirty-seven years old who loved dancing. It included Andonata, short, funny, and vulgar; his outspoken wife Bassalinde; and their two children, an older daughter and a son, Teliabo Kenge, who was eight or nine years of age and the leader of the children. It also included Herafu, whom Anne called the most sensitive and graceful of the pygmies.[22] Herafu had a motheaten notebook that he had bought at the market and carried around with him, often upside down. One day in camp after much vacillation he brought it over to Anne, who wondered what philosophical thoughts she might be asked to write down. Herafu pulled his chair up next to hers and, looking very serious, said in Kingwana (which she was just beginning to understand), "Madami, will you please write in my book that each time a white man takes my picture I want one franc."[23]

When Faizi's band of pygmies returned after a month (their usual stay in the forest), Anne went off with a second group, Cefu's band, which belonged officially to a nearby Bira (Bantu) village on the other side of the Epulu River whose chief was Saboni. They preferred Camp Putnam, however, and eventually moved in and built themselves a mud village next to Faizi's.[24] A month later, around the first of March, Anne returned to find that Patrick had gone to Stanleyville on business for an indefinite period.

[22] Anne to William J. and Florine Eisner, Jan. 28, 1948, Anne Eisner Putnam Papers.

[23] Anne to Pat, Feb. 25, 1948, Putnam Papers; also Anne to family, Feb. 16, 1948, Anne Eisner Putnam Papers.

[24] Anne to Allan, Aug. 23, 1953, Oct. 28, 1953, Anne Eisner Putnam Papers.

With Patrick away, Anne lingered at Camp Putnam, uncertain what to do next. She studied Kingwana and practiced it with the workers.[25] Several groups of expected visitors came for extended stays, among them a British duke and duchess, a French film crew, and Alfred Emerson, a termite specialist from the University of Chicago, and his wife. Emerson discovered many new species of termites and named two of them for Anne (*Odontotermes annae*) and the absent Patrick (*Microtermes putnami*).[26] Anne wrote Patrick cool letters; he wrote her warm, affectionate ones, encouraging her to serve as hostess at the hotel and trying to make everything all right between them. He had moved on from Stanleyville to Leopoldville, to look into the possibility of exporting derris root (for insecticides) and arabica coffee. He was not sure when he would return to Epulu. "I can't face it, I can't face it, I can't face it," he admitted. "For, except for those wonderful first three weeks or so, our time together at the Epulu has been, shall we say, not very pleasant, or, shall we say, Hell."[27]

Finally, in an unusually crisp and cool letter after he had been away for three months, Patrick offered resolution: he invited Anne to fly to Leopoldville, where he would marry her on the condition that she accept the situation at Epulu.[28] Anne agreed ecstatically in a letter addressed to "Dearest, dearest Pat."[29] At Epulu she and Mada drank a glass of beer together, pledged to cease quarreling, and arranged to share Patrick equally—one week with one, one week with the other. With this understanding, Anne Eisner flew to Leopoldville. On July 26, 1948, the anniversary of the date they had met in 1945 and of the date they had finally sailed for Africa in 1946, she and Patrick Putnam were married in the office of the mayor.

Camp Putnam now became Anne's home. She had her own separate house there, as did Mada. Anne threw herself into the life of the community. She was incessantly curious about the people and their lives, and she loved to argue with them. She learned Kingwana, but she always spoke it badly. Gradually a few of her linguistic errors crept into the general parlance at Camp Putnam.[30]

---

[25] Anne Eisner Putnam with Allan Keller, *Madami: My Eight Years of Adventure with the Congo Pigmies*, New York, Prentice-Hall, 1954, pp. 50, 60, 173.

[26] P. Putnam to William Mann, Sept. 14, 1948, Putnam Papers, Peabody Museum Archives.

[27] P. Putnam to Anne Eisner, April 24, 1948, Leopoldville, Putnam Papers.

[28] P. Putnam to Anne, May 29, 1948, Putnam Papers.

[29] Anne to Pat, June 5, 1948, Putnam Papers.

[30] Merlyn Severn, *Congo Pilgrim*, London, Museum Press Ltd., 1952, pp. 1787–184.

The Africans called her Madami ya Kaleli, which means the lady of lots of noise.[31] The nickname may just have been a reference to her exuberant spirit, but more likely it was an amused comment on her first months at Camp Putnam, for one African expression for the situation of a woman discovering her husband's infidelity is "a lot of noise." The pygmies remained Anne's special interest, as they had been from her first days there. In Leopoldville after their marriage, Pat quizzed her at length about her experiences in pygmy camps, and he had his temporary secretary, a Gold Coast clerk, type up some notes she had taken. From the library he got for her Schebesta's two books in English, and as a wedding present they bought themselves the first two volumes of Schebesta's major work on the pygmies, which was in German. Patrick read parts of it to Anne, and they compared her experiences with what Schebesta described.[32] Patrick Putnam could be selfish, but he could also be generous, and he wanted his new wife to love Africa as much as he did. He began to speak of her as a pygmy expert, and the pygmy camps in the forest continued to be her refuge—a place to go whenever life at Camp Putnam got to be too much for her.

Marriage didn't solve the problem of how Patrick and Anne were going to support themselves in their African home. Putnam continued to look for ways to make money. Among other things, he encouraged the production of crafts at Epulu. One of his employees, Pascall, made ivory carvings, mostly statues and chess pieces, for sale to visitors, and a forger (ironworker) settled at Epulu and made knives and arrow points.[33] His attempts to export African goods and products fizzled completely, though. The American market for African raw materials was a seller's market in 1945, but prices dropped as soon as the war was over and supplies of rubber, derris root, and plant fibers again became available from the Far East. Putnam was operating in a wide-open frontier where the winners were those who were swift, single-minded, and competitive, and he was none of those things. Importers in New York who had expected to hear from him in Stanleyville in six months lost interest when he did not write them for a year. Meanwhile more experienced entrepreneurs simply leased plantations, bought up available supplies, and established a monopoly over a product, leaving the details of production to others.

---

[31] Ibid, p. 184.

[32] Anon., "Outsider" (Colin Turnbull interview), *The New Yorker*, 42: 26-7, Aug. 20, 1966.

[33] Anne to Helen, Sept. 11, 1950, Anne Eisner Putnam Papers.

Putnam tried exporting African handcrafts such as masks, ivory and ebony statuettes, woven raffia table mats, and small musical instruments. But each piece had to be bargained for individually, for he could not find a reliable supplier of large quantities of high-quality goods, and his shipping was amateurish. He had similar difficulties when he tried to export animals: live ones to zoos and dead ones and skeletons to scientific researchers.

Putnam was torn between his need to earn money and his desire to be a colleague, generous host, and friend. He would let impecunious travelers who interested him live at Epulu for weeks and sometimes months for the cost of their food. He wanted to sell masks to museums or to Knoedler's, but he could not resist sending one of his best Ba Yaka ones as a gift to the Peabody Museum in 1948 in honor of his friend J. O. Brew's appointment as director of the museum.

Patrick's father urged him to stay home and save money instead of spending a fortune traveling around trying to make money, and Patrick finally acceded to the wisdom of this view. He had gone to Leopoldville in 1948 expecting to make a fortune exporting *Urene lobata* (for billiard balls), he admitted to friends, but instead spent every cent he had. He also knew that, due to his worsening health, the days of his grand journeys through parts of Africa or anywhere else, for that matter, were over.

As Putnam's illness progressed, he ironically found himself doing more and more hospital work. This, finally, was the source of additional income. A government medical mission visited Camp Putnam in 1949 and, liking what they saw, offered to make it an official dispensary under the Congo's new Ten-Year (health) Plan. Putnam was supplied with medicines and paid medical aides and given a stipend of $40 a month. The money was welcome, but the official status and abundant medicines meant an ever-increasing load of patients. The staff were soon giving a hundred injections a day, mostly for gonorrhea, syphilis, and yaws, all very common in the area. They also treated sleeping sickness, bilharziasis, trachoma, typhoid, and paratyphoid.

The hotel, averaging about two guests per day, continued to bring in some money—mostly for the workers who ran it, with a small amount going to the Putnams for maintenance—but business was very uneven. Anne served as hostess at the hotel, but Patrick was the authority. That was always his role at Camp Putnam.

Increasingly, Putnam was called upon to arbitrate disputes among the people at Epulu and the surrounding area. He had a fair knowledge of the local languages, and he understood the varying customs of the different peoples and could decide what was fair. They came too to talk to him about government directives. Should they plant more cotton, as they were being told to do? Putnam would set out the pros and cons as he saw them, so they could make up their own minds. The local Belgian administrators were not always comfortable, either with his popularity or with his free-thinking.[34]

When Putnam started a school for the village children at Epulu, the girls refused to attend, but the boys came and learned to count and to read and write in Kingwana. Classes were held at the hotel or outside under a tree, and the teacher was Lukamba, a mission-trained employee. The boys had slates, and Lukamba used chalk on a blackboard made from a hammered-out gasoline drum. He and Putnam had long arguments on whether learning by rote (which he favored) or by doing (which Putnam favored) was the better way. Lukamba was also put in charge of a *hotel des chauffeurs* that Patrick had his workmen build. It was a simple affair—two rooms, a veranda, and a cookhouse across from an old garage—but it provided a place where the native drivers who accompanied tourists could sleep and eat.[35]

Putnam's control over the pygmies was no greater than that of any of their other patrons. The pygmies went back and forth, playing their masters off against one another. When they tired of entertaining visitors at Camp Putnam, they would go visit Ngoma and Pakalili in Kopo's village until those two patrons got tired of feeding them. Then they would return to Camp Putnam. They brought meat when it suited them. For a time, when Moke was serving as the leader of a pygmy camp, he turned against the Europeans and for weeks refused to bring the Putnams any meat from the forest.

When nothing much else was happening, Putnam would create excitement. He had an old bicycle fixed up, and dozens of people at Camp Putnam learned how to ride, with roars of laughter every time anyone fell and with many requests for bandages and iodine. He sent to the United States for balls, bats, and mitts and, when they arrived, spent one Sunday afternoon teaching the men at Camp Putnam to play softball. His employees seemed to enjoy it, but at the end of the aftemoon they wanted to be paid for a

---

[34] Interview, Colin Turnbull, April 8, 1987.

[35] Helen Gould MS, Anne Eisner Putnam Papers.

half-day's work.[36] It was 1950, and the colonial world in Africa was coming to an end much more rapidly than anyone, including Putnam, realized.

Anne was involved in virtually every aspect of Camp Putnam, but her presence was felt most strongly in the art activity at Epulu, the planning and service of the hotel meals, and the pygmy shows, which became her particular specialty. Anne had instigated much of the Putnams' collecting of African art, and gradually the second room of her house, originally her studio, was transformed into a museum. After they had seen her painting and sketching, the pygmies took greater care with the paintings on their bark cloth, and the villagers began to carve figures and decorate their pipes. All this was new at Epulu.[37]

Guests at the hotel commented on the excellent and imaginative table that Anne set. First came drinks in the living room around the central fireplace, and then dinner in the open dining room overlooking the river. Dinner might be chicken broth, freshly caught fish, antelope stew with wine, boiled and riced manioc, hearts of palm salad, local coffee, and pineapple, papaya, and passion fruit. One of her specialties was a whiskey–hot pepper sauce made from the Duchess de Ligne's recipe. For hot baths she provided an Abercrombie and Fitch canvas shower bucket donated by Prince Ferdinand of Liechtenstein: the canvas bucket with a shower head on the bottom, filled with warm water and suspended from the sapling frame of a mongongo leaf enclosure, offered an excellent shower.[38]

But Anne's greatest contribution to Camp Putnam was her discovery of the special pygmy world in the forest. Feeling abandoned and humiliated after her arrival at Camp Putnam, for two months she had lived in the forest with the pygmies, and in so doing she experienced the pygmy world in a way that Patrick Putnam never had. He readily admitted as much. In 1949 he wrote to a would-be visitor: "I have lived in the Ituri forest a long time, and liked it, but have found so many things of interest in it that I have never become an authority on any one of them. My present wife, in a stay of a year, saw more of the pigmies 'at home' than I

---

[36] Anne to family, March 4, 1950, Jan. 29, 1951, April 11, 1951, Anne Eisner Putnam Papers.

[37] Helen Gould MS, Anne Eisner Putnam Papers.

[38] Oden Meeker, "The Safari Industry," *Harper's Magazine*, Oct. 1955, p. 48, pp. 47–52; Tay and Lowell Thomas, Jr., "Flight to Adventure," *National Geographic*, July 1957, 59–64, 73; also Wright and Jones in *True Magazine*.

have in twenty years." Putnam urged his potential guest to follow her example: "If you want the pigmies called in, that is perfectly feasible, but rather dull. If you want to go out to their camp and accompany them on one of their net-hunts, that is much better. Best of all is to take the folding beds and other equipment, and go out and sleep for a night or two in the pigmy encampment."[39]

When visitors chose, as most of them did, simply to observe the pygmy demonstration and perhaps also to go net hunting, Anne took charge. In a clearing down along the Epulu River the pygmies demonstrated the building of their leaf huts, setting up camp, making bark cloth, and tree climbing. In the evening there were songs and dancing, and the next day they went net hunting. To see it all required a stay of two full days and three nights, and some advance notice, since the pygmies would have to be summoned if they were far off in the forest.

The pygmies were sensitive to an audience's reactions and varied their performances accordingly so that no two shows were ever the same. It was amusing for them and for Anne, as well as for the visitors. They tried to outdo one another, and they were wonderful mimics. After some visitors from Argentina had been at Camp Putnam, the pygmies added the samba to their dances. But Anne insisted, as Patrick always had, on as much authenticity as possible in the pygmy shows.

In 1950 Merlyn Severn, an English journalist, was on her way to Mambasa with her driver and a servant when they were delayed by rain. Severn "remembered hearing about an eccentric American couple who conducted a holiday camp in the depths of the forest somewhere along this road," and when she saw the Camp Putnam sign they turned in. She found Patrick Putnam reclining in a lounge chair beside the fire in the living room of his house. His greeting was kindly but vague, and he immediately went back to the animated conversation he had been having with several Africans. When Patrick Putnam was not interested in a visitor, or had other things on his mind, he could be the most distant of human beings. Eventually, Severn was rescued by Anne Putnam, who made her feel welcome and offered to show her around.[40]

Anne told Severn that some recent well-known photographs of pygmies building a bridge of lianas over the river were fake because the photographer had told the pygmies what to do. She

[39] Pat to anon. [can't read], March 1, 1949, Putnam Papers.

[40] Merlyn Severn, *Congo Pilgrim*. London, Museum Press Ltd., 1952, pp. 1787–184.

recounted other frustrations with visitors. Later that night Anne Putnam urged Severn to stay for a few days, to go into the forest with the pygmies, live with them in a traditional leaf hut, and photograph their hunting and cooking. Merlyn Severn declined this suggestion, but Colin Turnbull, who arrived at Camp Putnam shortly thereafter, did go into the forest to live with the pygmies, and he wrote a best-selling book about them.

Colin M. Turnbull first arrived at Camp Putnam in April 1951. He was twenty-seven years old and on his way home to Scotland from India, where he had spent two years studying Indian music and philosophy. He was traveling with Newton Beal, a young musician and music teacher from Ohio. They took deck passage on a boat from Bombay to Mombasa, where they were met by Sir Charles Markham, the local agent of the international accounting firm for which Turnbull's father worked.[41] Markham advised them to get out of Kenya because of the Mau Mau unrest. He bought Turnbull new clothes, lent him money to buy a motorcycle, and suggested that in the Congo they look up a man he had known when he went hunting there, saying, "His name's Putnam. He's your kind of person. He likes the natives."[40]

Crossing Africa on their motorcycle, Colin Turnbull and Newton Beal saw the Camp Putnam sign on the road through the Ituri Forest and turned off, intending merely to spend the night. They pulled up in front of the large thatched mud house that was the hotel and suddenly found themselves surrounded by pygmies who were pointing at the motorcycle, talking, and laughing. The two travelers were startled, not by the pygmies' small size, for that they scarcely noticed at first, but by their large bright eyes looking directly into the visitors' faces as they talked, and by their serious demeanor alternating with shrieks of laughter. Turnbull and Beal stood there uncomfortably until Anne Putnam came out of the house to welcome them, happy to have visitors to talk to.

By 1951 Patrick Putnam was no longer the enthusiastic hunter he once had been. When he learned that Turnbull, although having

---

[41] Anon., "Outsider" (Colin Turnbull interview), The New Yorker, 42: 26–7, Aug. 20, 1966.

[40] Interview with Colin M. Turnbull, April 8, 1987. All remaining quotations are from this interview. Other sources for biographical information on Turnbull are Colin M. Turnbull, The Human Cycle, New York, Simon and Schuster, 1983 and The New Yorker interview (fn. 41).

come at the suggestion of a big-game hunter, was himself a student of Indian philosophy and a vegetarian, he was interested and opened up immediately. To Turnbull and Beal it was a startling experience to meet Patrick Putnam in the depths of the Ituri Forest. He seemed the prototypical proper Bostonian, still young-looking but immobile in his chair. They were interrogated politely and then welcomed as academic peers and given glimpses of his intellect and his ideas. They immediately got into a discussion of Indian philosophy and then music. Putnam said, "Oh, you've got to stay here. There's some of the richest music here, and no one has done any work on it." He offered to let the two young men live free in one of the small circular huts near the hotel and buy their food at cost.

Putnam talked first about village music, explaining the different styles of the Lese, the Bira, the Nguana, and the other tribal peoples who made up Camp Putnam, and what kinds of stringed instruments they had. Pygmy music in the forest, he said, was very different from what it was in the village. The pygmies agreed: after Turnbull had filled a notebook and a half with transcriptions of the songs they sang around Camp Putnam, they announced that that was not their real music. They told him that if he wanted to hear their real music, he would have to go into the forest with them.

Putnam made the same suggestion offhandedly. It was what Anne had urged much more overtly on Merlyn Severn. Newton Beal declined, but Colin Turnbull did go into the forest to a pygmy camp, and he was overwhelmed by the experience: "The first night out my mind was blown by what I heard! The comparison that came to my mind was some of the really great organ music that you hear in some of the better cathedrals in England." Turnbull was eventually able to distinguish four pitch collections used by the pygmies. He also found that they sing in parallel seconds and in hocket, where a melodic line is divided up so that each singer has only one note. Then they sing the same as a canon that overlaps so that everyone has two notes. They exchange notes by eye contact, saying in effect, as they look across at someone and blink their eyelids, "You take my note, I'll take yours." He found the pygmies' music spatially and structurally as complex as the forest itself.

Music had been Colin Turnbull's first choice as a profession. He studied organ at Worcester Cathedral while still in boarding school, but at an early date he decided that he was not good enough to have a satisfying career as a musician. At Oxford he concentrated on politics, economics, and philosophy. Then he went to Benares University on a two-year fellowship to study Hindu and Buddhist philosophy, for which the study of Indian music was a prerequisite. In heading home through Africa it was his stay at Camp Putnam, and particularly what Patrick Putnam told him about pygmy music, that started him on his career as an anthropologist.

The residents at Camp Putnam were as taken with Turnbull as he was with them. In many ways he seemed to be a twenty-years-younger version of Patrick Putnam. He was tall and thin, with a reddish beard and an engaging, outgoing personality of great charm. Behind that lay a quick, inquiring mind and something of a rebel spirit. That he was well educated they discerned immediately from his interests and his careful and precise use of language. He was also good with his hands and liked to tinker with cars, as did Putnam. And he was adventurous. He went often into the forest with the pygmies, and this became a special bond between him and Patrick Putnam, who, no longer able to go himself, wanted Turnbull to give him an exact description after each visit, of everything he had seen, heard or found. Sometimes Putnam would ask Turnbull to look in the forest for a particular kind of mushroom or plant that he was curious about.

Colin and Newton were supposed to have their own meals cooked for them, but Patrick invited them to dinner so often that it became a habit. He would grandly produce a bottle of whiskey or some imported Swiss cheese, items that Anne would hint they could ill afford. Then, after Turnbull and Beal had been there for several weeks and had exhausted their funds, Putnam told them that he wanted to build a dam across the Nepusi River. He offered to hire them for an African wage, enough to buy food, if they would supervise the construction. They accepted. Not until several years later did Colin learn from Anne that the dam had been a pretext, a spur-of-the-moment inspiration, because Patrick liked having the young men there and wanted to keep them around as long as possible.

The Nepusi was the small stream that ran between the hotel and the infirmary. Putnam had been having his employees carry him across the stream every day, stepping from one boulder to another. His excuse for the dam was that it would be safer to cross on a high dry bank. Once the dam was built and the water behind it had reached a level he liked, Putnam decided to try a hydroelectric project. He had the young men make a sluice gate in the dam, and he and Turnbull invented a kind of paddlewheel and rigged it up to a generator found on an old bicycle and a three-volt bulb. Putnam loved mechanical projects like these that required a certain logic and inventiveness. In great triumph they got the flow of water to produce a glow in the light bulb.

After the dam was finished, Putnam invented another project. Anne's old Chevy coupe had broken down and been abandoned in Stanleyville several years before. Putnam asked Turnbull if he would go to Stanleyville, repair it, and drive it back. Turnbull hitched a ride to Stanleyville on a passing truck. There he found the old car, put in a new battery and a few other parts, and got it going again.

In Stanleyville, Turnbull happened to meet a then relatively unknown post office employee named Patrice Lumumba. Turnbull had gone into an African bar and ordered a drink. When he was told they could not serve him, someone in the room called out, "Give him a drink," implying that though it was illegal to sell him a drink, it was not illegal to give him one. Glass in hand, Turnbull sat down next to a man playing a *mekembi* (thumb piano). The African noticed that he was listening intently and asked him in Kingwana if he could play it. Turnbull replied, "Yes, but not the way you've tuned it." The African handed it over, and when Turnbull had re-tuned it and started playing, he burst into guffaws of laughter. "That's how the pygmies play it!" he roared. He took it back and re-tuned it. "This is how the Tetela tune it. Now isn't that better?" Turnbull disagreed, and they argued back and forth for a few minutes. Then Patrice Lumumba introduced himself. He had seen Turnbull at the post office in Stanleyville, where he worked as a clerk, and he knew that Turnbull was staying out at Camp Putnam, because that was where his mail was being sent. Lumumba indicated approval and respect for Putnam, implying that he was one of the few Europeans around who cared about Africans.

On the final day of their visit, which had stretched into two months, Turnbull and Beal got ready to take off again on their motorcycle. Patrick, at work at the hospital across the Nepusi, where he directed the activities of his aides from his chair, challenged Turnbull to drive his motorcycle across the narrow dam they had built. Turnbull had misgivings, but he made it across. When he got to the hospital, Putnam stood up (the first time Turnbull had ever seen him standing), took four steps to the motorcycle, climbed on, and, gasping for breath from this exertion, told Turnbull to drive him back over the dam. Turnbull did so, to the great jubilation of the villagers who had gathered. Putnam's aides came running across the dam with his chair, and he collapsed into it on the other side, as Turnbull and Beal drove off. It was the kind of performance Putnam loved: a celebration of their visit, a triumphal farewell, and a way of avoiding sentiment.

Colin Turnbull and Newton Beal saw Patrick Putnam at the height of his greatness. He was no longer the cocksure but appealing vulnerable young man whose wealth, family position, charm, and talents all seemed to set him apart from the rest of the world. Thirty-five years later, Turnbull reflected on Patrick Putnam: "One of the best things that he's done... was simply as a foreigner in the forest, living all those years there, making a better name for us Europeans than any colonial administrator ever could." Turnbull added, "I mean that man was just so loved in the forest. And because of him, I was accepted."

*Ruth
Ellen
Kocher*

Ruth Ellen Kocher is this issue's Tom McAfee Discovery Feature poet. Her work has appeared in several magazines, including *Gettysburg Review, Antioch Review* and *African American Review.*

The Tom McAfee Discovery Feature is a continuing series to showcase the work of an outstanding young poet who has not yet published a book. The prize is funded by the family and friends of Tom McAfee.

PRINCIPLE / *Ruth Ellen Kocher*

Archimedes eats an apple and writes again. The volume of
    water
displaced by a body is not equal to what we assume
the mass of that body to be, but all the simple limbs,
the ribcage, the fingers spread out in ripples.

A sixty-pound girl would fill two buckets if she sat in a tub,
filled to the place where porcelain lips to a curve.

This girl is impatient, hair spilled over her eyes.
Perhaps, somewhere, she is expected. She hurries.
A crayfish, a rock, foot sliding in a stream,
the splash forking her leg.
She is the dream of a man,
a long beard, dropping pound weights
into vats of water, the overflow caught in tins
and weighed, measured, spilled again.
He hesitates, barefoot on granite, pools of water
swelling the dead skin on his toes,
pauses in the draft running over him,
but finally throws the last weight upward,
as he might toss a child, a small girl
into a pool, arcing the body first toward the sky
where form blackens to shadow, eyes
committed to memory, the nose, the ear
immersed in deep water loss of the whole.

THE FIRST MONSOON / *Ruth Ellen Kocher*

—for A.K.

Last week in Mostar, the fields were emptied.
The shot cows stiffened on their round backs,
balancing sky on the cleft angle of their hooves,
a sky that, all the while, sent clouds
into blue corners. This is not the story
of a woman in love or a girl who wakes beside herself
at 8:00 as the desert already enters her room.
Yes, a spine of ivy does rake the sun into splinters
that spell a name, then twist shadow into a girl,
but her mouth is dim and blind, comfortable
with closeness and being, full of her tongue.

The farmers killed outside of Travnik
did not know that today, the first monsoon would tear
the palm fronds into fringes while I heard you
breathe long vowels of mourning. I have lied again
to tell the story right. Imagine the limes which are green
but not ready to eat. The first fiber under the skin
could be stone, could be the grey promise of another
long season, the acacia already spent in heat,
the air waiting to break in thunder over the brown backs
of migrants who've caravaned up from the south.
They hang lanterns on their ladders, work the opal-deep
    dreams
of their children, filling baskets suspended on their hips,
remembering with one orange the smell of their grandmother's
    robe,
with another, the coffee for lunch, remembering words
swallowed with wafers, wine, with each orange layer
peeled back to fathers whose cigars were sweet-smelling,
the lover whose name has drifted into another grove, the
    wife, her
hair rich with mines and lemon. They don't know
the high peaks of Alaska where the glaciers
recognize your posture, cold against the cliffs.

They don't know the day of three mornings and one dream,
and three wakings which has brought you here to my house,
to my peppers hanging and the piano holding my whole life
in frames with faces smiling as though they know
something we should know of the women leveled this week
in their gardens near fresh winter radish.

In a pond near Mostar, three geese have found
a way to live through the silence all around them.
They are waiting for the United Nations' trucks
to bring them corn and white bread sent from America.
They are waiting for the summer and the end of the summer
when they leave and wait to be found by an accident
of direction, by a fluctuation of wind that began
a hemisphere away, the order of their movement
started in a storm east of where they've never been.
These are your figures twisted into a mortem pose,
emerged from your touch on the counter, the glass,
the bowl that is clear and empty
around both of our names.

GUSTAV'S ARC / *Ruth Ellen Kocher*

The old man who rides his bike around the neighborhood
has finally come to take the cans away
down a road that leads to the rest
of this small city,
dwarfed by large towns
to the west
which hug the earth's plate from the angry Pacific fault
all the way to cliffs craning up from the sea.
The waves there move as if they had no other shore to hold,
nothing balancing the other hemisphere
that spreads in mountains like knuckles
over the globe,
beneath an atmosphere paling in its own loneliness,
and too many miles away to comfort a raging Jupiter
who was once happy beyond the red eye of his storm
but now defeated and solemn, misses one
of the girls who's left him there,
one of his restless moons.

DROWNING / *Ruth Ellen Kocher*

It must have happened in the blue air
filtered into a summer night
so many years ago that no one
remembers
the green circle of algae
defining a pond's edge, an old boat
helpless against a steady rocking
that breathes a creak into her oars.
Every woman in my family
knows this fearful memory of water,
high weeds around the water shed,
a small perch,
backwards floating belly-up
in cattails,
the ancient drowning
stealing into each new year when the wet smell of
    growth
comes downstream weaving moss and lichen out of
    rock.
No one remembers.
Evenings, in the shock of sun
that spills last over a valley, you can hear
voices calling to some child stumbling near water
lost in the dizzying
revolutions of early years when blue choda
and coltsfoot clutter smaller worlds in deep soil,
June bugs and cicadas working their way
out of sleep
into an almost suffocating wind,
suffering the deep churning of age.
Not a fear of water, but a knowledge
of the lives inside, of their grandmothers
who couldn't swim, and all the obedient daughters
with our discipline of stones.

FEBRUARY LEAVING / *Ruth Ellen Kocher*

There was a thick summer.
There were cicadas and rows of grave markers,
mothers knitting and grandmothers
weaving their fading thoughts into combs of silver hair,
lightning bugs lost and flagging the woods,
homes that whispered to each other at midnight
the truth from their cellars,
three hundred arthritic joints creaking.
I could say that none of this lives in us
because at night there are fewer hands
to wind the air into our pockets,
that bats are nervous in their temporary waking;
I can tell you that the grass sorrows
if there is no thunder or the earth shudders
where people sleep or the mountains mouth
their wishes silently into snow.

The truth is, in winter, the earth rejects us.

What do you say with memory—
that the continents long for each other
just as children who are bundled ghosts
leaving their voices as trails in the woods,
that lakes are burdened with notions of ice
and heaviness, just like us.
The things we trust are less
and less true in winter.
I will say only that a cough,
deep inside you
at the heart of your lung
will turn you around just in time
to see the rock cliffs you've dreamed of,
the bull seals searching
for beaches to sleep, for rocks that hold
the moss long, long into the summer,
and a sun that's indifferent to the year,
to the herd, and to the ocean charging.

THE LONG ARM FORWARD
/ Ruth Ellen Kocher

The night I dreamed a crane
draped in a grey sheet stalked
my lover into the woods near our home,
the earth shook in Peru, covered a thousand
homes with mud and ash from a volcano
believed dormant. My lover was running silently away.
The crane was almost invisible under her sheet,
just the tip of flapping wings and long yellow legs.
In Peru, hands reach into rubble even now. The hands
    of dishes.
The hands of wood. The hands which are cold and
    warm,
sometimes wet. Hands that reach for a heavy hold,
that take us home, that speak somehow
and mold their forms into light like flocks of pale birds.
In this disaster, a woman remembers, a decade ago,
her husband drowning, and thinks,
through me you exist and fail. You
fail and exist again. Your mouth is full.
Leave me. Leave me alone.
She knows how easily lightning could erase her,
how the same water that carried
maroon legions of leaves past her home has changed
her life and the crane that haunts her sleep
so that it's not a crane, but a boy. A boy in a rain slicker
with muddy boots the color of mangoes
chasing storm through the woods until
he finds a stream. He is lost and the woman . . .
I am lost and her husband lost and leaving.
Yes, I am sleeping on long yellow legs and hear
through rain the rumble of mountains,
very far away, their red floes steaming mud.
I hear a mountain waking this world.

VARIABLE / *Ruth Ellen Kocher*

He calls thinking I can help him
but because I can't concentrate, because I don't really
   listen
when people speak and I'm remembering my own life:

the nurse with the deep cleft who was in love
with the sound of trains, who let me brush
her long, brown hair—the medicine bottle in her hands,
and her, confident she could calm me
in air that blued my nails cold:

I've thought of this
because he's called from a dark room to tell me
the cigarettes and the snow outside
remind him of me, that the cold
in his fingers reminds him of nights smoking
outside my home, my story of rhinoceros charging.

I imagine my nurse is there with him,
the room heavy with cigarettes he's smoked,
one after the other. He called to say he remembered
a man who hates him, who's somewhere
sipping coffee not understanding a wave of grief.
He listens for the familiar, the shape of my voice,
my hands, my shoulders which he can't remember.

I know he could love the nurse I think of,
her confident face, the large oak in her dreams
burdened with grackles. But he wants something
to level him, tells me I smelled like snow,
nicotine the last time we spoke so I say
no, it was you. Yes, he says,
and I say, there's a train near my house
that has no schedule but shakes the bottles
on my windowsill when it passes so that now
he knows I'm only a memory
and that somewhere a man remembers us both,

folds a newspaper under his arm and into his coat
pausing that moment before he pulls his collar closed
or that maybe a woman brushes her hair
and sees me at ten, coughing,
counting backwards to show off.
Between us all are lakes frozen into low sky,
orange-bellied southbound planes.
I'm torn, he says, without knowing
the division, the splintered,
the small reflections.

Two years later, this unfair firing was overturned by the U.S. Supreme Court, ushering in a new era for millions of disembodied Americans.

Robert Olen Butler

© Joshua Butler

Robert Olen Butler was awarded the 1993 Pulitzer Prize for his collection of stories, *A Good Scent from a Strange Mountain*, the first of which originally appeared in *The Missouri Review*. He has also published several novels, including *The Deuce*, and most recently the best-selling and controversial *They Whisper*, an excerpt from which also appeared originally in *MR*. In addition he is the recipient of a Guggenheim Fellowship and the Rosenthal Foundation Award. He teaches creative writing at McNeese State University in Lake Charles, Louisiana.

This interview was conducted in February of 1994 in Columbia, Missouri, by Kay Bonetti, Director of the American Audio Prose Library. The Prose Library offers tapes of American authors reading and discussing their work. For information contact AAPL at PO Box 842, Columbia, MO, 65205 or call 1-800-447-2275.

An Interview with
Robert Olen Butler

Interviewer: Your father was the chair of the theater department at St. Louis University and you grew up in Granite City, Illinois, the quintessential factory or blue-collar town.

Butler: I spent summers working in the Granite City Steel mill. As I grew up I was every bit as comfortable talking Cardinals baseball with fellow members of the labor gang at the blast furnace as I was talking aesthetic theory with my father's colleagues at St. Louis University. Granite City is not a racially mixed city but it's full of exiles from the Deep South. There were forty thousand people in the city at that time and one high school, and I was the student body president so I had good friends through the whole socioeconomic range. The sense of cultural collision that you find particularly in *A Good Scent from a Strange Mountain* I think flows from not just my experience in Vietnam but from my very childhood.

Interviewer: You went to school at Northwestern University, first as a theater major, an actor. Eventually you took a Master's degree in playwriting from the University of Iowa. What changed your direction?

Butler: I was more interested in acting than anything else when I was in high school. I went off to Northwestern in the fall of '63. Northwestern was, and still is, one of the premier training grounds for professional theater people. In that first year I was in four of the six major productions and had a major role in one of them, which was quite good. But into my sophomore year, I became restless with acting. I wanted to write, and since I was working in the theater I just assumed that the theater was what I should write for. On my twenty-first birthday, January of 1966, I was living at 626 Library Place in the top floor of a rooming house run by a very unusual old bachelor of a high-school English teacher. I looked out over the snowy rooftops of Evanston and said, "Well, if you really think you're going to be a writer, you'd better write something." So I sat down and wrote, in the next couple of months, a full-length play called "The Rooming House" about that house and the people there. By the time I finished my Master's at the University of Iowa, I had written a dozen full-length plays. The following eleven got worse and worse. I was a terrible playwright because I was in fact a nascent novelist trying to work in the wrong medium.

Interviewer: What's the difference?

Butler: Plays and movies are collaborative art forms. The writer is responsible for two things only: structure, and to some lesser extent, dialogue. But even that is a collaborative process with the actors. If you don't understand and embrace your limitation as an artist you will write badly. I think artists write because they encounter the chaos of life on the planet Earth and yet have some deep instinct of order behind that chaos. If what you see about the world is deeply embedded in the moment-to-moment sensual flow of experience, then you're not going to be satisfied as an artist whose sensual access to that material resides in a different artist.

Interviewer: John Gardner referred to fiction as the "whole hog," politics, history, anthropology, sociology, poetry; you get everything in fiction. Do you relate to that notion of the novel?

Butler: I was ready to embrace that idea, but when you started naming off those rational, abstracting sciences, I recoiled. I think

"Fiction resists and excludes the abstract and rational and philosophical."

fiction exists as a mode of discourse separate from any other because it resists and excludes the abstract and the rational and the ideational and the philosophical and the anthropological and sociological. All those things are the province of other modes of discourse. I don't think literature exists as a kind of elaborate word game where we sit around and talk rationally about what that work of art means. It's antithetical to the reason work is created and it's antithetical to the way the work should be encountered by a reader. There are 138,000 words in *They Whisper*. The only true answer to what that book means is to open the book up and read those 138,000 words again. The abstracting of our feelings, the interpreting, the analyzing, all those rational processes that we apply to our feelings are there in order to distance ourselves, to manage, to control, to shape, to vent off the direct, powerful hold these things have on us.

Interviewer: How does the writer shape then? The artistic unconscious delivers, but the writer has to shape.

Butler: It's the interlocking, the weaving together of the deeply patterned motifs of the sensual world, that conveys a sense of order. That's why art is organic. Every sensual object, every moment, every word, every action, every metaphor in a true work of art resonates into everything else, links everything else. The tiniest example for you: in *Countrymen of Bones*, on page two, Darell Reeves is out in the excavation site. He holds up his trowel, his basic tool. It's the thing that uncovers the past, and, in a way, uncovers himself to him. Now there are many different physical attributes he could consider at that moment, the heft of his trowel, the color of the blade, the texture of the handle, the pattern of earth clinging to the blade, but in fact he looks at it and notices

"The reason I can be effective in the realm of ideas and politics is that I ignore both when I write."

---

that its blade is as strong and flexible as a Toledo sword. That's a very vivid sensual image. We see the thing clearly, and that's one of the levels at which art works. A hundred and fifty pages later, one of the ranchers gallops into the excavation site and takes Darell and the two young graduate assistant workers hostage. That incident ends with Darell finally acting. And he does what?

Interviewer: He stabs him with his trowel.

Butler: Exactly. He picks up the trowel and kills the man with it. Now, I wouldn't expect any reader to hold that initial image consciously in her head until that moment, but the vision of the book is manifest in the sensual impact of that trowel as he holds it, as he contemplates its blade, as the blade enters the flesh of a man.

Interviewer: About eleven years ago you said, "I write novels to explore for myself and to reveal to others my vision of the fundamental patterns inherent in the flux of experience." Is that still your conviction?

Butler: *Explore* is the crucial word. I distinguish between literature and non-literature in this way. Stephen King, Danielle Steel, even people like Jean-Paul Sartre understand ahead of time what effect they wish to convey, what ideas they wish to get across. Then they construct an object to do that. The artist responds to the world directly. He has some deep vision of order, but has no idea what that vision is until the object is created. The artist creates the object as much to explore as to express his vision. That's the fundamental distinction between what artists do and what entertainers or ideologues do.

Interviewer: Anatole Broyard, the *New York Times* reviewer, spoke of you as a novelist of ideas, and Philip Biedler's study of the so-called Vietnam writers, *Rewriting America*, calls you the most political writer of your generation of Vietnam-era writers.

Butler: Everything I've been saying so far would seem to militate against both of those observations about me. But both men, I think, were on to something very important about the philosophical and political implications of art. The reason I can be so effective in the realm of ideas and the reason I can be so effective in the realm of politics is that I ignore both of those things when I write. I think it was Swift who said that you can't reason a person out of a position that he didn't reason himself into in the first place. The vast majority of the political beliefs that most people have are deeply irrational. We watch McNeil/Lehrer and read the *New York Times* in order to find some intellectual rationale for feeling the way we do. The work of art, because it ignores abstract ideas and touches the deepest irrational, sensual self, is better able to shape political ideas where they are truly formed.

Interviewer: Three characters from *The Alleys of Eden* each went on to become central to a subsequent novel. Was that by design?

Butler: No. When I was writing bad plays, one of the ways I knew I wanted to be a novelist, at least in retrospect, is that I kept writing cycles of plays, with the same characters continuing on. Ironically enough, I got intrigued with a couple of secondary characters from the first novel I wrote when I got back from Vietnam in the fall of '72. I called it *What Lies Near*. David Fleming was the central character and Clifford Wilkes was a minor character. By the time *The Alleys of Eden* finally got published I had written six novels, including *What Lies Near*. On the fourth published novel, I went back to David Fleming and did him right. So the sense of characters going on was created backwards. Every character I create, no matter how small, becomes enormously interesting to me. They branch out into some other corner or pocket or vein in my artistic unconscious and begin to work there.

Interviewer: Why did you move back to the past with *Countrymen of Bones* and *Wabash?*

Butler: I don't know. In a way going back to the fall of Vietnam was a kind of historical move, too. Going back to the energy crisis was a historical move as well, in a sense, because when I wrote those books we had gone past those events in some conclusive way. I've always been drawn to the large, external historical, cultural event that itself echoes the inner personal pattern of the characters.

Interviewer: Was a family story behind *Wabash?*

Butler: Oh, sure. My mother and my mother's mother and my mother's sisters were wonderful storytellers but there are no real-life counterparts to any of my characters. Graham Greene said that all good novelists have bad memories. What you remember comes out as journalism; what you forget goes into the compost of the imagination. All the characters in my work are creatures of the compost. Carlos Fuentes, I think, called the novel a pack of lies hounding the truth, and my books are the truest lies that I can tell. If anybody reads *They Whisper* looking for biographical details of me or my three wives or any other women I've loved or my son or my parents, they will be drastically misled. None

"I've always been drawn to the large, external historical, cultural event."

of us exist in that book. On a deeper level, I am nakedly present in *They Whisper* and *Ira Holloway*. I would hasten to add however that *They Whisper* is not an attempt to find the unified field theory of human sexuality. It is a partial vision of myself and of what I see. *A Good Scent from a Strange Mountain* is deeply and nakedly me, as well, in every aspect of every character in the sense that I am pouring my most impassioned encounter with the world and my most ardent search for its meaning into every word, every image of that and every book.

Interviewer: I read your novels in sequence and it seems to me that if there's a breakthrough book, a book where you found your voice, it was *The Deuce*.

Butler: I think you are absolutely right. It was the first book I wrote in the first person. The first five novels were my playwright self; from *The Deuce* on I've gone back to being an actor. I become the role, I become the character. In *A Good Scent from a Strange Mountain* it felt like I was speaking in tongues at times. I can't even imagine going back to the third person now. There's a great deal to explore with the first person. Look at *They Whisper*, the first-person voice of a man who lapses into the first-person voices of women, not as a kind of transsexual experience, but as the ultimate expression of heterosexual love.

Interviewer: I'd like to talk about *They Whisper*. Why did you choose to center the book around a character as dysfunctional as Fiona in taking on the task of exploring heterosexual love and relationships?

Butler: Fiona is not the center of the book, as Ira keeps pointing out. Fiona is one very important, but only one, sexual and sensual and

"In A Good Scent I felt like I was speaking in tongues at times."

female influence in the book. All the women are equally important in certain ways. Fiona's presence in the book, however, is as strong and dysfunctional as it is because she is the dark counter image to Ira. He sees sex as a kind of secular sacrament. Churches understand sacraments as a physical something that resonates into the cosmic sphere. For Ira, women's bodies are that. Though Ira loves many women, he loves them absolutely and individually. For him a woman's body is a sacramentally charged metaphor for the inner secrets of her unique personality, which he seeks even through hearing and taking on her woman's voice. For him there is a kind of holy grail that is unattainable: Karen Granger, the little girl that he loved one summer. For him, sexuality is a powerful life force. Fiona is the dark counter-image to that. She has had sexual encounters with many men. But they were part of a constant search for reassurance that she is not loathsome. In place of Ira's holy grail, she has from her childhood the dark malignant influence of her sexually abusive father. Instead of being connected to the life force, sexuality for her is connected to death. Fiona and Ira are the yin and the yang, it's the life and death, wellness and sickness, connection and disconnection, that come together in that union.

A critical aspect of this book is the women's voices. I hadn't even conceived *They Whisper* until I wrote *A Good Scent from a Strange Mountain*. Notably enough, Ira Holloway and I are strictly heterosexual, exclusively so, and yet I could not conceive a book, I could not write a book about the essence of male heterosexuality—what it is, how it drives a man, what the dark sides are—with the complexity it required until I found the woman's voice in me. Ira carries an inner landscape around with him in which dwell all the women he has ever loved, and as he meditates on them he lapses into their first-person voices. It is the ultimate act

Robert Olen Butler

of intimacy, to leave the self and to join the other in the inner self.

Interviewer: But at the end of the book, he still feels incomplete.

Butler: *They Whisper* does not intend to discover a unified field theory of human sexuality. But it says things that I think are deeply true about our yearnings. And it is not just the man who continues to yearn for that deep connection where bodies are the way in. Women do too. Society has been much more efficient in suppressing that urge in women, but it is there. The question is, if sexuality is a kind of search for glimpses into the infinite, is it possible for any one relationship ever to be so complete as to exclude any other yearning or any other need for connection?

Interviewer: Do you think that in any good story there is any such thing as a reliable narrator?

Butler: The work itself will encourage or discourage that half or full step back from the narrator. In *They Whisper* there is the tiniest little bit of distancing. We probably have our own independent sense—inevitably given the subject matter—of Ira's choices and decisions and priorities and so forth. But I think we trust him to be pretty thoroughly self-aware. He is prepared to feel guilty. He deeply regrets deception and pain and he tries rigorously to avoid deceiving anyone and to avoid inflicting pain in relationships and he is very conscious in trying to examine a profoundly mysterious impulse. Reviewers speak of Ira as if he were an acquaintance, a real person, and that's fine, that's good. To some extent to write about this subject matter you've got to build that into the process. If you get a half a dozen of your literary friends around a dinner table and say, "Let's name all the serious literary novels that we can about war," twenty minutes later you've got two hundred titles on the table. You say "Okay, let's name all the serious literary novels we can about family relationships." It's going to take an hour and you'll have five hundred titles on the table. Then you say, "Let's name all the serious literary works of fiction that we can about the essence of human sexuality. Not just books with sex in them, but that really go at that subject head on." There's going to be a lot of silence and you're going to stir your coffee and think and look out the window, and you probably won't get off the fingers of that one proverbial hand. There are reasons for that. This deeply personal reaction is one. Another is the limits of the language. Though the English language has more words than any other, the words for those most intimate of body parts involved in this most intimate of human activities don't carry with them the connotations of vulnerability and tenderness and cosmic resonance that many of us feel about those parts. They are either too clinical and scientific and bloodless or gross and trivializing and dismissive and pornographic. When I wrote *They Whisper*, with every word I felt as if I was reinventing the form of the novel and reinventing the language in certain ways.

Interviewer: You've made it clear that you think we should trust Ira. But the big problem with first-person narrative is that by definition every human being is limited; therefore the reader is going to recognize things that the narrator cannot. What are some of the main things that you would hope the reader sees in *They Whisper* that Ira can't see for himself?

Butler: That's a difficult question because you are asking me to reconsider the whole book in exactly the kind of psychoanalytical

"My deepest concerns led me not only into other cultures but into the other gender as well."

abstracting terms that I have resisted in writing it. You trust him as much as any single human consciousness can be trusted. By and large we are led to distrust Ira in the same ways he distrusts himself. At any given moment, a reader might well be able to anticipate Ira's conclusions about certain things. For instance, we might well sense that Ira is not whole before he is able to declare it. He is so close to the women he loves that it is impossible for him to get a perspective on the dark side or incompleteness as soon as we would. He is deeply in love with and caught up in that glimpse into the infinite present even in the fading fingertips of a waitress on a cold wineglass. As much as he is able to evoke that for us, we are still a little bit separate. There can well be a range of personal reactions to him as a human being which I think still fit within the frame of a book about human intimacy and sexuality. To keep that range of human personal reaction within an artistic frame is the best that one can hope for and may be something quite special on its own.

Interviewer: In her review of *They Whisper*, Jane Smiley wrote that men of the Vietnam generation live "the realities of imperialism, both abroad and in the home, without conviction." How would you respond?

Butler: On one level there is some validity to that but I think to limit it to men of the Vietnam era would be a big mistake. This is a universal and ages-old impulse of men that has existed since Solomon had two thousand wives and David lusted after somebody else's wife.

Interviewer: But Bathsheba was not allowed to lust after a lot of men and that's the difference I am getting at. We have a whole

"Every human being on the planet carries around the fear that each of us is utterly alone."

generation of men who accept that women have sex lives just like them, but it's a reality that you don't often find reflected in contemporary fiction.

Butler: That impulse needs to be understood and accepted and embraced by and for women, and we have to take out society's reflex aversion to that impulse in men. Men who continue to love women throughout their life and feel that they might well be in love with more than one woman at once are treated as absolutely reprehensible. But there are many men for whom that impulse to continue to love women is deeply serious. They revere the individuality and the uniqueness of each woman and are seeking that connection to the cosmos. But Ira and men like him are terribly vulnerable. And for the men who feel that vulnerability and can't live with it, one defense mechanism is to coarsen and diminish the impulse. They turn it into the reprehensible thing which is the objectifying of women and womanizing for the sake of power and possession, and these men ultimately kill that deeper self. It is terribly important to realize that the impulse exists in both men and women and that it exists in a serious and beautiful way.

Interviewer: It strikes a lot of your readers that you did a very, very nervy thing in writing not only *They Whisper*, but *A Good Scent* as well. You took a lot of risks.

Butler: That's true. The books are full of risks, and that's the only way I can continue to write. I just have to think about going deeper and deeper and deeper in. I only write from the place that my inspiration and my deepest concerns lead me. In this case it's led me not only into other cultures, but into the other gender as well. My conviction is that artists are in the business of breaking down those barriers between us. Every human being on the planet, I think, carries around the fear that, in spite of appearances, each of us is utterly alone. And it's the artist's job to take us out of ourselves and into the other. One should come to a work of art nakedly, as you would to a new lover, and say, "Take me. Make me part of you."

Interviewer: Was this your approach in writing *A Good Scent from a Strange Mountain* as well as *They Whisper?*

Butler: *A Good Scent* was really the book where I had to face down that inhibition that says, "I can't go there." I think that's best summed up in something that the great Japanese film director Akiri Kurasawa said, that to be an artist means to never avert your eyes. And if anything has guided me, that's it. With *A Good Scent* I found myself in that place artists must go in their unconscious where, lo and behold, we are neither Vietnamese nor American, neither Catholic nor Buddhist, neither Israeli nor Palestinian. We are all deeply, universally human. There is a place where all of us meet and share a self. And that's the place I think that all artists strive to get to. When you get there, you find that then you can project that common pool of experience from yourself, through yourself, but also from everyone else and through them. You can project back into characters and situations that on the surface seem far from you in those limiting ways of gender and race and culture.

Interviewer: How essential is learning the language of another culture to this process of reaching that common pool of experience?

Butler: I did need, in terms of my Vietnamese, to spend a year knowing the language fluently and deeply submerged in the culture. I took every opportunity I could. For the seven months that I was in Saigon, for instance, I would go out virtually every night well past midnight and just wander the steamy back alleys, where nobody ever seemed to sleep, and I would crouch in the doorways with the Vietnamese people, who were as a group the warmest, most open and generous-spirited people in the world. And they would invariably invite me into their homes and into their culture and lives. And I fell in love more than several times in Vietnam. And I had a wide range of friendships, from my favorite leper beggar on the streets, who was by the way the most cheerful man I have ever met in my life, to the highest government officials.

Interviewer: And you fell in love with the entire fabric of their culture and lives and language?

Butler: I was ravished by the sensuality of Vietnam. Fluency in another language, to really know another language is not just to develop equivalencies for words. You rename the world. And the sensual properties of that name echo into the object and the object echoes into the words and so with that other language, I was seeing the world afresh. I needed that.

Interviewer: What has the response in the Vietnamese community been to *A Good Scent*?

Butler: The most common comment is that my understanding of the Vietnamese and their culture is so intimate they could have sworn that I was Vietnamese. In Orange County, California, home to eighty thousand Vietnamese—it's called "Little Saigon," and is the de facto

"I was ravished by the sensuality of Vietnam."

capital of the Vietnamese in America—a wonderful man who's translating my work into Vietnamese arranged a luncheon with a dozen of the most prominent literary figures in the Vietnamese community in America. The thing they were so deeply grateful to me for was not the cultural accuracy of the book but the fact that I had portrayed the Vietnamese people as universally human. In Vietnam itself, an official in the foreign ministry, a fast-track young Communist, discovered my book and has translated some of the stories into Vietnamese. He wanted to do "A Good Scent from a Strange Mountain," the title story, but his superiors did not find that story politically acceptable. He went on to translate "Crickets," and his translation appeared in a weekly magazine in Saigon while I was there in '93 and caused quite a wonderful stir. Shopkeepers and cyclo drivers and so forth were stopping me on the street. "Crickets" has within it some pretty clear imagery.

There are two types of crickets: the large charcoal crickets, which are big and strong but slow; and the smaller fire crickets that are quick and wily. Even when a child had his own charcoal cricket in a fight, everyone, even that child, would root for the little fire cricket. Who was who was pretty clear in the story. Every morning I passed a man who sold lapel pins within a block of my hotel. I spoke a greeting to him in Vietnamese; and he spoke back. We had a lovely sort of very warm, passing hello relationship. This man was in his mid to late forties. He had a horrible mangled stump where his left arm had been. On the day after "Crickets" appeared, he waved the magazine at me and called me over. It turns out that he is a former Viet Cong soldier. We had a lovely chat and he went on about how much he loved all parts of the story. He says, "But you know what the best part was," and he gave this great rich, deep laugh, "I used to fight crickets and what you say is true. When the fire cricket fought

"The Vietnamese are extraordinarily pragmatic and eclectic people."

the charcoal crickets, we all rooted for the fire cricket." Kind of an eerie moment. Here literary symbol meets object of the symbolism, and he was responding, not in any intellectual abstract way but directly and emotionally to this imagery.

Interviewer: Your stories seem to strike an accommodation between Buddhists and Catholics in Vietnam that I assume is reflected in Vietnamese life.

Butler: The Vietnamese are extraordinarily pragmatic and eclectic people. Everything you need to know about the Vietnamese people—their beliefs, their attitudes, their politics, their religion, their character—you can understand by learning how to cross the streets of Saigon. Those wonderful old wide French boulevards are filled at almost any hour of the day or night with ten, fifteen, twenty, twenty-five lanes of traffic in each direction. I say lanes but it's very amorphous. Virtually all of that traffic is motorcycles, motor bikes, bicycles, some cylos—pedi-cabs that is—a few taxicabs. To cross the streets in Saigon you stand on the corner and look across to the far side where you want to go. If you wait for an opening to get all the way across, you will die of old age on the curb. If you dash to an opening and wait and then dash to the next opening and so forth—you will die in the center of the street within seconds. In Saigon, what you do is this. You look to the left—the first small opening, you step into. And then you do not stop. You do not slow down. You continue to walk at a very moderate pace across the street toward the place you want to be. All those lanes of traffic bearing down on you will not stop, they will not slow down. But the vehicle that's about to strike you at any given second will at the last moment veer into the next lane. Without looking. Whoever is in that lane, understanding this process instinctively, moves into the next lane and so forth. You will continue to move through that traffic and it will ripple and flow around you until you are at the other side. If JFK had sent his chief of staff to Saigon in 1962 and said, "Learn how to cross the streets and tell me what you think," that general would have learned two important things. First of all, we could never win the war. Second of all, we didn't need to win the war, because as soon as the failures of the communist system were clear to the Vietnamese, they would go around it—which is exactly what happened.

Interviewer: In many ways the title story of *A Good Scent from a Strange Mountain* serves as a touchstone for the whole collection. Its function in the book echoes the structure of many of the individual stories: it makes you go back and think about the collection as a whole.

Butler: Yes, that story was written last, and it does indeed have a kind of over-arching vision of life and the world and human aspiration and exile and choice of self that echoes through the whole collection. There's no question about that. John Clark Pratt did a very careful analysis of *Good Scent* in the *Colorado Review* last year. He sees it as a kind of quintessential post-modernist novel, working in montage. And I think he has got a point. Every story in the collection is carefully placed. "A Good Scent from a Strange Mountain" was consciously written at the end from a specific sensual inspiration, but it stands in the book as an over-arching vision of the whole.

Interviewer: How did you decide to order the rest of the stories?

Butler: It was a deeply subjective thing. I was looking for a rhythm of tone, of emotion, of gender. I positioned the stories so that there would be a kind of wave form, of hope and despair and cynicism and aspiration and so forth. It was a way of modulating the rhythm of emotion through the whole mosaic of voices.

Interviewer: Certainly a story like "The Trip Back" is about the ways of memory. One of the first things the narrator says is, "I'm not a poet. I'm a businessman." Yet it takes a poet to tell this story, and the coming to be a poet is tied in with memory and action.

Butler: There's a certain paradox, yes. The narrator definitely feels that failure in himself; his potential to be a poet is latent, and the action he takes at the end of the story is the consummate artistic gesture.

Interviewer: It says to his wife, "I'll be your grandfather. I'll be your brother, I'll be your friend, your father, everything to you." It's a great act of the imagination and it's also an embodiment of sensory memory.

Butler: Thanks. But part of me inevitably balks at analysis and generalization of that kind. We sit here to talk about the work like this, but ultimately the work is only itself. It is only the act. He puts his wife on his back and runs with her. The impulse to step back from it and say, "Ah, now he's telling her that he's everything to her" is a reductive act. When I teach literature we look at the subtext and articulate it in terms different from the terms in which they sit there on the page. But I always tell my students, "The only reason we are doing this terribly artificial thing

"To be a real reader means to close the book and sensually resonate to the vision of order there and be at peace with that."

is that the process may help you to thrum more completely or harmoniously with the next work of art that you read. In order to do that, when you leave here your last assignment is to forget everything we've said here." To be a real reader means to close the book and sensually resonate to the vision of order there and be at peace with that. That's enough. That's everything.

Interviewer: Like many of the stories in the book, every detail in "Mr. Green" comes together and works perfectly with the ending. It answers the question "What then?" and also is a response to her grandfather's "Not possible" on so many levels. Every detail. What role does revision play in bringing everything to such a fine pitch?

Butler: There was very, very little revision in any of the stories. My editor did not change a comma in that book. I do not leave a sentence until it is as close to being finished as it can possibly be. I revise as I go, so there was, of course, revision from sentence to sentence, but there were no drafts of any story, nothing had to be pulled through the whole process again and again.

Interviewer: Do you ever have fun writing? Was "Love" in *A Good Scent* a fun story to write?

Butler: Of course it was fun, and parts of *They Whisper* were great fun. The Karen Granger stuff, the synthesized voice at the grocery store checkout counter, the handwriting on the girl's restroom walls. There is actually quite a lot of humor in *They Whisper* and those things are fun to write. But there's a deeper fun, bound up with fear and trembling and pain. It's the deep satisfaction of going as far as you can into that utterly sensual unconscious and

*"Vietnam for me has always been sim-
ply a matrix of concrete sensual experience
that holds the deep human issues I'm concerned with."*

---

shaping it into a vivid and clear vision of the world. I walk away
from my computer every day with an exhilaration. No matter how
difficult, how troubling the vision is, the articulation of it is joyful.

Interviewer: I know that you have in your head right now several
more books. Can you please tell us what that means?

Butler: My unconscious is telling me that if I sat down tomorrow
and began to focus entirely on one of the four novels and two
books of stories I have in mind, eighteen months from now it
would have an existence. It's an accretion of sensual details and
relationships and localities and characters who yearn. You drive
down a street at night and you know everybody on the block in
some way. All the picture windows are open and you look to the
left and somebody's sitting at a table and somebody is just moving
into the room with her hair up in a towel and her bathrobe on
and he turns and looks over his shoulder. Over in this house
there's a child climbing onto the back of a father and down at
the next house something else. You know that all you need to
do is stop your car and go knock on the door and they would
let you in and you'd sit in there for a year and a half and walk
out with everything. It's images. It's that sense of lives together
in a place that you can access.

Interviewer: Now that a whole body of Vietnam war literature
exists, is there anything productive to say about that literature and
your place in it?

Butler: If one writes from the artistic impulse I've been describing,
then to call me a Vietnam novelist is like calling Monet a lily-pad
painter. Vietnam for me has always been simply a metaphor, a

---

location, an instigator of action, a source of characters, a matrix o concrete sensual experience that holds the deep universal humar issues I'm concerned with.

Interviewer: You've been quoted as saying that to avoid madness, you had to turn yourself into your writing pad or computer and write, not think about prizes and fame and glory. Now you've won the Pulitzer Prize and you're one of the best-known writers in the country. I guess I would like to ask Mr. Green's question: "What then?"

Butler: The nice thing about the Pulitzer is that it will be there forever. I think the monkey's off my back now. I'm always the Pulitzer Prize winner now and it just makes it easier to write the books that I'm given to write. I was going to do that anyway, but the great and blessed difference is that people will actually buy the books and read them. I've always known that I would find a much wider audience someday. My books are devoted to the proposition that literary fiction does not need to disenfranchise itself from strong storytelling. Though the artist must focus ultimately on exploring and expressing his or her own deep vision of the world, the very act of expressing reveals a deep yearning to touch and to connect to others. It's also an act of lovemaking. When I write a book I am making myself naked to the world and saying I wish to touch you. I wish to connect deeply with you. The wonderful thing about the prize is that now others will respond.

Interviewer: Earlier we touched on the question of wanting to make the reader see your vision of the world. If you were backed to the wall and had to say, "this is my vision of the world," what would you say?

Butler: The only true answer to that is to take my eight book and read them to you again. And then to read you every boo I write from this point on. Ultimately, after all this talk, that i my vision of the world. It is irreducible.

Jack Kerouac

Courtesy of Ed White

LETTERS FROM JACK KEROUAC
TO ED WHITE, 1947–68

The accepted thumbnail portrait of Jack Kerouac depicts him as soured and embittered in his later years, turning his back on the ideals of the Beats and most of his old friends. In a *Paris Review* interview of 1967, he said:

> Oh the beat generation was just a phrase I used in the 1951 written manuscript of *On the Road* to describe guys like Moriarty who run around the country in cars looking for odd jobs, girlfriends, kicks. It was thereafter picked up by West Coast leftist groups and turned into a meaning like "beat mutiny" and "beat insurrection" and all that nonsense; they just wanted some youth movement to grab onto for their own political and social purposes. I had nothing to do with any of that. I was a football player, a scholarship college student, a merchant seaman, a railroad brakeman on road freights, a script synopsizer, a secretary.
>
> ...The community feeling was largely inspired by the same characters I mentioned, like Ferlinghetti, Ginsberg; they are very socialistically minded and want everybody to live in some kind of frenetic kibbutz, solidarity and all that. I was a loner. Snyder is not like Whalen, Whalen is not like McClure, I am not like McClure.... There's no "beat crowd" like you say.... what about Scott Fitzgerald and his "lost crowd," does that sound right?

Whether Kerouac was ill and disillusioned when he made these remarks or not, he was telling the truth. He mythologized the Beats but he never fully embraced them. He certainly did not present the Beat life as a formula for happiness. *On the Road* ends with a turning away from the road, as the narrator Sal refuses to leave on another journey with Dean Moriarty, and has a final vision of him as a lost man, ragged and freezing in his "moth-eaten overcoat." It was somewhere between such incongruities, and partly because of them, that Kerouac's writing really lived—between his rhapsodic acceptance and his criticism of the Beat ethic, between the group as a self-conscious literary avant-garde and a post-war condition, between himself as a mythologist and an objective novelist.

Even more than most writers, Kerouac was a bundle of contradictions. He sometimes yearned for the stability of a middle-class life but was never able to maintain it for long. Primarily a heterosexual, he flirted with homosexuality. An intense and at times predatory woman chaser, he was also a lifelong momma's boy who regularly cared for and went back to live with his mother. An Easterner, he fantasized about the West and moved to Denver, and several times to San Francisco. A Catholic, he became deeply interested in Buddhism for many years, before returning to Catholicism at the last.

As someone who had grown up a working-class kid of French-Canadian ancestry in a New England mill town, he seldom strayed from a conservative bias in his personal politics. Yet like many of the leftist writers of the 1930s—Jack Conroy, Mike Gold, Edward Dahlberg, Henry Roth—he wrote about people who floated around, often broke, with laboring jobs or no jobs at all, and no futures. The seeming unconcern of his characters about security or their futures was their definitive difference, the very thing that made them so fascinating. However, it only went so far, and at those times when the uprootedness and poverty began to bite, when the future went particularly bleak, their stories are surprisingly like the desolate novels of the thirties.

Kerouac's great hero was Neal Cassady of Denver. Cassady was the model for Dean Moriarty, and he reappeared under the name Cody Pomeroy in several of Kerouac's later novels. Cassady was variously described by those who knew him as a con artist, a "psychopath," and genius. He was a car thief of epic accomplishments, who had boosted some five hundred cars during his teenage years. He was also an extraordinarily well-read autodidact, a taker of bennies, a manic seducer of women, as well as the lover of a few men, and a writer who was seldom able to finish things. He was an extreme character, even among the Beats, and several of them roundly disliked or disapproved of him. In appearance, he and Kerouac looked like brothers, both of them handsome, muscular, strong-jawed. About Cassady's influence on him Kerouac said:

> I spent my entire youth writing slowly with revisions and endless re-hashing speculation and deleting and got so I was writing one sentence a day and the sentence had no FEELING. I got my idea for spontaneous prose from letters from Cassady. He, too, began his early writing with slow, painstaking, and all-that-crap craft business, but got sick of it like I did. All his letters to me were about his younger days before I met him, a child with his father.... There was a 13,000-word piece that became his novel *The First Third*.

The big letter though was 40,000 words long, and it was the greatest piece of writing I ever saw, better'n anybody in America. Ginsberg loaned it to a guy on a houseboat in California in 1955. His name was Gerd Stern, lived on a boat in Sausalito, and he lost the letter, presumably overboard. All about Christmas weekend in the poolhalls, jails, hotel rooms of Denver, with hilarious events throughout. We also did much fast talking between us, on tape recorders, way back in 1952, and listened to them so much, we both got the secret of LINGO in telling a tale and figured that was the only way to express the speed and tension and ecstatic tomfoolery of the age.

Neal Cassady's one major published work, *The First Third*—part novel, part autobiographical essay—was a classic lumpenproletarian account of his growing up in Denver in the thirties, the son of a flophouse drunk. Reading it, one understands how close the Beats were to the streets of down-and-out America, and how their radical questionings derived naturally from the bald realities of Depression and war-era childhoods.

Neal Cassady was one among several of Jack's connections from Denver. At the end of the war, when Jack was back from the sea and living in New York, hanging out at Columbia, he met Hal Chase through Jack Fitzgerald, a Columbia student who lived in Poughkeepsie. Chase, originally from Denver, had been in the ski troops during the war, and he was Jack's original contact to the circle of Denver friends that eventually widened to include Neal Cassady, Al Hinkle, LuAnne Henderson, Justin Brierly, Bob and Beverly Burford, and Ed White, as well as another Easterner who circulated with the Denver crowd, Allan Temko. Over time, Denver proved to be one of Kerouac's spiritual "home bases."

He was adept at handling lack of recognition as a writer and living in relative poverty. After the modest reception of his first, conventional novel, *The Town and the City*, Kerouac was unable to sell a book for six years, yet he continued to write, carrying his novels around with him literally in a duffel bag. During that period, he wrote a heroic eight novels without acceptances. From 1948 to 1952 his "road book" alone went through five versions. What was published in 1957 by Viking Press as *On the Road* was the fourth version, and *Visions of Cody*—which Kerouac always believed to be his masterpiece—was the final version, not published in its entirety until after Kerouac's death. In 1957, all in a flash, Kerouac achieved notoriety for a book that he had written six years before.

Suddenly, there was money, adulation, scandals, television and radio interviews, and often virulent controversy.

Everything conspired to make Jack Kerouac, the "King of the Beats" (a phrase he despised), a soft target. He began to receive telegrams, letters, telephone calls, people started dropping by his house at all hours—mostly young men expecting "Jack Kerouac" to be exactly like the Sal Paradise of *On the Road*.

He simply was not built to play the role of living legend. He wasn't cool and objective enough; he wasn't calculating enough; and by that time he had relied too long on alcohol and pills. For Jack Kerouac, personally, literary acceptance and acclaim coincided with disaster.

The *New York Times* editor who had published the review welcoming *On the Road* as a major American novel arranged a fete for the author, but Kerouac called after the party had already started, lamely asking his friend John Clellon Holmes to make excuses for him. He told Holmes that he had been drinking so much that he had the DTs. Holmes went to visit him and later reported that Kerouac really wasn't all that drunk, he was just worn out. "He had been interviewed to death and was terribly confused." He would never, according to Holmes, fully regain his compass settings.

Kerouac tended to be naive about interviewers, thinking that he could really communicate with them. He was attacked verbally and, surprisingly often, physically. Many people hated him before they met him. "All the men wanted to fight him," said Holmes. "It was dreadful. I decided I never wanted to be a famous person."

Despite his problems, Kerouac's last decade of life was productive, both in terms of publishing his unpublished manuscripts and writing new novels. But the dual curse of alcoholism and notoriety was compounded by a destructive orneriness that prevented him from maintaining a good editorial relationship. Malcolm Cowley had fought bravely for him at Viking, but Kerouac eventually broke with him, and he never again had a trusted editor who could stand up to him as well as for him. He began to believe too much in the myth of "spontaneous" composition, as if writing books in ten days or three days was a virtue in itself.

Jack and Ed White maintained their friendship through all these vicissitudes. White became an architect, later well known for designing the Denver Arboretum and other notable projects. Citations about White in the Beat literature and folklore portray him as one of the good guys in the crowd—generous, thoughtful, and less extreme in his habits than many of them. When Jack was working on *On the Road*, Ed made a suggestion that turned out to be crucial in Jack's writing. As an architect, Ed carried around notebooks on which to sketch interesting buildings, and he suggested that Jack begin to do his own quick "word sketches" in the notebooks that he carried. This suggestion, along with the example of Neal Cassady's letters, was the basis of the spontaneous prose style in his novels.

Kerouac was never very good at playing the role of the Great Writer. Despite the fact that he had a "steel trap mind," he was both too candid and too limited by his alcoholism. "Notoriety and public confession in literary form is a frazzler of the heart you were born with, believe me," he said in 1967. As much as anything, his fame, when it finally came, bewildered him and contributed to his retreat from the world. Among these letters, he shows himself to be an enormously sincere correspondent, with an abiding urge to communicate with his old friend, even when he was down.

He also shows himself to be a fiercely dedicated writer, whose motivation was never money, and who had to painfully grope toward solutions in his art. "The wish for fame and fortune is the greatest obstacle, initially, to work," he says, "and work is just ragged and sad." Kerouac was naturally endowed with what Buddhists call "beginner's mind"—staying open to the moment, being amazed even by the commonplace. "What a panorama these Fifties will present," he wrote to his old friend, and he was right.

SM/KAS/KDS/JBG

Sept. 17, 1947
P.O. Box 819
Marin City, Calif.

Dear Ed—

I'm afraid this isn't going to reach you in Dearborn in time, but I'm sure Jeanie is going to send the letter on to you at Columbia. However, you spoke of a message to Edie, and if you're in Michigan as you read this now, tell her I want to know when she's going to go and live on the farm in Dexter, Michigan.[1] This is a mysterious enigmatic question that will dumb-found her for a week. Also, you might mention what I've been generally doing, and ask her what she thinks about that. You must at all costs be clever, so that you will be able to give me an interesting report on her.

Edie is the only thing in the world I have to figure out. Everything else is charmingly clear and also charmingly paradoxical—but my comprehension of Edie is stormy, unwilling, and, also, insane. What can you make of that?

I wrote a letter to Hal to distract him in his illness.[2] I quoted excerpts from Balzac to amuse him. Also I wrote a letter to Brierly, c/o of Ed White, Jr., at the Cherry Street address, not knowing our cultural tycoon's address.[3] I hope no one will take it as a sly joke. The world is very sly and always on the watch for slyness— even me right now. But you and I are very honest with one another, and that's a strange thing—I think we're trying to outdo each other in honesty. That's a strange and good fact. Yet pardon me for digressing in the mail.

I haven't seen any of the Burfords, but maybe I'll hear from them.

Write again, and tell Livornese to drop me a card.[4] I discovered a great unknown Tristano out here whose very name eludes me. But tell Tom, and mark it yourself, that he played "Louise" with two fingers in the most truly beautiful thing I've ever heard. Two fingers, sometimes three, doing the melody very slowly, with intricate yet simple combinations never straying far from the melody-note—I wish I could explain it technically. But I'll work it out on the piano.

If you see Fitz, give him my address and my admonitions to write.[5]

And so on. I'll write you a long letter on a typewriter next time— and, be sure to study hard this year in spite of everything luring you from all sides. I'll never get to know Washington if I don't have a friend *wheeling* around there someday. Also, you must raise the Denver Whites to the heights practically single-handed. "The honest American families are disappearing too fast," my father always said, a little dogmatically and with Peglerian undertones, really, but in a specially important way, true.[6] Morally there's nothing you or I can say, but emotionally, for me, and aesthetically also, I like the old American types, like your father, best. You can see from the way 90% of American industry is being extorted or extorting with the extorters, through a thousand devices means legal *and* illegal, raising cain with the economy which was once fundamentally *honest* (they make too much of the word *solid*), that the family is the root of it. The sons of chicanerous price-raisers, monopolists, tyrannical unioneers, and general unscrupulous businessmen operating in disorganized communities, will never grow up with a keen interest in professional ethics. It will all fall apart like Rome if there isn't a renaissance in American feeling. Our modern art depicting life-dissatisfaction certainly isn't helping. But this is all too much for me right now. Signing off, Jack.

On receipt: Oct. 29 1948
Ozone

Dear Ed,

The Paris plans seem wild to me and I still can't believe it is possible to take off like legendary figures in Scott Fitzgerald and Temko and actually hit the bistros and the Haute-Savoies. However, this is only because of loneliness. It should be easy for me to transfer from the New School to the Sorbonne, I mean my papers et cetera, and I will give this matter a shot in the ass this week.[7] I'm not using up much of my G.I. bill, just four months, and that only to pay the rent. If by February I haven't got some sort of advance on my book(s)—(started a second novel)—I wonder if I'll really go.[8] But then, I could very well go tonight if somebody asked me. Anyway, time & circumstance heal...these solitary abrasions.

Tom is so busy trying to marry his charming Julie Metzger that I rarely see him. At a Tristano concert last week I saw him sitting up front with Julie and the vice-president of Decca Records. I had the composer David Diamond with me. However, Diamond was a little professionally jealous of Lenny & quintet, and pissed off Tom a little bit, and I haven't seen Tom since. As you know Tom is a mad romancer, and all of a sudden one day he will come to my house and wipe his brow and sigh. When he's in the middle of a romance he runs around with a great deal of fury and you don't get to see him. I'll prod him about the Paris deal when I see him.

I'm looking for Hal, but not cleverly enough: that is, telling Arizona to give him messages may be too shrewdly self-confounding. Hal's own address Arizona does not divulge. I roam the campus once in a while. I call Warren Hall: Arizona answers the phone, when she's in. But I'll find him. The funny thing is that all this melodrama is nothing but pepsi-cola. I particularly wanted to find Hal this week (isn't that a crazy statement!) on account of Jack Fitzgerald wants us to drive up to Poke and stay at his new house filling and re-filling boms.

You with your Denver of brothers and sisters and parents and buddies and houses a-building, and mountains, how I envy you. I think it is fine for a Phi Beta Kappa man to relax building houses, and prepare to go to Paris. Soon there'll be a war, I guess, and you will have got some good years under your belt. As the old Jews say in delicatessens, "Enjoy, enjoy." This is better than the madman I saw last night in the Brooklyn el who spent ten minutes talking to himself and gesturing and laughing, and smiling his secret locked-up enjoyments, just enjoying himself, by himself, with himself, mad as mad can be, then leaving the train and shouting: "So long gang!" Everybody in the train was indignant, including me, because we realized that it was we who had driven him mad. Enjoy, enjoy. (The last addressed to myself particularly.)

The title of my second novel is "Doctor Sax."[9] It is sub-titled: "The Imagination of Kids." It's about kids, and you will love it. My "Town & City" 1100-page ms. is now at Little, Brown, in Boston. MacMillan has not rejected it; they want to read it in its entirety (they had read selections). I also have Knopf, Houghton-Mifflin, Harper's, Random House and another place I can't remember waiting for it. The Leland Hayward agency wants to handle it. I am hard to get. The legend is being bruited about (publishing and agency grapevines) that I am a little bird that you have to put salt on; and actually, though, I only sit home writing sad letters like this.

The big romance didn't last. The girl was sixteen, and beautiful; she wanted me to treat her rough and I couldn't do it. It seems that her mother was a martinet and she had no father, and she had the tragic sense of being left out in the cold by her two sisters who went to Paris. It's a girl looking for someone to stick pitiful needles in (her little needles are so sad). Well, it hurt me to part from her—I'm still devising schemes to see her again. We had a wonderful day last summer, and nights. Looking at the thing objectively may I suggest that our prophecy concerning 16-year-olds was in no way inaccurate. How I felt like old Karamazov himself!—(no piddling Dmitri). Shortly after that I hooked up with a woman more than twice her age, and was disgusted. Little Jinny (16) had slanted green eyes, little bangs on her brow (which perspired), a little slight body (in slacks), and a way of clinging to my bared wrists on subways and buses that was like desperation. I still don't understand it.

Then I went down South to woo a nurse who looked like Joan Fontaine. I overlooked the fact that she was engaged to a young medic and made all kinds of plans. She finally had to break the news to me gently. In the end, I wrote a letter to Edie telling her it was important that we should see each other again. No answer. This has been a bad year (as they say in Grenoble). My mother laughs at me, she says I'm behaving like an old man. Well goddamit I feel like an old man. I want a little girl.

Of course the New School with its ugly Jewesses and generally ugly intellectuals is making me sick. The lectures are interesting, though—the only trouble is that some of those guys there are bald-faced enough to deem they are privileged to re-interpret everything from the Bible to Melville and Sartre. "Job was the scapegoat of his culture," etc. All with Marxian overtones and under-rumblings. Finally, being so bored with some of these lectures, I began making notes about the New School itself and its tendency to revaluate according to superficial "modern" standards... a separate study, for which I won't have to take an exam. But it is an old study with me... of the psychology of psychology. One guy, William Troy, says that old great literature follows these patterns, 1) Conflict, 2) Pathos (suffering), 3) Dismemberment (sparganos), 4) Symbolic death, and 5) Epiphany (restoration to the culture). But such a clod-headed American as Dreiser cannot be fitted into these formulae... something will have to be done about *that*! A new research department will be set up to squeeze Dreiser into their theories, as Dreiser moulds by the old stonewall. Mouldy Dreiser with his juicy tears of the grave. On one occasion, describing Sonya's little sister in *Crime & Punishment*, the prof, instead of reading Dusty's own words about this little girl who says she will pray for Raskolnikov (in a dim hallway too), goes on to describe her as a "sweet nymph of orisons" or something like that; which, to me, is proof that modern symbolism is simply an escape from the reality of real little girls and real Raskolnikovs and real dim hallways. He was substituting the human value of the little girl for a poetic value; and as a rule they go on to substitute social values for personal values, such as by saying that Job is a "scapegoat of his culture" when after all he is only an old man who had misfortunes. Everything has got to be symbolic of *what they mean*. Dig? "What they mean" is what they want, of course, and this is acceptable to me as a force in historical will-to-destiny, but it is not scholarship. And what they want is not what *I* want, of course. The New School is a battleground for European ideas-of-disintegration, as you already know, but direct constant experience of it gives me a fresh feeling of mistrust and loathing.

Consider these banalities as you put up another beam to your house—house-building is the thing itself. I sit here by my typewriter in the late afternoon with its long reddish slants of light, always a symbol to me of my childhood solitariness (previous to football), and I too want to build houses and get out of this fatal late afternoon light that falls on the bed I sleep too much in. Doom and death,—so we'll go to Paris. Jack

Nov. 30, 1948
Ozone

Dear Ed,

Read your fascinating, great, and kind letter. In it you show more than wisdom-in-moderation, but an "excessive" knowledge of what everybody's doing. The poem you quoted: was that from Alice in Wonderland? I did as you instructed, applying everyone to the various roles in the roundel, and it gave me the weird feeling that we're all alike and all doing the same thing, much as Dostoevsky indicates continually. There can be no "false dichotomies" when we realize that everybody's madness stems from the same sanity of intention. When I placed Jesus in the place of the protagonist of the poem—"I told them 'This is what I wish'"—it like to tore my guts out, it was so unusual a vision or perception of him/Him. It reminded me of Rembrandt's Christ, the woeful one leaning from a post in the gloom (have you seen that?)—the Christ which Ginsberg perceptively designates as "Not knowing either."

Well, these heavy, gloomy subjects sometimes wear me out. I saw Jack Fitzgerald two weeks ago, spent the weekend in Poke, and had one of the greatest times of my life. We are now exchanging letters in which we have created a myth out of our dead fathers— Old Mad Murphy and George Martin—wherein they sit up in the oversoul, the clouds, heaven, and look down, much as Melville's father might have looked down on Herman when he wandered around Liverpool trying to decipher his father's out-dated map & guide-book.[10] Old Mad Murphy calls my father you "old bastard" and they swear and spit and finally Old Mad Murphy says they might as well have a few beers up there, it's too much down here. But they think of their sons, who will be fathers themselves, and try to guide them. Fitz, by the way I now consider the freshest, most original mind of them all, and the finest boy in the world, like you, and don't be offended if I say Neal also (for different reasons). Fitz is just great—and very much the sad mime of "Children of Paradise." His wife Jeanne is indescribably fine... their baby is an angel.

I have recently met another family much like the Fitzes—people I envy, because nothing is more enviable than a great man and a great woman with beautiful children. This person is an artist called Alan Wood-Thomas whom you would be pleased to know. I only wish you were in New York now so I could hear you and Wood-Thomas discuss art and "lines" and so on. I met another fine couple, John and Marian Holmes, a novelist and poet.[11] The thing that distinguishes these people from my old Carr-Burroughs-Adams-Ginsberg crowd is that they try their best to be humanly good, while still "knowing as much," in a way, as the others. I don't feel cold and lost among them. Wood-Thomas recently had his preview.

Finally I've made the acquaintance of several—actually two— very fine girls. One is Wood-Thomas' model, a married girl with a baby, Pauline. A very beauteous thing: Lombardian, tall, sloe-eyed, Edie-naive but not bitter, a girl with a background perhaps like Neal's (no breaks). This girl moves me in every possible way but I don't like to interfere in marriages so much and I'm just glad I know her. The other girl is an eye-popper but not so spiritual, though sorta sad. In black Persian slacks she sat in the windowsill and told me she needed a friend. Meanwhile I have been gunning innumerable women so much that I sometimes confuse them in my sensual thoughts—an orgy of arms and legs: all kinds of mad creatures, most of them from the Middle West strangely. Except for the 17-year-old one Fitz had for me in Poke, a high school type, mad, mad.

I have written to Monsieur Goy in Paris and have dropped in at the Cultural office. It seems to be a cinch. The problem is boat fare. Also I have fine connections myself to get there—Diamond is going in April, knows everybody; and I know a novelist who is also an official of the National Maritime Union, in case I should want to work my way over. And we ought to write Temko and tell him to pave the way. I got a letter from him full of Haute-Savoies, or did I already tell you? He's a good kid. He gave me a list of names so I could sell my book. He's finishing his own novel now, dabbling leisurely like a continental novelist. He will finish the last draft in the Midi, I expect. He said he saw a "rotten bullfight" in Arles. So this must be the end of his Hemingway period in an odd way.

My sister and her husband the Southerner and their kid may move in with my maw and I in Ozone, which would be great. Then I wouldn't mind so much going to France with you-all, she wouldn't be alone. Things may happen by February too. Any day I expect news on my novel and a story, and I'm getting G.I. checks soon.[12] Besides, by the way, my mother is very keen on my going to France—she says a writer mustn't stagnate at home—and finally she feels she won't worry if I go with that "Fine, decent Ed White and his pals." No doubt Burford would sweep her off her feet if he ever gets to meet her, too. As Hal says, he would "cut a fine figure in her eyes," and that is so, too.

Which gets us to Hal. I haven't seen him yet. My feeling is utterly sad and lost about this. The more I think about it the less I understand it, because I love Hal like a brother. I guess it's just a passing, incomprehensible phase in a murky season. I'm afraid I'm beginning to hate Ginger overly, with the passion of a Balzac villain, and that too is murky, meaningless. Time will eat it out, and then we will all die anyway. I think Hal is in a state where too many people confuse his intentions...just as, at a party recently, where there were 25 people all of whom I knew well enough to be involved with, I went out of my mind because it was all so superficial...jumping from one thing to another like kingfishers and forgetting it all next day. The world is too big. Even Ginger I miss. The world is too big.

I saw Tom on Thanksgiving. Tom has whipped up a fine trio: he and Julie his girl (a bass player) and a guitarist. He showed me a few of their routines. It sounds just like the Page Cavanaugh trio. At the opening I will sit at the front table and watch Tom up there, draped in a vast blue jacket, bow-tied, sharp, white teeth shining, as he leans eagerly from the keyboard whispering the songs they sing together as they play . . . and the smile of the trooper. "Picture . . . you . . . upon . . . my . . . knee . . . it's . . . tea for two . . . and two for tea." And Julie in black slacks plucking away, Tom hitting his new chords—the tinkle of glasses and voices in the club, the smoothness, the drinks, the smokes, the smooth music. Tom and I were going to fill a "bom" one night and suddenly decided instead to go on an eating jag. We ate dozens of White Tower hamburgers and vast banana splits in a famous soda fountain in Richmond Hill. Then Tom folded up and went home . . . wandering absentmindedly out of the house leaving his coat behind, and books, and a quart of ice cream he had bought for his father. I yelled him back just in time. I wonder if Tom is well, the way he folds up so quick at night, like a collapse of some kind. He never sleeps. The finest boy in the world— how many times can I say that? Why don't they think up a new expression for these feelings.

Did you go on with the house during the big snows? How's Jeffries?[13] Did you know that I never met Jeffries? But I think I might have seen him around the campus plenty, and will recognize him. Finally—I might be in Denver when you're ready to entrain to New York in February. I might very well be. But more on that later. At-random me another letter soon, boy.

Jack

p.s. Do you remember the time you told me about Trollope and how he wrote apparently "without emotion." I was so struck by that—mostly also by the way you yourself described it. Well, lately, working on two new novels, it seems I am practically doing the same thing. The other night I found myself writing a very funny scene with a frown on my face, nay a scowl, as though I knew perfectly what I was doing and why it was funny yet felt no inclination myself to laugh. I never even cracked a smile—much as a radio comedian is blank-faced in the midst of his funniest jokes. The same thing applies to "tragic" writings . . . a kind of irritable scowl that just wants to get it over with. The one advantage of this is that I'll never again spend three years on one work, and also one doesn't become "wasted."

pp.ss. I have already acquired a demoiselle's address in Paris: Claudie Renault, 2 Rue de Florence, Paris 8—Phone Number:- EUR 44-58. How's that sound? I got it from a Pan American girl who will also be in Paris in ze Spwing.

Dec. 7, 1948

I delayed sending this off because it didn't seem worthy of your last letter.

J.

March 29, 1949

Dear Ed,

Well, boy, guess what? I sold my novel to Harcourt Brace— (after one rejection from Little, Brown)—and got a $1,000 advance. Mad?—I tell you it's mad. Mad?—me mad? Heh heh heh. As Hal says, I'm just chuckling all over... *chuck*-ling, that is. Also, my personal editor is the boss of H-B himself, Robert Giroux, a fine young man of 35 or so, prematurely gray-haired, who read my novel (it almost seems) with *my* eyes. Ah Ed, I feel good. My mother and family feel good. I am redeemed in so many ways that I realize now I've been living under a cloud of inferiority complex. But aside from that kind of bull, just think what it means to me and the family. Later, I'll have saved enough to buy a homestead, get married, etc., and I have nothing but books to write. Shit!

So there you are in France, and here I am in Ozone Park, and— presto!—why aren't I in France? First, how long will you be there? Knowing this, I can plan. I keep thinking I may get a fellowship within a year; maybe I ought to wait for that. I have a school-year of G.I. left, however. I have a long time to try and get a job on a ship. Many angles. Ask Bob about what he thinks.[14] How's Buck Jeffries? I'll bet you are having one hell of a time, one such as has never none-suched so...etc. etc.

In your letter you said you watched the children in the parks and gardens. That's for me—to sit in a Baroque park, at red dusk, in Paris, watching the amazingly charming children play, with you: & *commenting* like we did that day on Central Park West. With Burford get the great girls that are there (let him do the open-field running, I'm the coach). With Jeffries do whatever he does greatly (which I don't know now). And all together, one, two, three four, sweep down to the *Cirque Mediano in Montmartre* and see the circus as it was intended, the French-Italian circus of rueful, cosmic, Shakespearean clowns. And scraggle in the streets of Rancy, where Céline raged. And what about this here Côte d'Azur? Jumps? Women in diaper suits? Fine, I'll take one. Ed, who have you seen? Temko? and Walter Adams? Do you know that I have known Herb Benjamin in N.Y. for a year without knowing you knew him? Tom is great now (he's muttering up a revolt from his straits. Also he's auditioning his trio). No see Hal, who can come and see me any time he wants, of course. Yes, I sold my novel, and I'll come to Paris sometime; just let me know your plans. Right now Giroux and I are working on some revisions in his office, in the evenings. (By the way, the chapter you and Hal didn't like is undergoing a cut.) My contract includes a Hollywood clause—What? Lana Turner and me? bosh! I command you, as King of the Thousand Dollars, to write me a *long* and informative epistle, Sirs. BET-A-THOUSAND

Mon. May 9, 1949

Dear Ed,

There seems to be a note of sadness in your last, fine letter. Without mentioning it you indicate that the 3 musketeers are somewhat scattered across the continent: Jeffries in a kind of pleasant absentminded pilgrimage through strange joys & places; and Burf in what sounds like a tragic, precipitate *affaire d'amour*.... [15] With all this, then, you appear, through your own printed lines (or between them) sadly cogitating over Pernod at some café...not even certain whether it should be Pernod or a martini or Cinzano. There is a gigantic aloneness somewhere in the letter...and a gigantic sadness; I know not what. Ed, by God, perhaps I'll join you in the Fall. Every now and then I get drunk and it seems the only logical thing to do. After all I am not always going to have a chance to go to Paris—a war might come again in the 50s; and Paris might change someday into some monstrous Housing Project. It seems to me, too, that for Americans—serious yet needful of some Dyonisian splurge somewhere along the line—like you and I—Paris and the gigantic, sad French night that must be there, and all the appurtenances of boozy wonder and the nostalgia of real though strangely different men and women—etc. etc.—all the things there are, known and unknown—it seems to me that this at one point becomes every bit as important as the other necessary activities, love, work, marriage, etc. In short, a year on the continent is a necessary activity, no matter how aimless it might appear while it's going on, or sad, or aught.

I've been writing to you as if to the 3 of you, not knowing that actually you were alone. Therefore with great pleasure I revert to the old-fashioned letter—since Burf and Jeffries, tho great guys, might not catch on, somehow; tho of course I know they would. I am in a great gigantically sad mood to write a long letter anyhow—and I think you need one at this point. I can see you when you receive this letter. Perceiving its immense bulk, you'll make great preparations before reading it. You'll repair to a sidewalk table, order a Pernod, spread the sheets, light up a butt, glance around leisurely a moment, and begin reading. And in this letter you'll see all the wild thoughts of a buddy 3,000 miles away who sits in his room at midnight, madly drinking coffee and smoking, typing away faster than he can think—and you'll think of the gigantic sadness of the Atlantic Ocean at night where shrouded waves toil in the salt hoods of water (or hurling salt shrouds in the hooded Atlantic night). I must copy down some of my *poetry* for you before this letter ends. . . .

But first. About Hal. I went up to see him several times at his new room at 1165 Fifth Avenue, but he wasn't in. I wanted to see him anyway, but specifically (and knowing that he likes specific reasons) about Denver and accommodations possibly in his brother's mountain shack for me and my b-in-law while we scout around this summer. Finally I wrote and explained. He wrote back a swell letter. "It is to the point to say that I dreaded meeting any of the old crowd. I had vowed to myself that I would not revert to the aimlessness of '45 and '46. Much of my recent activity feels like manufactured interest to me, a kind of scholastic busy-work to fill the time till my unknown love comes along. There is nothing now to compel me to come to grips with anything that I feel to be real in the world. The term for this is 'hanging on by the teeth.' " These are quotes from his letter. He figures it will be alright about the shack, etc., but the most important thing to me is that he is trying to get a $1000 grant from the U. to go digging in Colorado, and is trying to get work done, and has been doing so all this time. I feel that I have been unfair to him in my innermost thoughts, since after all I buried myself away for 3 years in Ozone and only came out when I felt like getting drunk, and always had my workaday lonely room to go back to for work; whereas, he, as in Livingston on the 11th floor, always had so many distractions (he can't work among distractions as you can, for instance). I guess this is a pretty fair estimate, isn't it? At any rate, I'll see Hal in June and may even drive him home to Denver come that time. He mentions that he may have to work on a farm this summer; that his father almost died, but recovered. I only hope I make enough money to help Hal someday—after all his needs are slight, and I believe my income may eventually be rather bloated out of proportion (God knows why), or as Lucien says, I have been elected the Queen of the May, and have been given Grace (of that kind) for strange Fateful reasons.[16] I don't know, finally, what gives with the Ginger element in Hal's life.

I have just returned from a weekend in Poughkeepsie with Jack Fitzgerald and wife and friends. It was one perpetual beer-drinking dream. Every time I looked up I saw old Fitz sitting there with a glass of beer in his hand, and every time I went to the icebox for another quart it seemed that our original supply of 30 quarts was diminishing in an unorthodox way, that is, with great rapidity. With an old friend of ours Duncan Purcell we went tearing around Poughkeepsie on a Saturday night underneath the soft Yokum's Moon of the Hudson . . . to Tulip Street (famed after that great story of Jack's called "Snatch and Dratch and the Tulip Street Belles"). We hit many bars. At home we continued to drain quart after quart. It was funny and great and sad. As a matter of fact you must have noticed that I used the term "gigantic sadness" about five times in this letter; it is Jack's expression, casually dropped at dinner table Sunday as he sat there looking out the window at the slanting red light, reflecting that if it were true that "life on earth was actually heaven itself, that we were all angels with wings, that when we died we were buried here in heaven forever," if so (as I had been maintaining through beer-glasses) then, by

God, "I know a lot of dumb sonofabitches who're going to be fucked when they find out there's no heaven after this one to finagle for." He said, "I like people who are conscious of the gigantic sadness of the whole mad thing—the dumb bastards," he added. He is writing a novel called "Mighty Mike and Mad Murphy," and I've heard all about the story and hope to hell he writes it, for it is wonderful. There was much screwing in the night also—mingling various belles. Finally on Monday morning (I was still there dumbly wondering how to get back to N.Y.) Fitz refused to go to work and began drinking beer again. He said, "Someday everybody in the world will refuse to go to work on Monday morning and then the whole mad, gigantically sad thing will change. Into God knows what, the dumb bastards." We had his truck and went tearing down moonlit roads; we even took his one-year-old son to various bars in the afternoon; almost got picked up by the cops for crazy driving; and had a great time. Every time I go see Jack Fitzgerald I come home feeling different— as though the world was full of sad, dumb bastards who are at bottom amazingly funny to behold.

But eventually my own morbid nature reasserts itself, and I sweat in the night with my own perspiring vision. Here is an example of what I've been thinking of lately. Mostly my ideas are now springing out of actual nightmares—well, dreams. At Jack's house last Saturday afternoon I had an awful and beautiful dream. It took place in the late afternoon somewhere...among many excited people, friends, lovers, relatives. Dozens trooped into front parlors and argued and harangued about something. God knows what it was but I was the center of it all. I was trying not only to pacify everybody but actually to make a separate peace with each individual. This involved many difficulties—since some relationships were more intense than others. But that seemed to make no impression on my dull, beating brain. All I wanted to do was win the mad approbation of everyone. I pulled strings, I laboured, I rushed around shouting—and all of it in a strange, eternal, red light of late afternoon, under really beautiful trees. There was one house on a dirt road in the country; and another kind of dormitory in the town. It is one dream I can't reconstruct, except the feeling it gave me—of my own falseness. The sum of it was: how could all these people be so blind to my monstrousness, how could they be fooled, why couldn't they see? At one point I remember stealing a baseball bat in a store, with a sly grin, and sneaking out with it in front of everybody (impressing them immensely with my daring), only to learn later on that my mother had paid the owner of the store for it. Things like that. In which everybody seemed to be mystified by me, except my mother who bore my madness sadly and "paid." In this dream I realized that each of us has a really horrible sense of personal falseness that is almost mortally dangerous—it's hard to imagine how we can manage to stay alive with this sense of loneliness and terror. Yet when I related this dream to Fitz and Jeanne they said they dreamed the same things, and wondered why no one noticed how horrible they were. It seemed to me, then, why don't we call it a day sometime and confess all . . . a big confession before the seat of Judgment Day. But let me elaborate further, in more detail.

Here's the way I wrote up another dream and series of thoughts attending, in a journal of mine called "Rain and Rivers" . . . (in conjunction with the third novel "The Myth of the Rainy Night").

The night of the eclipse of the moon, 11 P.M., April 12, 1949, I had a dream and a trance in my queer house in Ozone Park . . . that is to say, it was suddenly the same ambiguous house of my dreams, with many meanings and existences, like a great well-placed word in a line of poetry—or prose. It was that very house that sometimes rattles . . . and is set on the edge of the world instead of Crossbay Blvd, with all the windows open and all things within immediate reach. Down the street: whole continents, and the sea of night; up the street, strange cities, and rain, and shouts, and big hubbubs of crowds; and lights—and all the familiar faces of all men and women. Jesus. Earlier in the day, however (to elaborate) he who is known by name, Allen Ginsberg, and I, discussed the "shrouded stranger."[17] This is a concept stemming from a dream I once had of Jerusalem and Arabia long ago. . . . Traveling by dusty road in the white desert (where some men walk in satisfaction and drink up dust, while I stagger and look for soft trees, the Oasis), traveling from Arabia to the Protective City, I saw that I was being inexorably pursued by a Hooded Wayfarer Without a Name, who carried a Stave, and slowly occupied and traversed the plain behind me, sending up a shroud of dust slowly. I don't know how I knew he was following me, but I thought if I could make it to the Protective City before he caught up with me, I'd be safe. As much as I hurried and staggered and ran, he, sauntering, kept catching up slowly—or if not sauntering, it was a kind of shrouded movement on the plain he made. It was out of the question: I knew I was doomed. So I wanted to waylay him in a house at the side of the road, with a rifle that became a rubber toy as he drew nearer. And the Protective City was just over the hill, too.

Allen G. was much interested and wanted to know who this was, and what was meant by this.

I proposed that it was one's own self merely wearing a shroud.

For where do we come from? Isn't it awfully true that we come from the darkness before-birth, which for merely being *dark*, is therefore hell—and arrive here in life in the LIGHT of earth, which, for merely being LIGHT, is heaven. Following this, then—what are our ambiguous intentions for being alive, each of us?—for why should we deign to live anyway? Isn't it true that each newborn babe is a new ambiguity for this queer world. Immediately, at the tender age of several months, you begin to notice the way in which he is able to get what he wants . . . the way he cries, or sulks, or mopes, or coys, or cuddles up. You stand there amazed by the maturity of his *soul*, even before the brain is developed . . . (for what is even a Beethoven, if not a soul peeking from the mighty darkness of his own creation?) And peeking at what? At US, US all. . . . What secrets has the babe?—what means he?—what does he *want*? What does he know? What will he admit? Only a Celestial tongue can tell, someone wearing White Robes Flowing and writing with a Golden Pen of Fire. In my trance following the dream of the Shrouded Stranger, as I sat there half-awake in this queer house, I saw that there is definitely another world . . . the world which appears to us from out of our own shrouded existence which was given in darkness, before the light of life arrived. But though we're born in darkness of the womb (of time etc.) it is true that we die in light. I have some doubts about my extension of this, i.e., is the darkness from whence we come, hell?—and is the Earth heaven?—or just purgatory? What is the Shrouded Dream after all? It is perhaps the vision of hell from which we came, and from which we tend, towards heaven, here, now. It all needs further explanation, and is the most serious matter I can think of. Or is there an actual celestial heaven incarnate in the sky? (just mysticism?)

What is Love? The meeting of two souls in a tangle of shrouds? And so on—(here I am dishonestly, merely copying some notes). I'm in a very mad and nervous mood and actually don't quite know what to say, except that I want to say everything at once to you. But the realest thing I felt when I woke up from this dream was that what we are doing here (in all this) is trying to do our best in whatever world we find ourselves. In the world that appears or is made flesh in a dream, we dumbly lie there arranging and rearranging the memories of other dreams, other existences; like file-cards, and so on. And in the daylight "rational" world we rush around...bleeding and weeping every blessed heavenly moment. Why? What I want to do is explain it all some day, and get that mad cark out of my heart (and the reader's heart) thereby...so that we can proceed to greater things somehow. I don't know. For instance, just imagine what it means for me (or anyone else) to write a line like this, as I did in *Town and City*—that, why did I write it? What did I really mean?—"George Martin arrived in the riotous tinkling night of Times Square a dusty, shabby traveler from the desert of the night (that Cyrus-like spread camping to incomprehensible horizons)." Within the parentheses are additions made on the spot, just now, just for the hell of it.

Or consider this from my diary of the trip to California last January:

"Trip from N.Y. to Frisco, 1949. Across the tunnel to New Jersey—the Jersey night of Allen Ginsberg, rolling in the rainy night on tidal highways. We in the car jubilant, beating on the dashboard of the '49 Hudson...headed West. And I haunted by something I have yet to remember. And a rainy, road-glistening misty night again. Big white sign saying "WEST" and "SOUTH"— our gleeful choices. Neal and I and Louanne talking of the value of life as we speed along, in such thoughts as "Whither goest thou America in thy shiny car at night?" and in the mere fact that we're together under such rainy circumstances talking heart to heart. Telling ghost stories even. Seldom had I been so glad of life."

Well, enough of all this. What I've been trying to do in the past 2,000 words was to mass up enough stuff to show you some of my recent considerations. It is all a disorderly mess. I'll straighten it out.

If I were in Paris with you I'd have all the time in the world to explain. You would see, then, that it is not all exotic or esoteric, but merely the thing we all feel—as soon as I knew how to universalize my notions. I can't describe these things logically, or in a dialectic of any kind (and many more). The only possible way to suggest what I mean is to re-arrange life in an artwork that will demonstrate what I mean and what I think we all mean. (How ironic it is that the critics will say I don't realize what I'm saying...altho it's true, of course; and true for the dumb bastards particularly, that is, the critics.) For me the truth is not formularable, if such a word exists. For me the truth is rushing from moment to moment incomprehensible, ungraspable, but terribly *clear*. It rushes so fast across my disordered brain sometimes that I realize that I'm only a workman in an old motheaten sweater, complaining, sweating, hustling to catch the fresh dream, the fresh thought—a writer is a fisherman of the deep, with old, partially useful nets. All the gold that spills by my little thimble. The writer is only the guy who cares to bail and bail with his little thimble, and then in solitude hack away with the little chisel on the great iron mass....What burdens. What joys too by God. Also it is not important for me to formularize the "terrible clarity of truth" as I see it, because, and even if it is true that it cannot be formularized of course, any formula would give a picture of false clearness, like glass reflecting a reflection only. The reflection is the clarity itself and must not be looked at through a glass which may be false for all we know. Formula is just this glass (the formula of easy critiques), and may be warp'd. It is the fire itself I will show. Its hue is its secret, and formula gapes dumbly like glass warp'd & dull. I don't want to dumbly mull and file away Theorems, either; the only good line an "intellectual" friend of mine wrote was "I see metaphysics through my desk." Through my desk with its pigeonholes waiting for file-cards on reality, instead, I want to go off, like Shakespeare and like all the good ones, and dance on the edges of relative knowledge, dance to all the plaints, a rueful dancer, a clown...dancing the rueful dance....

My whole point sometimes resolves itself in: "What are we going to do?" And in a statement: "There is no need to care, but care is man's only need." And don't I love to talk about myself. What a gigantic loneliness this all is.

"But the Mississippi—and my Montana log that floats Odyssiac by craggy Missouri bluffs down along the wide night-shores by Hannibal, Cairo, Greenville and Natchez, and by old Algiers of Louisiana—the Mississippi and my log journeys by Baton Rouge, where, miles to the west, some underground, supernatural phenomena of the flood has created bayous (who knows?)—west of Opelousas, southeast of Ogallala, southwest of Ashtabula—and there in the bayous, too, and therefore, across my patient soul's-eye floats the wraith of mist, the ghost, the swamp-gyre, the light in the night, the fog-shroud of the Mississippi and Montana and of all the tidal earth: to bring me the message of the log. Ghost by ghost these bayou-shapes swim by in the hanging night, from mossy palaces, from the mansion of the snake; and I have read the big elaborate manuscript of the night. For what is the Mississippi River? It ends in the Gulf—called Mexico—likelier Night: and my riven, wandering log, all water-heavy and sunken and turning over, floats out to sea—around the keys...where the oceangoing ship (like an eternal ferry) passes again its strange destiny like a wraith. While I, a careless poet, I, an eye, a man, a wraith, a watcher of rivers, night, panorama and continents (and of men and women), in San Francisco scribble. For the rain is the sea coming back, and the river—no lake—is the rain become night, and the night is water and earth and infolding look—in other worlds are stars, etc."

Finally do you notice how my images have grown progressively "poetic"? This is only because they go further now, get more complex, and it is only a challenge to clarify them at last. (Don't worry about my mind, even though this is a mad letter.)

Only after spending a few days with those wonderful kids up in Poughkeepsie do I realize how alone and foolish I am—that is, I tried to tell them all these things in person, but couldn't—was certain I could if I went home and wrote them in a letter. And now telling it to you, even then it's incoherent. All dreamtalk. But it is that Carlylean earnestness, and the only thing I fear to lose in all life.

Tommy is renting an apartment in N.Y. for the summer. Actually it's John Holmes' apartment on Lexington Ave. I'll see a lot of him. How strange he is. Still hung up on that bag too. He's not particularly mad about music any more, tho he plays extremely well now. He wants to make money. He wants to live in his mad way.

Those two painters Roche and Moberg sound...so lost....Why do they tear their hair out? Why do we all tear our hair out? It's as Fitz says, we're all a bunch of dumb bastards and we might as well all get drunk like Mad Murphy and forget it. Either with beer or Pernod. Tom wants Pernod.

You must elaborate further about getting thrown out of the Communist rally—about your girl—about the big night out there. About the play. About Burford (I detect a note of disappointment in you there). I haven't heard from Beverly. Actually I don't want to now that she's married. It's all too fucking sad. I wonder if Burf is getting married because his sister got married—for it all makes us feel so old. Where is Central City? Les neiges d'antan.... And that time Temko acted like a Hemingway character all afternoon as we recruited 100 chorus girls to sweep the miner's shack.

You see, in this letter I feel like chatting away as though we sat over a "bom" and it's simply merely impossible.

In Denver I want to look up that literary man on the *Denver Post*. Send me his name next letter—the guy Temko conned for the job. I want to get a little sportswriting job on the paper if possible. I'd give my right arm to make a few bucks a week while waiting for my royalties just sitting around watching the Western League ball games...the Denver Bears: and writing them up. Or even covering grammar school basketball. It's all the same, all sad and wonderful.

We want to rent a house outside town, or even inside ...anywhere, to begin. Already Hal says he will scout around. We're going in June. I am very happy. I picture myself taking a stroll in the Denver streets after supper, then going back to my room to write. On weekends having big wonderful parties like the old Burf parties. In the summers swimming, drinking brew, going up to the mountains, fishing and hunting with my brother-in-law—in the winter skiing. Chatting. Living. Going out with the fine gals out there. Eating ice cream. Screwing up at Pecker's Knob. Eventually raising a family out on the farm I'll get...having a shack on the Western Slope where I can go and be mad alone, out of sight—or having 3-week bats up there with the crowd. Is there not a St. John the Divine hiding in the mountains even now? A beerdrinking mad fool...something, anything. I look forward to Denver as something of a salvation. I only hope you will live there someday, but I guess you won't. I'm going to make it my hometown. It reminds me a lot of Lowell anyway. Perhaps you will live there; I only hope so. One or two or three great friends is all I need. I think of Colorado also as a great place to raise my kids. There is a gravity there...as in Lowell...that N.Y. lacks: a Carlylean, earnest gravity. And the most wonderful guys I know all seem to come from there.

I look forward to Denver with the kind of joy that is not present in this crazy letter. But I'm only writing it to while away your sad hours at the café—perhaps you may even read it of a dawn to your mistress, O Baudelaire...and listen to the rumble of her stomach as he did.

By now, at dawn now, this letter wears thinner and thinner...yet I feel reluctant to leave off. Ah well. It's like dawn, all this. Sad, mad dawn: the gigantic sadness of the breaking light. Soon the sun will rise, and become the pearl of heaven flaming on high, and all will see.

Read this description of the mobsters in jail listening to the Gangbusters on Saturday night, in my 2nd novel "On the Road": "They even sat encircled in darkness like children, with eager regards, bending their ear to the human voice on the radio, the very voices so pathetically dedicated to the unravelment of some absurd plot about crime and eventual punishment at the hands of the law—the stern-voiced law that never failed; they sat in rings of darkness, by the warm orange eye of the radio dial, press'd together fondly in fond absorption, filled with the glee of night and the mysteries of safe, soft darkness that lay as in winding-sheets about their heads; they sat, and at their feet, on the very floor of the cell, or in corners, or places where the bars were runged in steel, and in the little places where mice hide, were all the dark-toed goblin things that occupy the night in any dwelling of any human kind, wherever men are (criminals or children: which is man).

"They sat back and sighed and wondered when the story was interrupted at mid-point by a commercial, and discussed the various points eagerly, and then leaned forward with mad anticipation when the story was resumed: they bit their fingernails, frowned with misunderstanding, cocked their heads, laboured to hear, nodded, shook their heads with dawning smiles, chuckled, laughed, roared and were incalculably and magically pleased by the whole thing. Even the cop in the hall with the *Sunday News* listened in a scowling reverie, and himself chuckled with delight whenever anything tickled his understanding.

"It was as the children, as little boys and girls, in that very moment by radios all over the Saturday-night America when Mom has finished shopping and is sewing little Billy's pants, and the old man is smoking a cigar and mixing drinks with his friends in the kitchen, and Big Sis is out dancing at the Rainbow Ballroom with her date, and the dog dozes on an old sweater on the parlor floor, and the Sunday papers are being brought around by boys with wagons in the thrilling darkness outside: it was the same dark room, the same warm glow of the radio's eye, the same engulfing drama of deeds and gunshots and shouts all swirling in the goblin dark, the dark that hid like glee all around and in the little shrouded corners... the titmouse corner, the migs-and-marbles corner, the corner where Billy's rubber ball was hid, the places where ragamuffin dolls and little dusts did lie: all child-sweet.

"Yet the difference was there—maybe merely for a pathetic reason of some kind—that these men in jail were the criminals themselves; the fugitive himself, the hero of the tale, the adult, crazy-hearted, murdering thief who snarled in a radio darkness at the stern-voiced law. And here in jail he listened to himself: out there he was listened to by the children. And he knew that insofar as payment went, crime many times paid, and crime was everywhere: while the fresh-eyed child believed that crime did not pay and gloated for joy, and cackled.

"Yup. Crime does not pay!" quotes little Billy riding back and forth in the rocking chair contentedly.

—But in jail, now, the Brain spoke up:

"For krissakes! Who in the hell ever heard of pulling a bank caper in a city like St. Louis in broad daylight without at least two cars, one carload out front with ready heat. Phew! I don't know where they dig up such ideas!"— Etc.

These lines express a lot of what I meant to tell you—in a true, though roundabout, way. How I feel... about it all. Come on, Ed White, spin me another letter. Excuse the madness. But at least c'est un divertissement, non? Who gives a fuck anyway. Write a madder letter if you can. So long boy.

                                                              Jack

                                                    Jan. 28, 1950

Dear Ed,

It's Saturday night. As I write this at home, a big party is raging at Walter Adams—with Temko, John Holmes, Victor Tejeira, Jinny Baker, Simpson; a party I avoided so I could think & work.[18] Last night I came home drunk on beer, and read your letter in the kitchen over my eggs; at dawn, actually. The letter concerning the eerie weariness... you & Buck, and the scene in the Colfax bar. I was moved by this note, and I know that the events moved you even more. Knowing nothing about the details, nevertheless I can feel & conjecture what it is...particularly from your saying "The day the well went dry, J. beat up his old mad father..." Doom comes in parcels, as in Ecclesiastes. Your own experience, designated as "furtive" but probably just restrained by essential goodwill & ethical sadness. Well, what can any of us do. I had the impulse to zoom to Denver at once.

Temko is on his way Monday. Your comments share my own. The wish for fame & fortune is the greatest obstacle, initially, to work—and work is just ragged and sad, and not at all like fame and fortune. I was just reading what Molière said, that it is easier to express one's noble sentiments than reveal the folly of others. But is there such a thing as folly when all the world, including you and I, is foolish? You might just as well reveal the folly of the air. T. is foolish, in his tortuous rationalization of bitterness, in blaming it on an abstraction, America; of course.[19] But this feeling reduces me to vague sympathy with his plight, and each our own eternal plight, which I suppose is mortality & feeblest understanding & death. A bom solves these things, and some of the aristocratic liberality of good wishes the Guinea has. What good is knowledge that hurts & impedes? Let's discover a true optimism, based on facts, and ask your brother Frank if facts are not equally "true" from any vantage they operate (relativity). —So a party rages at Adams. The last time I saw him he repeated his idea that the only criteria among us, is, Who can beat up who? We pulled wrists. We broke the table. I won. He decided I'm a good novelist because I have muscles. He wanted to arrange a fight between me & Neal, me and Lucien, to arrange his hierarchy of values. He stumbles [line missing] mad girl lost on the moors, in a corner. They talk. At midnight bottles start breaking. What a panorama these Fifties will present!

Ed, I'm coming earlier than I planned. Got somebody to sign at school for me—rent money—and am as free and "as mad as the mist and snow." I want to go where the wild goose goes. In March I begin to smell what must be going on in the great Missouris and Yellowstones and even Yukon rivers of the north—a muddy exhalation of the earth which in summer becomes like a tropical isle of vales—and I gotta go. Early in March, then. In April I want you to help me in several matters—info about Denver, such as when the Platte floods, and how and where it inundates. I've got to find a flood this April. One of my main characters in "On the Road" will be a young alcoholic Lucien-like newspaperman whose only love is great floods which inundate the silliness of cities. He goes driving in the night to cover them for the paper. Rivers play a big part. In New Orleans, the hero, Red, ponders over the rail of the Algiers ferry and sees a log coming down on top of the brown old flood—and the log is coming from Montana, where his father is (somewhere in Montana, he does not know exactly till he goes to find him).[20] Rainy nights, hitch-hiking; rivers; floods; states, towns; bop in niggertowns; freights; the plains— and hoboes singing: "Home in Missoula, home in Truckee, home in Opelousas, but ain't no home for me. Home in old Medora, home in Wounded Knee, home in Ogallala, home I'll never be, home I'll never be." I invented this.

Well, what am I rambling on about. I hope everything turns out OK for you & Buck in your present melancholies. I look forward to *knowing* Jeffries, whom I only met once. I enjoyed your joy with my book, and the comments on Francis not being an Ivan. I'm curious to know whether you noticed that the conversation during the funeral between the 3 brothers, while fishing, about "slaps in the face" was connected with the slap in the face Francis gave Peter when they were little kids.[21] Perhaps Hal would like to read the book. Lend him copy I sent you. Perhaps it will revive in him the goodness of our past friendship, although I absolutely refuse to "rout him out" when I go to Denver. He must make the first overture. I can be just as Sorelian as he.[22] In his present state of mind (Navajo rugs & such) he's probably no longer interested in the qualities that united us anyway. I don't care unless he shows signs of care. I have all the world and I have nothing, and it's all the same. And besides, what the hell's the difference? I sent copies of my completed book (cover, pix, etc.) to Beverly and to Bob Burford;[23] to Tom & family, and to a woman & her daughter in Denver, sort of Okies, you'll meet when I get there. Being a proficient typist, tendency is to write you rambling notes like this. Don't attempt to answer since you write by hand, and consideredly; that is, don't attempt to match my wordage. "What the hell's the difference" only means we all die anyway. Such bleakness man in infancy hath seen. Yet a nudder think may change the sea—How sweetly shrinks in my mind—Kind is Kind, and Goodness All. So I guess that's truer. I'm anxious to know what your "Oriental" experience was. You wrote weariness instead of eeriness I think because you see too clearly to see eerily. Nothing is strange; therefore all is strange. Jack

---

Cerrada Medellin 35-B
Mexico City, D.F.
July 5, 1950

Dear Ed,

Sir, what gives and why have you not communicated with us at our new address. Things are going a-pace and you are not here. I wrote to Justin the other day. Is there the possibility you might come down with him (and Dan) this summer? It would be a wonderful reunion in a wonderful city, and an interesting fivesome of talk & cervesa.

Frank is writing full tilt and shows a natural talent to avoid unnecessary pitfalls as beleaguer most new writers.[24] He is not as happy as he was in France, I think however, because the girls are so hard to meet & make...beyond the whores.

As for me, I am doing what I came down to do—investigate all the levels of Elitch's Gardens, Mexican mile-and-a-half-high version, particularly with reference to the many problems and considerations of that second novel I have to write.[25] I have come up with many interesting new discoveries—or, say, I have dived deep for them. What I want to do is take inescapably true subconscious subjects and bring them to light of objective clarity. For instance, why do I feel so strongly about "a rose of the rainy night journeying on the river to the sea"? These thoughts are incommunicable in the novel, yet I don't want to write another novel unless I discover the way of communicating them. I want to work in revelations, not just spin silly tales for money. I want to fish as deep as possible into my own subconscious in the belief that once that far down, everyone will understand because they are the same that far down. The things of the night that never reach the light of noon...and of print. Why else should I write? Money is not my aim, only a means to that aim. With my inexhaustible supplies of Elitch I daily dive again into these dim regions, and crawl to the surface with the stub of a pencil, sweating, to record what I have observed.[26] I feel like a scientist. All becomes true when one wakes from a nightmare and considers it, half-asleep; similarly with Elitch. And similarly with those feverish talents that beset one in the middle of hot work. For instance, I was not Elitched when I wrote some of the mad parts of *Town & City*, only what they call "inspired"— made mad, made sane, all one. Now I'm unfolding whole new areas of work and life. For instance: you know, as I once told you, that I sometimes think deep subconscious thoughts in the French language, which takes me back to childhood revelations of the world. Consequently, discovering other aspects of this on Elitch, in my more sober moments I erect a form to rack this in. The form in this case obtains from the creation of a hero who is a French-Canadian (no Peter Martin), but one well-versed in "English" uses & style—and in order to bring in the pure French-C. element I create a fellow traveler, his cousin (whom he calls Cousin, in Quebec literally meaning among countryfolk, "my kind") who chastises him continually and is not bubbled-up with "English silliness" and therefore acts Panza to the hero's Quixote.[27] I have also come up with an idea for a technique; in that every moment of life, every scene, is fraught with a prophesy of the next moment, and this is indicated by signs and hints that everybody knows it's so.

Sufficient example, this, of what I am thinking; yet how Elitch prevents one from writing clearly. I will go back to New York laden with this new work and proceed, as of old, in old sweaters and sober moods, and make it. Right now I can't explain clearly enough, or at least, not in the short space of a letter. There is no need to write any more unless man has stopped discovering—and that he has not; nevertheless 2,000 American novels are published every year repeating the same old formulas that have failed and failed and failed.

What there is in my individual life that makes hope for my own individual future—what strange things they are!—(nothing so sensational, maybe, but the remembrance of a sun-whitened street and what happened there, never to change, forever fixed and existent, with all its messages and hints of what may yet happen *on that level* and finally on all levels possibly)—these things that make for hope in my subconscious gropings, may possibly after all be the same for everyone in the world...Mexicans, Africans, Chinese, who knows? So that there could emerge a great world religion based on the hopes and images of childhood and made into form in the rational vigor of adulthood. Down here in Mexico, high, I've seen innumerable places I saw before in my boyhood in Lowell; the same street, the same afternoon...*except that it was Mexican*, of course, and that's my point—and point of departure. What will I do with this strange material? This is how I'm spending my time; working in the material, thinking, Elitching.

For instance, I know that I will die and I know that you will die, nevertheless on a rainy night, when God hovers over blowing rain on my rooftop, I am soothed and I do believe that none of us will really die in these wide, rainy, fore-ordained spaces with their freight of mysterious and beautiful time. Something is bound to happen, some revelation is bound to appear to me soon, like light; like a scientific discovery; but not in a formula; so that, in my work I will be able to reflect these mysteries in a glass—a glass not warp'd and dull like the glass of formulas—but a fiery glass. A pen that spurts golden fire and winds white shrouds around the man. I guess I want to be an angel of some kind. That is a fact. Not for immunity, but for the right to be near God. I even pray Him to make me more devout than I ever was. Somewhere along the line it will happen. Romantic as it sounds, I would like to fall on my knees like Handel and pray for a work to appear to me; and then, lo and behold, there it is appearing in my window, hallucinatory visions of Bethlehem and the Star... fit images and pictures for an Oratorio which is to be called the Messiah. Why can't this happen to me, except that I would not call forth Bethlehem and the Star, just a rose in the rainy night and the faces of people, and a dark room much like holy Roualt's room in the picture called "Out of the Depths Have I Cried to Thee O Lord."

Every night the phrase resounds to me..."What Hath God Wrought?" This is no quibbling matter. American life is my subject because I love no other life; but at the bottom of American life is the universal light, and the prophecy, of something that will happen... perhaps on judgment day. I don't recommend fire for America, like Guru Wallace, but I recommend rainy nights and pattering rooftops for the sleeping babe, the dreaming babe... and whatever happens from there on, let it happen to me, so I can seal my prayer when this consistent husk leaves off in dirt.[28] Does any of this make sense or is it pure Elitch? That too is another problem I'm dealing with.

Meanwhile, much fun; whores; steaks; sun. Please try to come down. I'll be leaving MC in the middle of August, via Havana. Write soon. Tell yr. mother it has taken me all this time to realize how delicious those Sunday afternoon desserts were... remember? Mint ice cream and hot fudge? Give my love to Bev. Is she mad at me for coming & going & not thanking as I should have? Ah well—

A la vue, mon ami,

Jack

P.S. Frank inserts missive.

Dear Ed,

Just received yr. latest missive, sir, which I shall present to Madame Beverly in the evening. Tonight we are attending a big party at John Holmes' house. What you said about the long-distance call holds true. . . . Tom did come; but the evening fizzled somewhat because the girls we had for him turned out to be real cherries (in the social sense). The evening ended weirdly with a ride to Brooklyn in search of a certain *field*, an Elitch field, with its fronds waving under the nose of passers-by on a busy street. Presence of innumerable gendarmes apprised us of the possibility that its harvest had been nipped in the ripest bud. Our guide, a little hipster character, apologized profusely for the wild goose chase but Tom enjoyed the madness of it. This little hipster—let us name him Irving—had his personality analyzed for me by a local friend: "The trouble with Irving is that he found a field." Isn't that one of the most beautiful remarks in this ugly century? Irving found a field. . . . Sir, it puts one in the mind of Tennyson and allied bards. Agh, agh, agh. Tom just missed your call by minutes. We watched him from the 12 story window parking his big 49 Buick among the aggressive New Yorkers. We watched him hurry up the street; as usual he was an hour late. We yelled at him from above; he danced in the street below. For my part, Ed, I had no idea what to talk about on the phone, primarily because it was Bev's call and Bev's bill, but I did have a vision of you in Denver making ready for an evening of casual riot. I was mulling something to say to you in French and leaped to the phone just as you were telling Bev to tell me to take care of her, and malappropriately said, "Toujours ton amie." However, a good joke was had by all. Today, Sat., I feel gloomy and inappropriate for life. I wonder what Bev and the big party will unfold tonight. Ah well, life is brief, health is brief, joy is brief, and brief is as brief be. Think of the pathos of the fact that all of us, poor children of God, have to sleep eight hours every day, as though we were hardly fit for this world and God was only trying us out for endurance initially. Sometimes I am fascinated by this pit of night we live in, [ends here]

April, 1951

Dear Mr. Eduardo White—

What are you doing, m'boy? Has Justin told you of our get-together in N.Y.? It was amusing—(certes?)—and in the past ten days I've written 86,000 words almost finishing "On The Road" and finishing it by this Sat. night April ?—[29]

I don't know the date nor care and life is a bowl of pretty juicy cherries that I want one by one biting first with my cherry stained teeth.—how?

Sir, if I am to understand that you're coming in June then I am to understand joyously a coming event of first-rate superior importance to me. And if so, remember the moment you get off the train you rush at once to 454 W. 20 and throw a pebble in my dusty window—to get drunk with me or never—to celebrate dull life and make the cherries dance the Kerry dance which is the Kerouac-White dance of life, no Ellis—Right? American women are making it awfully easy for American men in the city of N.Y. this Springtime.

—As ever yr. copain, Jack

August 1, 1951
(p.s.—Am completely re-writing Neal-Epic)[30]

Dear Ed—

Believe it or not, this is all the paper I have. I'm in the Kingsbridge VA Hospital recuperating from my fifth attack of thrombophlebitis since 1945—the worst; so I have to stop smoking altogether, take blood-thinning pills and penicillin and take care of myself the rest of my life, or, if the condition spreads from legs upwards, I get brain, heart or lung thromboses that prove fatal anytime.[31] I just received yr. marvelous letters yesterday via John Holmes, who visited me here last week (been here 3 weeks, previous to that laid up a month in No. Carolina.) Yes, my (pregnant) wife has flown, and good riddance, I've work to do and fun to concentrate on. Your coming to New York is going to enrich my life. Bravo for fate in this case!—she finally got us in the same town. I'll be demeuring at my mother's house at *94-21 134th St. Richmond Hill* as soon as I get out of the hospital next Friday. Of course, a bom celebration is in order for us battered Knights of the Cross. Really, Ed, I'm *exhilarated* you're coming; think of the fun; I have mad new places to go to (tell you later); and women galore all over. Yes, I think you made the right choice in architecture—architecture is better than teaching and all that sissy shit—architecture is a noble thing—it was Faust's last dream—and *you* are a born *architect*, sir! Think of the honor, sir, in this age, of being the exact opposite of a psychoanalyst! I look forward to meeting you at the train— shoot me the coming-time. All's well. Sir, to be your admirer is not to be meek.

                                                    Sam. Kerouac Esq.
Sir, I'm not about to die

                                                    Monday, Aug. 31, 1953

Cher Edourard I mean Edouard pas accotumé au français:—

Notes written drunk last night to you, by brakeman's lantern at my bedroom window:[32] Dear Ed:

I love my ceiling more since it is a dancing floor—lost opportunities with Ginger and Dusty in the Village that night you and I—boy don't you remember?[33] I've tried to hide in vain underneath my counterpane. Well, new seasons, and I'm going to Paris before fifty-four—at last—to rail in other bars, other bellies. Trumanote me that, Cap— Hurry back to N.Y.—order from Copain Jean Louis.
    Sir, 'ere you build my house'll you design my crypt. I want a crypt with wish fulfillment in stone, a cock in a cunt—a dick in a woman's mouth—the pelvis out, and it empty—empty except of juices and sweet walls, sir— With that furtive ammoniac smell. Black pussy's the same as white, Ed—taste buds *democratique*. Glints off automobiles burn into our sad eyes, this is what we know before we die— In this crucified universe. Dreamt last night of Hal, as follows: "There've been big events and family reunions in NY and I got $1000 from the publishers at the same time I was offered a job selling books in a company car and some other job with it but I go to Mexico to "start my homestead," by bus. On the bus are Hal and Ginger and their 3 little vagamuffing blond kids who cry and play with passengers and are neglected by their parents as suddenly when I'm doing something (dozing

somewhere) "near Kansas" I hear a commotion, the bus stops, I go on dozing but wake up finally just in time to see the little boy is brushing something off the floor near the driver's clutch handle, brushing up grit, crying in a strange emotionless strangled despair inhuman unreal and short, just one cry—apparently he's puked (wasteland grit he puked) and this stopped the bus and his mother who's been in the back seats talking and playing guitar with people is letting him clean up himself far from helping him. I think "No wonder he puked after those pickles and those shmioles at noon and God knows what he had this morning (what his fool mother gave him)"—when we've stopped Hal the father all blond and white has stepped out to pee, he too unconcerned, and now as the bus is ready to start up again he steps back in arrogantly down the aisle gliding floating digging all the ladies with a perfectly defined hard-on in his blue slacks sticking way out and he knows it—I despise him—I think how he thinks I'm going to Denver again on some fiasco plan but I'm only "going thru to Mexico" I think proudly and I won't even give him the satisfaction of knowing this—of course we haven't talked at all on the bus—suddenly I despair and want to go back to NY and take that book job and park my car on Wall St. while I'm picking up my samples and selling my books to my "driving students" clients while I'm at it, and make it, take care of my children if any with concern not like these wretched conceited Hal Chases and Gingers but it's too late, the bus is almost in Kansas, we've been traveling for days, hard, slow travel & trouble—even if I cash in my ticket at Kansas I'll have lost $36 and leave me $80 and it's all a stupid big fiasco, and there Hal with his egomaniacal hard-on flouncing down the bus aisle—the world is drearily repetitious of itself . . . " end of dream.

Burroughs is in town, is a big celebrity among the subterraneans, a new gang of village heroes Ginsberg latched to: their names: Bill Keck, Anton Rosenberg, Mason Hoffenstein, Mark Rasovsky, Stanley Gould (hipster of "Portrait of a Hipster" by Anatole Broyard in Neurotica 1949) and Peter van Meter who is a beautiful blond Al Hinkle liked by everyone.[34] Burroughs having arrived with his dried telepathic vines is being lionized and loves it and by the coolest in fact coldest most intime interior hip group of all, they hang out in Fugazzi's on 6th Avenue and Minetta Lane.[35] The one thing I would commend both Burroughs and Ginsberg for is they continually dig the new elements in new generations and do not stagnate—and this new group tho interesting and modernly cold, as soon you'll definitely be hearing of cold jazz and cold peace of course, bugs me because of limitations in education—I have just had an affair with one of their chicks, Alena Lee, who is [a] beautiful brown girl but refuses to trust in my madness like William Blake's wife and so—will have to get along with the cold.[36] And I sir, I am headed for hot Paree—incidentally it is very hot the weather is in NY right now, the seventh straight day of over 90 degrees temperature makes the very wooden chair you sit in a bloody radiator, sir it is too much, an insult to the north— I look forward to your rearrivals in New Yorkio, we will light up the bom and blow up the night, sire—of course, in fact I don't know where you got the mad idea I'd be in Denver this summer, just because I hitched thru there last summer for the umpteenth time aigk I made it, I'm thru with hitching this goddamn America, I'm going hitching in Brittany.

I'll tell you more news of everything when I see you. It's too hot to write a long letter, all I want you to know from this letter is that I do think of you and am waiting for your rearrival and have not stopt corresponding with you or communicating with you by any name ever. I'm writing that railroad novel madly now, "Wine in the Railroad Earth" so far the title is, and it's all wild, I'll show it to you in cold glad October over brews at the bloody good west end sire.[37]

Where is Maria the Mad Italienne, Beverly's in NY?[38] I'll call and find out this week later. Shoot me yr date of arrival. . . . Give my very best to dear old Justin, tell him to come back to NY soon and not expect us to take him to turkish baths—well, we'll do it if we're drunk and even then circumspect—them bloody Arabian pleasures are alright for eunuchs, I say, but cunt rules my thoughts and world, sir, Cunt, as ever, yours,
    à la bom,
      à la straj,
        à la cunt
          à la vue
           amigo

                    Jack
                    Jean
                    Louis
                    le
                      Brice
                      Baron
                        de

                                    Kerouac
                                    de le
                                    Village
                                    de
                                    Kerouac
                                    en
                                    la
                                    Bretagne
                                    Okay

                        PS Dear Ed
                        With you I would *very much*
                        like to get drunk tonight!

                                    April 28, 1957
                                    Jack c/o Glassman
                                    554 W. 113 St.
                                    New York, NY

Ho Ed!

Yes my good friend I got your fine letter in Tangier, Morocco[39] less than a month ago and wanted to write to you from Dr. Johnson's house in London when I got there but got too engrossed in the British Museum and staring at El Grecos in the National Gallery so here I am back in NY and leisure to write you.... [40] Very interesting, your notes about Buddhist art, in fact in the Brutish [sic] Museum they have a Stupa from the Deccan south India showing empty places for the Buddha in the old sculpture.... [41] En route from Tangier to Paris... well first, in Tangier are Bill Burroughs who has just written a great book WORD HOARD and Allen Ginsberg whose poem HOWL has just been banned in Frisco.[42] There I had a room overlooking the straits, a patio, for 20 bucks month, and went mountain climbing to isolated Berber villages, etc. and smoked tea out of pipes with shrouded Arabs in cafés.... Then, after Marseilles, I tried to hitchhike through Provence, outside Aix, where Cézanne painted, ended up hiking 20 miles but it was worth it... sat on side of hills and pencil sketched drawings of the Cézanne country, dull red rusty rooftops, blue hills, white stones, green fields, hasn't changed in all these years... mauve tan farm houses in quiet fertile farmer's valleys, rustic, with weathered pink

---

powder roof tiles, a grey green mild warmness, voices of girl, gray stacks of baled hay, a fertilized chalky horseshit garden, a cherry tree in white bloom (April), a rooster crowing at mid day mildly, tall Cézanne trees in back...etc. just like Cézanne nein? Then a rattly old bus through Arles country, the restless afternoon trees of Van Gogh in the high mistral wind, the cypress rows tossing, yellow tulips in window boxes, a vast outdoor café with huge awning, and the gold sunlight....I haven't had chance to tell you but I've begun to paint, hence all the excitement about painting, started in Mexico City last October, first with pencil, then chalks, then watercolor, then paint...my first painting: God.—So I went to Paris and in the Louvre stuck my nose up against Van Gogh and Rembrandt canvases and saw they are the same person....I dug Pittoni first, as I walked in, expressive gestures...Tiepolo, *Last Supper*, perfect dog attitude at bone, the final white paint touches on Christ's face...Guardi, always the Doge, insane for detail and architecture but Canaletto is the master for that (*View of Venice*) splashing light on building and plazas and on corner, one thin line on corner edge (the Venetian 18th Century school)...and so on, and thru David, Girodet Trioson, Fragonard, Gros, and suddenly face to face staring at me, a Rubens! A big smoky Rubens (*La Mort de Dido*) which got better as I lookt, the muscles' tones in cream and pink, the rim shot luminous eyes, the dull purple velvet robe on the bed....But ah, THEN, Goya's *Marquesa de la Solana*, could hardly be more modern, her little silver feet shoes pointed like fish crisscrossed, the immense diaphanous pink ribbons over a pink face, a woman a French workingwoman said "Ah c'est trop beau!"...but then, walking along thru Gentileschi's little Jesus and Castiglione who paints a raging Christ distantly in a blue robe scourging the vendors in the Temple, throatslit lambs on the floor, confusions of ducks, baskets, goats....Ah then Brueghel! Wow! His *Battle of Arbelles* has at least 600 faces clearly defined in impossibly confused tight mad battle leading nowhere NOWHERE like real life, no wonder Céline loved him! Complete understanding of world madness, beyond which we see thousands of clearly defined figures and swords, above it all the calm mountains, trees on a hill, clouds....everyone LAUGHS when they see this insane masterpiece, they know what it means....Then O Rembrandt! Dim Van Gogh like trees in the darkness of Crépuscule Château, the hanging beef completely modern with splash of blood paint...with Van Gogh swirls in face of Emmaeus Christ...the floor (in Sainte Famille) completely detail'd in color of planks, and nails, and shafts of light on Virgin's tit. . . . St. Matthew being Inspired by the Angel is a MIRACLE, the rough strokes, so much so, the drip of red paint in the angel's lower lip making it so angelic and his own rough hands ready to write the Gospel (as I will be visited). . . . Also miraculous is the veil [of] mistaken angel smoke on Tobiah's departing angel's left arm. Finally, not least, Van Gogh . . . his crazy blue Chinese church, the hurrying woman, the spontaneous brush stroke, the secret of it is Japanese, is what for instance makes the woman's back, white, because her back is unpainted canvas with a few black thick script strokes (so that I wasn't wrong when I started painting God last Fall in doing everything fast like I write and that's it). . . . Then the madness of blue running in the roof of the church where he had a ball, I can see the joy red mad gladness he rioted in that church heart. . . . I have a headache from all this. . . . His maddest pic is of those gardens Les Somethings, with insane trees whirling in the blue swirl sky, one tree finally exploding into just black lines, almost silly but divine, the thick curls and butter burls of color paint, beautiful rusts, glubs, creams, greens, a master madman, Rembrandt reincarnated to do the same thing without pestiferous detail. . . . HISTORY OF ART: from Egyptians & wall cavers to Meissonier-types (where was finally mastered exact imitation of nature) (of DeHootch, Treck, Van Velsen, Kalf and all the Dutchmen and Italians who could do exact silver spoons and hams) back to Van Gogh and Renoir and Degas and Cézanne (Gauguin really a cheap cartoonist compared to these masters), (via Goya, Greco, Velázquez and Tintoretto this movement back), to exact *painting* (not imitating) of nature. . . . So I will paint what I see, color and line, exactly FAST . . . Paint being the holy blood. . . . (St. Matthew's Angel with the smear red mouth MOVED when I lookt!!!)

And of course Ed I visited Notre Dame, Montmartre, etc. all
    that jive,

And so, Ed, another letter later, write to me,
    and I'll tell you more about Paris than
        just museums. . . . I had a ball,
    it is greater than I thought it would be
but now I'm going to
                    California . . . .
            if you want to write to me care
                    of this address pronto, do it

by return mail as I am
leaving in 8 days....
alas, won't pass thru
Denver but thru El Paso.

Till I hear from you,
as ever
sir, your
humble
servant

Jack

Regards to your loved ones.
How's Justin?

By the way, you started whole new movement of American
literature (spontaneous prose & poetry) when (1951) in that Chinese restaurant on 125th street one night you told me to start
SKETCHING in the streets...tell you more later...this is big
historical fact, you'll see...(weird sketches).
And how in Dickens did you know always I wd. become painter
somehow?

1958

Sir,

Truth is, you hadn't answered my long letter about museums
of Europe, no wonder you didn't know where I was. That letter
came mostly from my notes made in Europe and will be grafted
into a piece *Holiday Mag* just bought, called "Tangiers to London,"
due to come out around Xmas 1958. For that, sir, I received
the handsome sum of a thousand clams not pounds. It seems
the writing business has begun to earn my living and I need no
longer cable our friend Brierly from the depths a Kansas for further
monies with which to reach the fair Denver.
Did you read *On the Road*, and *The Subterraneans*?[43] Has Hal
Chase read any of these two books? Tell him to read them, and
to vouchsafe an opinion about the prose in *Subterraneans*. Tell Hal
when you see him I still feel the same about him and he can

go right on the way he's been doing—that I at least appreciate his putting me down BEFORE I was famous. Ask Hal if he will remember that morning in a bar on Columbus Avenue, 1946, when I told him I was going to be famous young.

However now I'm old. I see you have a boy. What's his name? Are you going to have any more children?

The address on the envelope is my agent's. I'm staying with friends in Long Island meanwhile, looking to buy a cheap old house for me and my mother.

Gone are the pure days when I used to get excited in life, now I need wine for excitement.[44]

I have a new book coming out in the Fall, "The Dharma Bums," that I would like you to vouchsafe an opinion upon, sir. I am a veritable Boswell of busyness. Still another book comes out 1959, either "Desolation Angels" or "Doctor Sax." (I prefer the latter, sir, because it is a dark myth of Gothic New England and would take me off the "hipster" hook.) "Desolation Angels" is rather well-written but deals mostly with the peregrinations and machinations and musings and lipstrokings of our Friend Howl Allen Ginsberg and other poets including Gregorio Corso yet the central figure seems to emerge again as Neal Cass, I love to write about that crazy sonumbitch, in this book we go to the racetrack and what a wild day at the races! Hilarious, sire, to say the least.

How is our friend the aristocrat from Puerto Rico?

I have not written to Miss Beverly, sir, for the reason that she had me live with her a week in Sausalito in 1956 and then sent me a charming letter from a TB hospital, enclosed with a letter from her doctor, saying that I was now a TB Cousin. In fact I had developed a rich cough. So I slept outdoors for 6 months in the grasses of Marin and in the heights of the Cascades (fire-lookout) and got rid of it by that propitious method, and I do feel that Miss B. was rather sloppy not reminding me that TB is contagious. A slight hint of woesome malice, sire, but not enough to condemn her to the dogs of eternity: rather, I prefer silence now anyway.[45] Having my hands full of pretty young golls.

Jack

August 7, 1961

c/o Blake, PO Bx 700, Orlando, Fla.

Dear Ed

Just got home from Mexico & found your note. Yes, that Joan ex-wife, after throwing me out, got herself pregnant, then got me arrested & has been harassing my life (and my ma's) all these years.[46] She's a victim of litiginous paranoia as well as of hatred of everybody. I want a blood test to try to prove paternity, for one thing, and then testimony about my actual assets (which ain't what you read about). (as usual). Also, as you say, my mother's "maintenance money" shouldn't go to her, her new husband, her new twins et al, either. Her real name is Joan Aly, not Kerouac, but she uses the name anyway. Besides blood tests, they also have new kinds of "anthropological" tests. My doctor told me last winter my fertility rate is abnormally low; my uncles Ernest and John were sterile. I am going to NY to face that rat-hole court in a month or so. It will be awful. Sposing the judge suddenly starts lecturing me on my evil influence on American youth or something? Supposing the jury is prejudiced against beatniks? My lawyer Gene Brooks (Allen G's brother) had the silly "King of the Beatniks" clause stricken out of the Complaint, as tho that had anything to do with the case.[47] My income this year will come to about $100 or maybe $90 a week, which ain't a king's pay.

Hay. Well, it's been a long time since you told me to "sketch" in that Chinese restaurant on 125th Street, which started me on all my new writing techniques after *Town & City* style. Did you know you were the one who gave me the idea about my new prose? Just sketch "from memory" etc.

Well, maybe you can take a vacation some day and build me a log cabin in the Vermont hills, with bookshelves, woodstove, kerosene lamp and outhouse (and a well).

Just now in Mexico I wrote half a new novel, came home, looked at it, felt sick. Not that it's bad, but I'm getting sick of writing true stories out of my own life, they get so sordid sometimes & scare my family (my mother, sister, etc.). I'se without honor in me own house, sir.

Sometimes I feel like just dropping dead. But I think I'll manage and not only that, a bright Fall will come, Autumn, golden hills, me on a hill in a mackinaw, me with a bottle of wine beneath the moon, a new world, a new start. It's been terrible. I shoulda been an architect. But somehow I feel it will suddenly all work out. Also there won't be no war, I'm feeling that too. So don't worry about your kiddies.

How simple it was when I was in Denver that cold September when you drove me to the viaduct to sketch all day, remember? (1952)

Incidentally, Neal Cassady told me to write to Bev Burford a year ago in a letter from San Quentin, but I was getting hundreds of letters and just throwing them away.[48] But that was nice of old Neal. Neal is now reduced to tire-recap backbreak work in his hometown, even walks to work while kids are driven to school. But he's somehow calm & even wisely gay. A plus tard,

Jack

April 21, 1968

Dear Ed:

Carolyn Cassady called me up collect from California in and around Feb. 4 (supposed date of Neal's death) (my ma's birthday) and told me he'd been found dead by a railroad track, in a T-shirt, in the rain, in San Miguel, south of Mexico City.[49] But Neal's girlfriend had "refused" to mail his ashes to the widow Carolyn. So I asked Carolyn to check with the local consulate and confirm death if any. No answer. It may be just a trick to get welfare payments for Carolyn while he runs around with said girlfriend. I hope so. His buddy Ken Kesey pulled the same stunt, if you'll remember, or if you didn't know, a few years ago, leaving his writing-bus parked over a cliff at Big Sur, with a suicide note in his typewriter, and the cops found nothing in the surf below and presumed he was washed to sea or eaten by sharks.[50] But Kesey turned up in Mexico a year later.

Ginsberg, who is usually shrewd, laughed on the telephone and said something about "no body around, even."

I really don't know, Ed.

So tell this to Justin, it's all I know. There've been obituaries or obituary type writings about his "death" in certain avant-garde publications that make him out one who was destroyed by trying to live up to his image as Dean Moriarty.[51] Even hinting it was all my fault. Earlier writings said that a girl at a big hippie party asked to see his famous truncated thumb (of *On The Road*) and that she wanted to kiss it, and that he let her kiss it and presumably whipped out the alter-thumb because it then says "the party really got going."

We'll see.

All he has to do is grow a beard and wear beads and go to Madrid.

I just got back from Lisbon, Madrid, Munich, Geneva, Stuttgart. Traveled there with a bunch of Greek in-laws and friends. Had balls in Lisbon and Madrid: Stuttgart is severe and parochial. Am moving my family (paralyzed Ma, new wife Stella, 2 cats) to Florida as soon as I can sell this house.[52] You Can't Go Home Again.

Reason I haven't written to you is that I'm so busy and drunk too all the time, and befuddled, and my wife tore up my address book but I made her pick up all the pieces and write me up a new one.

I'll send you my new Florida address when I gets there (it'll be 5169-10th Ave. North, St. Petersburg, Fla., so make a note of it now). But it'll take a few months. I'm borrowing money from my publishers because all of a sudden, in this crucial time of my life, the money has stopped cold: altho I thought *Vanity of Duluoz*, latest novel, would make a hit. The reviews were as usual but my gripe is that the reprint (softcover cheap edition) people have so far refused to buy it: is it because I said Roosevelt had an ugly wife? Yet I say thank God that America still has a Literature otherwise everything would read like Romney, Reagan, Nixon, Kennedy, McCarthy, Humphrey B.S.

Ton copain, Jack As always, sir

Selected Bibliography

Cassady, Neal. *Grace Beats Karma: Letters from Prison, 1958–60.* New York: Blast Books, 1993.

Charters, Ann. *Kerouac.* San Francisco: Straight Arrow Books, 1973.

Cook, Bruce. *The Beat Generation: The Tumultuous '50s Movement and Its Impact on Today.* New York: Quill, 1994.

Donaldson, Scott, ed. *Jack Kerouac: On the Road.* New York: Penguin Books, 1979.

French, Warren. *Jack Kerouac.* Boston: Twayne Publishers, 1986.

Gifford, Barry, and Lawrence Lee. *Jack's Book.* New York: St. Martin's Press, 1978.

Ginsberg, Allen. *As Ever.* Berkeley: Creative Arts Book Co., 1977.

Huncke, Herbert. *Guilty of Everything: The Autobiography of Herbert Huncke.* New York: Paragon House, 1990.

Hunt, Tim. *Kerouac's Crooked Road.* Hamden, CT: Archon Books, 1981.

Jones, James T. *A Map of Mexico City Blues: Jack Kerouac as Poet.* Carbondale: Southern Illinois University Press, 1992.

Kerouac, Jack. *Desolation Angels.* New York: Coward-McCann, Inc., 1965.

— — —. *Big Sur.* New York: Farrar, Straus and Cudahy, 1962.

McNally, Dennis. *Desolate Angel.* New York: Random House, 1979.

Schumacher, Michael. *Dharma Lion: A Biography of Allen Ginsberg.* New York: St. Martin's Press, 1992.

Special thanks to Ed White, who made this project possible, and to Jim Jackson who helped get it started.

Endnotes

1 Kerouac met Edie Parker through Columbia University friend Henri Cru. Parker's well-to-do family and friends considered her relationship with Kerouac slumming. In 1944 Jack was held in the Bronx City Jail as a material witness in a homicide case. His father would not post the $5,000 bail, saying a Kerouac had never been involved in a murder. Jack and Edie agreed to marry in order to ask the Parker family for money. To pay back the debt, Jack took a job in a Michigan factory, but grew bored and frustrated with the routine. After two months of marriage, he hitched a ride back to New York.

2 Hal Chase, a Columbia student from Denver, told Kerouac mythic tales about a mad genius who was into car theft and romancing women. Chase called Cassady a "Nietzschean hero of the pure snowy wild West" and passed around letters Neal had written while he was in reform school. Kerouac and Ginsberg read the letters before actually meeting Cassady in December 1946.

3 Brierly played an active part in Denver society, moving in art and music circles. He worked as an attorney, served on the school board, helped truant boys, and screened local applicants for admission to Columbia University, his alma mater. Brierly encouraged Cassady academically and was one of his early intellectual influences.

4 Tom Livornese, a mutual friend of Kerouac and Ed White, was a Columbia student and jazz pianist.

5 A native of Poughkeepsie, New York, and also a writer, Fitz was the person who originally introduced Jack to Hal Chase.

6 Wesbrook Pegler was a right-wing newspaper columnist. His writing dealt extensively with the labor movement. Kerouac respected him and valued his integrity.

7 Founded in 1918 by dissident academics tied to the *New Republic*, the New School was designed to be an alternative to the American university system. The instructors were freelance intellectuals and artists with a theoretical bent, who stressed interdisciplinary study. In 1933 the "University in Exile" was added to the New School as an academic sanctuary for scholars exiled by Hitler and Mussolini. Since its founding, the New School has been a controversial center for New York cultural life. Its steadfast liberalism has been criticized as naive and overly optimistic for its faith in scientific rationalism and political democracy.

8 Kerouac's first published novel appeared in 1950. *The Town and the City* was heavily influenced by Thomas Wolfe at a time when Wolfe's popularity was fading. The novel fictionally recounts many of Kerouac's own early life experiences through his alter egos in the Martin family.

9 In the novel, the young protagonist becomes friends with the mysterious night wanderer, Dr. Sax, a character equal parts Dracula and thirties radio serial crime fighter The Shadow. While the novel retains comic book flash, the relationship between the protagonist and Dr. Sax becomes a metaphor for the artist discovering his creative voice.

10 Jack's father Leo was the model for George Martin, the father of five sons in *The Town and the City*.

11 John Clellon Holmes' sensational novel *Go* was the first to define the Beat movement for the general public. His parties were the center of the hip scene at the time, but the Beats were as diverse spiritually and politically as they were economically. Though Kerouac admired Holmes, he sometimes resented the degree to which Holmes' novel borrowed from his own letters, conversations, and unpublished work.

12 Kerouac enlisted in the U.S. Navy in 1943. He was discharged for psychiatric reasons when he dropped his rifle and wandered off to the base library in the middle of a drill. Though he continued his service in the Merchant Marines, he was in constant conflict with even the relaxed discipline of the civilian service. Despite his poor military record, Kerouac received money under the G.I. Bill.

13 Frank Jeffries was a friend of Jack's from Denver. His journey from Denver to Mexico City with Jack and Neal was detailed in *On the Road*. Jeffries appeared as Sam Shepard in *On The Road* and as Dave Sherman in *Visions of Cody*.

14 Bob Burford was a Denver friend of Kerouac's, and one-time editor of *New Story Magazine*. He served as the model for Ray Rolands in *On the Road*.

15 Jeffries, Burford and White.

16 Edie Parker introduced Kerouac to Lucien Carr at the West End Bar on Broadway and 114th Street across from Columbia University. Kerouac's first impression was that Carr looked like "a mischievous little prick." In 1944, Carr claimed self-defense in the stabbing murder of David Kamarer, a Columbia hanger-on who was sexually obsessed with him. Burroughs advised Carr to contact his family, get a good lawyer and turn himself in. Instead, Carr and Kerouac dropped the murder weapon— a Boy Scout knife—down a subway grate and then went for drinks, before reporting to the police precinct. Both Burroughs and Kerouac were indicted as material witnesses. Burroughs posted his bond immediately, but Leo Kerouac refused to help his son. While in custody, Kerouac created a buzz among the other prisoners. He was visited by curious guards and inmates, including members of New York's notorious mob hit squad, Murder Inc., who wanted to find out if Carr was indeed "queer." Panicked, Kerouac created outlandish stories about his friends' voracious heterosexual appetites to prove that he was straight. Carr was convicted of first-degree manslaughter and sentenced to up to twenty years in the Elmira Reformatory. He served just over two years before being paroled.

17 Kerouac first met Ginsberg at Columbia in 1944. The two became close friends, but Kerouac was troubled about being linked to Ginsberg and a Beat movement that he believed never really existed. In a 1968 *Paris Review* interview, Kerouac dismissed Ginsberg as an annoying social gadfly.

18 Prior to the publication of *The Town and the City* on March 2, 1950, Kerouac had temporarily gone on the wagon. He quit the weekend party circuit, ended his relationship with his girlfriend, wrote steadily and joined the YMCA to get in shape. Unfortunately, the work he called "a perfect Niagara of a novel" failed to make the impact he had hoped. It opened to mixed critical reviews and sold poorly. Later Kerouac attributed the book's failure to its "dreary prose." The novel's lack of success ruined his love life; he thought he was too poor to date.

19 Kerouac's friendship with Alan Temko went all the way back to Horace Mann Prep School in New York, where they had both been students. Temko described the prep-school Kerouac as a poor country boy in ill-fitting clothes. Though they shared a similar education—they

political beliefs. Temko also had reservations about Kerouac's friends; he couldn't understand the fascination they held for Jack. Temko remembers that Jack "thought they were America...Neal was Huck Finn and Bob Burford was a smart-aleck Tom Sawyer." Temko was portrayed as Roland Major in *On the Road*.

20 In the second version of *On the Road*, Kerouac shifted the novel's emphasis from Ray Smith, renaming him Smitty, and created Red Moultrie, the novel's new hero, who searches for his father. As an ex–minor-league ballplayer, ex–jazz drummer, ex–London University student, ex–seaman, and ex–truck driver, Red envisions his life as a work of art. A lone bus ride across America inspired Kerouac to pay close attention to the American landscape. He recalled that during the journey home, he had "nothing to do but read the land." At Three Forks, Montana, Jack decided he had located "the source of everything." He also conceived the image of a log floating downriver, a symbol he would use in several of his novels.

21 Kerouac and the Columbia crowd avidly read Dostoevski and discussed the eternal questions raised in his novels. By saying that Francis in *The Town and the City* was not an Ivan, White was differentiating Kerouac's character from the atheistic intellectual brother in Dostoevski's *The Brothers Karamazov*.

22 Chase's destructive nature often alienated him from his friends. By calling Chase Sorelian, Kerouac may be commenting on his propensity toward violence. French social philosopher Georges Sorel's best-known work, *Reflections of Violence* (1908), describes violence as the creative power of the proletariat to overcome the economic dominance of the bourgeoisie.

23 To celebrate the publication of his novel, Jack planned a long trip to Denver. Ed White and friends gave a book-signing party at Daniels and Fisher Tower to meet the visiting New York novelist, whose advance publicity capitalized on comparisons to Thomas Wolfe. Beverly Burford and her brother Bob, among the guests, remained interested in Jack's work until his death. Bob viewed Kerouac, Cassady and the others with an editor's detachment. Of Jack he said, "Kerouac did have immense talent. It was only a question of where you put him. Kerouac was always in a lousy situation. You never saw him at a party where he was really having fun all night, or for many hours. He was never consistently having fun." Beverly had a brief affair with Kerouac, and afterwards remained a staunch supporter of his writing and a loyal friend.

24 Frank Jeffries, who appeared as Sam Shepard in *On The Road*.

25 Denver's Elitch Gardens, an amusement park that was deserted at night, provided Jack, Frank Jeffries, and Neal Cassady a haven for smoking marijuana. The word "elitching" became their secret code word for this activity.

26 While in Mexico, living in Burroughs' apartment, Kerouac returned to his notes for a novel he tentatively titled *The Shadow of Doctor Sax*. He used Burroughs as a model for Sax. Because of his past experience with the police, Burroughs worried about the smell of pot, which Kerouac was using heavily to recall memories of his boyhood in Lowell and the fears and fantasies of adolescence. To quiet Bill's concerns, Jack wrote in the bathroom. He remarked years later that editor Malcolm Cowley noticed that the novel "continually mentions urine, and quite naturally it does because I had no place to write it but on the closed toilet seat in a little tile toilet in Mexico City."

27 In Kerouac's notes for the second version of *On the Road*, he frequently referred to Smitty, the novel's narrator, as too innocent and naive for this world. Kerouac also likened Smitty to Sancho Panza, Pip and Boswell in that his narrative stance was that of an observer, rather than a participant.

28 Kerouac might be referring to Henry Wallace, a politician who ran unsuccessfully for the presidency as the candidate of the Progressive Party in 1948. Wallace denounced Truman's foreign policy. He wanted to end the Cold War with Russia, and believed the Russians wanted peace.

29 Inspired by Neal's Joan Anderson letter, Kerouac went to work on the fourth version of *On the Road*. He rewrote the story as a fast-paced, Cassady-style confession, keeping all the characters' real names. "An autobiography of self-image," Kerouac called his new technique. Kerouac didn't want to interrupt his flow by changing pages in the typewriter. In order to pour the story out in its natural order, he glued the sheets of onionskin paper together to make one big scroll. About April 5 he began typing. Spurred on by Benzedrine and coffee, he averaged about a hundred words a minute. After three weeks of nonstop work, Kerouac presented Giroux with a single-spaced, 175,000-word, 120-foot-long paragraph and declared, "I don't make any corrections." The April 1951 version of *On the Road* was finally published in 1957.

30 Instead of revising *On the Road*, Kerouac went to work on "inserts" for the book. The scenes he sketched of Neal's childhood were alternately referred to as *On the Road* and as "the book about Cassady." The six-hundred-page character study of the hero in the road book later became *Visions of Cody*, published in full in 1973.

31 After several months of furious writing, Kerouac experienced a flare-up of the phlebitis that afflicted him off and on throughout his life. He never forgot that if the clots reached his brain or his heart, it would kill him. He used his time in the hospital to reread Proust and start a hospital diary in which he attempted a Proustian recollection of his own past. In the diary he also outlined a series of books that would comprise the legend of Jack Kerouac. He was convinced that remembering his personal odyssey through life would lead to a new burst of creativity.

32 In January 1952 Cassady helped Kerouac get a job as a brakeman for the Southern Pacific Railroad in California. Kerouac began his training in the Oakland yards. He later carried his brakeman's lantern with him to write by when there wasn't available electricity.

33 Hal Chase's girlfriend, Ginger, was a ballet dancer who lived near the Columbia campus.

34 The word "subterranean" was a loose, and at times derogatory label that Kerouac and others hung on the players in the Village scene. Kerouac was less than enthusiastic about these hipsters, who he regarded as avant-garde *poseurs.*

35 Fugazzi's, a Village bar, was a popular hangout among the Beats. Joyce Glassman (now Johnson), an aspiring writer at the time, and a one-time girlfriend of Kerouac's, later recalled that the women were locked out of the intellectual dialogue and sat on the periphery of the group, keeping their mouths shut. There was never any participation by the women as artists.

36 Kerouac's two-month tryst with "Mardou Fox" in 1953 was the focus of his 1958 novel, *The Subterraneans.* Mardou was an attractive, half-American Indian and half-Black girl he met in the Village. Kerouac was infatuated with her because of her exotic looks and bearing, but his mother's objections and Mardou's affair with Gregory Corso ended their relationship.

37 This "novel" Kerouac writes about eventually became the essay "October in the Railroad Earth," detailing his life as a brakeman. It is one of Kerouac's finest sketches.

38 Maria L—, a student at Barnard College, was the younger sister of Tom Livornese.

39 After years of contemplating a trip to Europe, Kerouac finally made the journey on February 15, 1957. Though plans to trace some of his family history in France fell through, Kerouac was successful in helping Burroughs, who was then living in Tangier, organize and edit the manuscript that became *Naked Lunch.* Ultimately, Kerouac's visit to Tangier was marred by Viking Press's rejection of *Dr. Sax* and *Desolation Angels,* and by the nightmares and physical illness that he suffered as a result of his experimentation with hashish and opium.

40 Kerouac saw parallels between his relationship with Neal Cassady and that of Samuel Johnson and his understudy/biographer James Boswell.

41 Kerouac's interest in Buddhism and philosophy flourished in the aftermath of his breakup with Mardou. His interest in Buddhism was further stimulated by Gary Snyder, a young scholar in Oriental languages at Berkeley, whom Kerouac met in 1955. Snyder was a Zen Buddhist, preferring organized meditation and haiku, while Kerouac appreciated the more traditional Mahayana teachings. Their differences aside, Kerouac

and Snyder shared the same favorite saint, Avalokitesvara, the Buddha of the human voice. Kerouac went on to write about Snyder in *The Dharma Bums*, a novel describing his friendship with Snyder and their stays in the mountains with Snyder's wilderness-loving friend, John Montgomery. According to Ginsberg, the group was particularly drawn to three Buddhist themes: suffering, transitoriness and egolessness. Kerouac wrote *Some of the Dharma* in 1954–55; it became a collection of his Buddhist notes and sketches, and was published posthumously.

42 Allen Ginsberg's poem *Howl*, which was dedicated in part to Kerouac, played a major part in the 1956 reading that sparked the "San Francisco Poetry Renaissance." While in Tangier, Ginsberg learned that 520 copies of *Howl* had been confiscated, and that undercover officers had bought a copy of *Howl and Other Poems* at the City Lights bookstore. A warrant was issued for Ferlinghetti's arrest, stating that he knowingly printed obscene writings. By angering the close-knit literary community in San Francisco, the banning of *Howl* in that city boosted both the sales of the piece and Ginsberg's poetic reputation.

43 Kerouac was very interested in what his friends thought about his writing, though he was sensitive to any type of criticism. When friends or editors suggested changes, Kerouac grew angry and claimed his "spontaneous prose" style could not be edited.

44 With his thrombophlebitis plaguing him constantly, Kerouac stayed drunk on wine in order to relieve the pain. At times he was forced to bandage his swollen legs and type in bed with a portable typewriter in his lap.

45 In *The Dharma Bums*, and more explicitly in *Desolation Angels*, Kerouac describes the job he took in 1956, as a lookout for wild grass fires on Desolation Peak in Mount Baker National Forest, Washington. Gary Snyder, an experienced outdoorsman, influenced Kerouac to take the job. He spotted no fires in his area in the eight weeks he was alone on the mountain, and the complete solitude was not the Walden-like experience he had hoped for. He was lonely, depressed, and could not wait to return to civilization.

46 Kerouac married Joan Haverty, his second wife, on November 17, 1950; he separated from her the next year. Joan got pregnant around this time, but Kerouac insisted that the child was not his, citing his infertility. A paternity battle ensued when Joan demanded child support. Kerouac's lawyer, Gene Brooks (Ginsberg's brother), argued that Kerouac was unable to work because of thrombophlebitis. The judge dropped the case. Kerouac later admitted to Ginsberg that the child, Michelle Kerouac, looked like him.

47 San Francisco journalist Herb Caen coined the derogatory term "Beatnik" at roughly the same time the Russians were launching Sputnik. Because

Kerouac wrote about the Beats and Beat life, the press insisted on calling him "King of the Beatniks," an epithet he despised.

48 During the years when his alter ego, Dean Moriarty of *On the Road*, was becoming famous, Neal Cassady was in jail. In May 1958, he began serving a five-year sentence in San Quentin on two counts of possession of marijuana. Cassady was set up by suspecting Federal narcotics agents, who purchased two marijuana cigarettes from him. He spent two years in San Quentin before he was paroled.

49 Carolyn Cassady called to inform Kerouac of Neal Cassady's death on February 4, 1968—Jack's mother's birthday. Stella Kerouac would not put the first call through, and Carolyn had to call a second time. Kerouac comforted her, but ended the conversation by telling her that he didn't believe Neal was dead.

50 Neal Cassady began a friendship with Ken Kesey, author of *One Flew Over the Cuckoo's Nest* and *Sometimes a Great Notion*, after his release from San Quentin. It was at this time that Cassady, Kesey and others began experimenting with LSD, a drug Kerouac tried only once. Their group, the Merry Pranksters, acquired an old school bus, remodeled it and travelled around, mainly on the West Coast, with Cassady at the wheel. (Kerouac's reference to Kesey's faked suicide is related in Tom Wolfe's *The Electric Kool-Aid Acid Test*.) Kerouac never felt part of the Merry Pranksters' antics.

51 Dean Moriarty, the main character of *On the Road*, is based solely on Neal Cassady and the real-life events that surrounded his cross-country journeys with Kerouac. Some of their mutual acquaintances later felt that Cassady's effort to live up to the fictional character was one of the reasons for his early death.

52 Kerouac married his third and final wife, Stella Sampas, on November 19, 1966. She was the sister of his boyhood friend, Sammy Sampas, who had died at an early age. Stella became Jack's protector in his last years, and on occasion would turn curious fans away from their door.

THE BYERSON TEST / *E. S. Goldman*

CHESTER BYERSON WAS SOMEBODY I knew in the elevator and the coffee shop. A man who sells something substantial, I thought: carloads, bonds, yachts, properties. Jutting from his breast pocket like a third cuff was a squared handkerchief with the erratic weave and edge of handwork; I took this for a trademark. Men don't show breast pocket handkerchiefs much these days. Well-barbered thready bronze hair frizzed to an Abyssinian beard behind his ears.

On a morning when people from the convention hotel on the corner were swarming for breakfast he motioned me to the open seat at his table. We said no more than was polite while we explored how much interruption of the *Times* was enough for civility. He read as I did, scanning page one, lingering at Business before returning to other sections. We found it congenial to sit together, turning pages, making circumspect comments on the news, and continued to do so other mornings when our breakfast times coincided.

Byerson is a partner in a public relations firm. He is more gregarious than I, natural for someone in his line; but I am not taciturn, so our conversation expanded over the months to include by disclosure and inference as much information as most people in more intimate relationships exchange in a lifetime. He is Philadelphia and Princeton. I am Akron and Western Reserve. He says *At this point in time,* which for me implies a whole cultural landscape. He is separated from Ann Marie but they are friends. His trick right knee made him draft-proof. He considered going for political science while at Princeton. He thinks he is vulnerable to colon cancer on account of a family history. Bernice and I are divorced. The children cling to her side of the family, which makes it rather morose for me sometimes. During Vietnam I did biology at Western Reserve and now I'm a science writer. We have stocks. We know scores, game scores, not music. We travel. We know hotels.

We had had this relationship for several months when Byerson said, "I have business in France. I'll be gone for a couple of days next week."

I said that it seemed to me he had been in France not long ago.

"We have clients there, a cosmetic house and a drug company. We show the flag now and then. Do you get to Paris?"

"As a matter of fact—," I began without the firm intent to say what the fact was. I had a mission in Paris for somebody but was not entirely comfortable that Chester Byerson was the person for it.

Understand, the friendship between us didn't extend a foot beyond the breakfast table. For one thing, to put a word on it, and looking at it only from my side, I didn't trust him. I liked him but didn't trust him. I liked him for breakfast, think of him as a cereal, but I'd never asked if he wanted to meet with our dates at Bradley's or volunteered to pick up a pair of tickets for the Knicks, nor had he asked me.

We didn't have the kind of workplace friendship I had with Claude Prennis. Claude and I saw the world with the same biases. I could say to Claude, "The president has no business sending American troops to Kuwait. It's out-of-date oil diplomacy," and anticipate his agreement. Or I could say the opposite and Claude would write it off as temporary insanity. But to Byerson I never ventured an opinion that couldn't be tempered, softened, put aside for another subject. On the same evidence that I would say flatly to Prennis that Kuwait was no business of ours, I would say circumspectly to Byerson, "I see the president is committing more ground troops to Kuwait," and the accredited observer from Mars wouldn't be able to say if either of us seriously thought that was a good idea or a bad one.

It frustrated me that if Claude's wife weren't so militant they would live at a more convenient address and we would fit into a comfortable after-hours relationship. Maybe that is a matter of trust, too, that Sarice just doesn't want relationships to get too white, the explanation I prefer because it is abstract enough to have no personal reference to me. Sarice certainly has no reason to distrust me as an individual.

But what had I to trust Byerson with? He was not my lawyer, my dentist, my broker. If he ever disappeared owing me anything it would be no more than he borrowed to get him through the morning of a day he mislaid his wallet. Some of my wariness may have been that of a medical journalist for a publicist of drug and cosmetic companies who might want to use me. But if you really required me to justify distrust to your satisfaction, I wouldn't be able to. Knowing my test you would ask, How about me? Do I pass? And how would you know if you could trust my answer?

The trust test occurred to me unsought, as it may have to Sarice, assuming she has such a test. I was reading Anne Frank's diary and a question strayed off the text, causing me to follow it for a moment: to whom would I go for refuge? For a necessary hour? For a day? A week? For a long time?

That is to say, would this person—Chester Byerson—risk going to jail, maybe even being shot, on my account? That is all there is to the test, and you can see why I am reluctant to discuss it. This is apart from Whom have I the right to ask? to which the answer is Anybody. Anybody has the right, in a matter of life and death, to ask me. The question is not the right to ask, but who opens the door.

Such questions really come up only when the police are going through the neighborhood with a list. These things happen surprisingly fast once they reach critical mass, which can be quite small. Reading Holocaust literature, I continually wonder how so many responsible men of means, heads of businesses, men who know human nature, allowed themselves and their families to be trapped with no exit except through the camps. Of course, in this country no one would think of using ovens; if such a time comes here, categorically rejecting ovens will be a bid for moderate opinion. This country has an instinct for the center.

Think about a coffee shop like Charleston's, a place on West 54th Street with greenery and louvered white blinds, and walking room between the glass-topped wrought-iron tables, and a side door into an apartment hotel. Say that in the newspapers and on television there's a worrisome din of speeches and marches. OpEd writers discover that beasts no longer slink toward Bethlehem, they lift their heads and lope. People get out of their way. But even animals who come to this oasis on West 54th Street respect the rules.

Now, say, you are in the middle of your meal when the critical mass of four pushes open the door and commands the room. They holler at selected people. They upset your table in your lap and holler at you. For some diners the situation does not exist, it is no affair of theirs. Others look displeased by those who go too far. Elnora comes from the kitchen and expresses with a severe look that she does not approve of a disruption of her business. With your pasta in your lap, you feel a measure of guilt to be even indirectly the cause of somebody's emotional distress.

Have you been in the subway when one hoodlum cows a car full of ordinary people who think mostly of moving to a better car? Nobody rides the subway anymore because things like that happen. You see? The solution is to stop using the subways. It isn't that people aren't sympathetic, it's that sympathy is all they have. Do you blame a poor man because he doesn't take a taxi? With what? He is sympathetic to the idea of taking a taxi.

When, then, in fewer years than you think possible, it comes down to the police going through the neighborhood with a list, I see myself with this problem: On whose door can I knock with confidence? Will you take my daughter in? I'm working on something to get her across the border. I am a proud man and won't ask it for myself. Although we don't know how proud we are—do we?—until the police are going through the neighborhood with a list. For my daughter, who doesn't call or write except a card two weeks late for my birthday, for her I will not be too proud to ask. Maybe, secretly, I wish only to show her how she had wronged me with so many years of ingratitude. At such times we don't inspect motives. Yes, I guess if my former wife asked, I would do the same for her. We had good years. Of all sentiments, loyalty is the most peculiar.

Having come this far with you and my absurd test, I may as well say I wouldn't have invested much trust in Chester Byerson. He might be good for five minutes while I stood in his foyer and he thought it over.

I continued tentatively, "If you're going to be in Paris and you're not locked up in meetings—"

"Is there something I can do?"

As he had asked—"You may have time to solve a mystery for me. Do you know the memorial to the *Martyrs Français de la Déportation?*"

"Isn't it on Rosiers Street in the old Jewish section of the Marais?" His face did not conceal its pleasure that a man of his background knew something a man of mine would not suspect.

Rosiers is a street and also the generic name for a neighborhood, like Wall Street. When I was in Paris last year my hotel was just beyond Rosiers, on Place des Vosges, and I had walked the sidewalks of small shops, eating places, bookstores and walk-up apartments, although I had not seen the memorial. Byerson had correctly foreseen that I would not expect him to be familiar with a Jewish neighborhood—so modest in the scale of magnificent Paris—and remember a memorial.

My distrust softened. It had not, after all, been distrust of his probity as much as of his sensibility. I rated him up to an hour.

In a pinch, while I made other arrangements, I might trust him to keep my daughter for an hour. Not bad, when you've read history and think about people you know. Some of your friends—relatives, for that matter—you can't imagine even coming to the door if they have an idea of what's going on out there. An hour is a long time to keep somebody in a closet the police want to see at Penn Station at three P.M.

However, my subject was not Rosiers, and the Déportation memorial I was speaking of was not in Rosiers. It was behind Notre Dame cathedral, a taxi ride away.

"Chester, it's interesting that you know the Rosiers memorial, but it's the wrong memorial."

All coincidences are by definition curious, and among the more curious must be that the day before Byerson told me he was going to France I had received a scribbled note on the letterhead of *Amicale des Anciens Déportés Juifs de France* to whom I had—at the suggestion of the cultural attaché of the Embassy of France in Washington—written an inquiry about the memorial I had visited behind Notre Dame. From recognizable syllables I got the point:

Cher Monsieur,

This reply has been delayed. The writer, whose name is signed, not legibly beyond Henry, has been on vacance for four mois. *The memorial to which you refer is le Mémorial du Martyr Juif Inconnu on rue Geoffroy-l'Asnier.* On my walk through Rosiers I had seen that street sign but not explored its resources. *I will send your letter to the director of the projet, who is known to us—*

"But Henry," I had protested to the letter as I read, "I asked clearly about the memorial behind Notre Dame. Rue Geoffroy-l'Asnier is in the Rosiers section, nowhere near the cathedral, a forty- or fifty-franc taxi ride."

I recited this to Byerson when his memory produced a shrine on Rosiers.

"So there is a Rosiers memorial," he declared, vindicated by Henry's letter.

"Apparently, but it isn't mine. To get to my memorial, the memorial with the mystery, follow the landscaped walkway on the river side of Notre Dame to the next street. On your right is one of the short bridges that loop over the Seine like running squirrels. Cross the street behind the cathedral to a small park. In a waist-high stone wall is an inscription: *Martyrs Français de la Déportation 1945.* The memorial itself is below ground. The entrance is down a narrow stairway between stone walls, like going into a burial vault."

The building and grounds had an aspect of newness, the cement seams glistened; no more than three or four years old when I was there last April.

Byerson said, "I don't think I know it."

"Sometimes I have the feeling that I'm the only one who knows. The riverboats for tourists go by without the public address mentioning it. *Martyrs Français de la Déportation 1945* isn't listed with other places of interest in the itinerary handouts. They mention Notre Dame, of course."

"Well, Notre Dame...." Who could overlook Notre Dame? A question had been dangling from Byerson's tongue. "Tell me something. Why do Jews seem not to want to share their monuments of the Holocaust? It seems to me that blacks think they're eligible for inclusion in the Holocaust monument in New York, and there was some discussion about including Indians in the Washington memorial. Blacks and Indians think everything that happened to Jews happened to them. But Jews want to go it alone. Doesn't that seem strange?"

Strange got away from him while he looked for a better word. He didn't know if he was in an area where he might inadvertently say something not quite sensitive, something unidiomatic to an ear better trained than his for discourse about Jewish memorials.

He went on, picking his way among the words. "Rather than cultivate isolation, wouldn't it be better to be present as a matter of right—to horn in, even—at the funeral service for a common relative? Wouldn't it be advantageous to be seen as the most authentic part of a more general grief?"

I corrected him. It wasn't altogether true about going it alone. "In the Washington memorial Jehovah's Witnesses and Gypsies and some others on Hitler's annihilation list have a part. I believe I've got that right."

"But not to include blacks and Indians in a memorial on American ground—"

"You have to bear in mind that Holocaust memorials refer to Europe, not America."

"Ah," he said, glad to have a reason to be in error.

"I'm not a member of the establishment that decides these things. They are people with strong feelings. They express themselves arbitrarily. They are deferred to. People who have nuanced reservations are reluctant to enter that kind of controversy."

"I can understand strong feelings in the circumstances," he said.

"It's easier to understand when you don't have to live with it." I implied that I had endured such conversations.

"I know what you mean."

"I shouldn't have said strong feelings. One man's feelings are as strong as another's. It's a matter of undisciplined expression. Heaven protect us from having to subordinate judgment to assertion. However, it happens."

He still had a problem: "But why two memorials in Paris to the deported?"

I guessed: "People with *very* strong feelings."

I had no problem with the scenario of dispute and schism. I imagined hectic volunteer activity on l'Asnier, bulletin boards covered with notices of readings, programs, lectures, membership drives. Some arbitrary people thought things should be done more professionally, in a less orthodox way. New cadres of bereaved, of philanthropy, of faction, of public relations formed. I didn't say it was what happened. I was speculating about how they may have got to the austere second shrine behind Notre Dame.

Reconstructing my descent into the vault, it came to me very much in the mood of the Washington Vietnam memorial. Simple, dignified, direct. Be quiet here. Think of what was done to human beings by other human beings. Pray, if you are so minded. The high space was enclosed by stone walls. I remembered a memorial light; chiseled in stone, the names of the death camps to which the *Martyrs Français de la Déportation* had been consigned; an inscription PARDONNE N'OUBLIE PAS.

I was the only visitor until a young couple came down the stairs, took in everything at a glance, expected somewhat more, spoke quietly to each other and climbed out. Surely they had just come from the throng in the cathedral and found this unexciting. I was again the only visitor.

Behind a door, barred like a prison cell, was a long gallery of drawers or niches, floor to ceiling. Visualize a Chinese apothecary chest or shelves of shallow safe deposit boxes, each with a button of light where a keyhole would be. There must have been on the order of a quarter of a million of these, for somewhere was a statement that the martyrs numbered that many. I made a rough count—so many rows high, so many inches wide, the corridor so many feet long—and got to well over 200,000 keyhole lights. I seem to recall a biblical inscription, but the sense of the room was the less said the better, everybody knew what had happened.

I did not record everything as exactly as I might have. I must have had the expectation that there would be a brochure to remind me; an account of the historical event that was the structure's reason to be, the name and address of the sponsoring institution, the architect. There should be a visitor's book to sign, a functionary—caretaker, guard, receptionist—to take questions. None of that was evident.

While my frustrations accumulated, a black man came down the stairs purposefully, and before I realized he was the functionary I looked for, he unlocked another jail door that was like the door to the corridor of lights and got a leg into the passage. I interrupted him—

"*S'il vous plaît.* Is there a pamphlet? A brochure?"

He appeared to have never before had the question. He thought while his knee held the door ajar. Taking from his breast pocket an envelope, he pointed to the corner card which I copied:

Ministre à Ancien Combattant
Secrétariat: 10 Ave Val Fonenary
Paris 94125
Fontenay Sous Bois Cedex

If I have more than a word to say in another language I have to organize for it like an arthritic getting out of a chair. Not having quite composed a sentence, I offered *Merci beaucoup, Monsieur;* and knowing I was not competitive enough in the system to get a phone number and a connection and make my interest known to the *Ministre à Ancien Combattant* if reaching him, I decided to hand the problem to the French Tourist agency which operates under a banner on Champs Elysées near the Arc de Triomphe. At the counter of a lobby shingled with pamphlets I got the attention of a clever girl whose English was at least as good as mine.

"*Ma'mselle, s'il vous plaît.* I have been to the impressive monument to the *Déportés* behind Notre Dame."

She nodded that she knew.

"There is no literature there. I thought there might be a brochure here?"

"We should have something," she agreed. She came around her counter to get to one of the pamphlet walls. She frowned a pinch not to find the brochure exactly where she knew to look among the hundreds racked around us.

I told her I had been given an address. "I am leaving Paris tomorrow. I'm not very good on the phone here. Perhaps you could call and they will send something to me in America? I would be glad to cover the shipping costs."

"That shouldn't be necessary. They will send it."

English spoken by a French girl can be a considerable improvement over our rendition of the same thought or even the same words. The most commonplace things said in French have the flavor of something memorable. She found a number in a directory and dialed. As soon as the connection was made and she asked the question, she began to shake her head, and stayed only long enough to hear the other side out. It was the wrong place.

"This address is a suburban office. Way out. They have another office in the city."

The second office was not more helpful. She hung the phone on her shoulder while pantomiming profound regret being expressed at the other end and thumbed a notebook that had the name of an authority of next resort. The authority gave a number to call that did not answer. My friend pointed to her watch. It was late, they were doubtless closed. She hung up and sang an address while she wrote:

Association Israélite de Paris
17 rue St.-George

To prepare Byerson for his assignment in Paris I debriefed myself of those uneventful events and those that followed after I had returned to the U.S.A. First, though there had not been time to call at the *Association Israélite de Paris* before leaving Paris the following afternoon, I had acted on what I thought might be a better idea. I had gone to a bookstore on Rosiers. Surely a house of books in the heart of the neighborhood from which so many had been taken away would have something about the memorial.

The store on Rosiers was satisfactorily worn and dimly lighted, crowded with books on shelves and tables, and on the floor awaiting vacancies at higher levels. Titles that didn't fit elsewhere lounged on leftover inches above the rows. Madame, in a gray knitted garment that appeared to have grown its own shawl, examined the disorder of French coming from my mouth. She looked at me as if saying, Is this what you call making love in your country? and abruptly rejected any implication that she knew of a memorial behind Notre Dame. It is a couple of miles from here, I argued. I was there yesterday. She had no more time for me. She did not mention, alternatively, a memorial of the neighborhood on rue Geoffroy-l'Asnier that would travel well, and I did not know to ask. She left me formulating puzzlement.

It is impossible for me just to walk out of a bookstore. I scanned a few shelves and found *Déportation et génocide* by Annette Wiéviorka. The index had no entry for any variant of *Martyrs Français de la Déportation 1945*.

Byerson said, "There is a character in a story who returns to his hotel and is told there is no such room as the one he slept in last night."

"I think the story is there is no such address, there is no such hotel. A really good story like that abandons its author and acquires the variations of a myth."

But this was not a story in which a stone building could be made to disappear in an amusing way. The memorial was there. It could not have been made to disappear overnight. I returned to New York fired by the need of information. I wrote to the *Association Israélite de Paris* and got no reply. Well, I thought, they do not choose to deal with my English. I called the French Embassy in Washington and reached a cultural attaché who referred me to a new resource, *Amicale des Anciens Déportés Juifs de France* at a Paris address. I wrote. No reply. That is to say, none for the months that passed until a few days before Byerson left for France.

"It is as if my inquiries are about a member of the family who has done something disgraceful," I said to Byerson. "Nobody will discuss the scandal. All this time, with due diligence, I've not reached one person who knows anything about the memorial *Martyrs Français de la Déportation 1945* behind Notre Dame, and now this letter from Henry changes the subject to something I never heard of—although you have—on rue Geoffroy-l'Asnier."

I said to him, "The mystery for me is why there is no pamphlet. The mystery for you is why there are two shrines. So if you have time in Paris, you may want to see what you can find out."

While Henry had converted my memorial behind Notre Dame to his memorial on l'Asnier, he had also put me in touch with Dr. Francine Masliah who was omnicompetent in memorials. On the heels of Henry's letter, while Byerson was abroad, another arrived from Dr. Masliah, director of the *Mémorial du Martyr Juif Inconnu, Centre de Documentation Juive Contemporaine, 17 rue Geoffroy-l'Asnier*. Mindful of my evident language disability, Dr. Masliah affirmed in English: *Both Memorials deserve our reverence and admiration, but they have a different history.* She recounted the history of her memorial. *The Memorial to the Unknown Jewish Martyr was planned just after the liberation when the unbelievable was proved to have actually happened. Ashes were immediately brought back from the camps and were buried in the shrine of the crypt at 17 rue Geoffroy-l'Asnier for the world to remember.* One of the architects had survived Auschwitz. There had been articles in *Le Monde.* A program of events and facilities was enclosed. Of my memorial she had not a word.

So when Chester Byerson returned from Paris I knew what Dr. Masliah's packet had told me. Of the stone vault at Notre Dame, the newer one, bonded with fresh cement, which I had visited, I still knew nothing. The head waitress associated me with Byerson and saw me to his table.

"I see you're back. I hope your trip was successful?"

"All right, thank you. Good morning." He was impatient to tell me, "I've seen your memorial. There is still no attendant. There is still no brochure. Tell me, what made you think it's a Holocaust memorial?"

"What else could it be? The Nazis took over. The Vichy government cooperated. Jews were rounded up and sent to the death camps. It was what the Deportation was."

"I don't think so. I would say it's a memorial of the French nation for all the deported. They were not all Jews."

"It's something you found out? It never occurred to me."

"I didn't find out anything. I went to the memorial behind Notre Dame. I didn't have much time. I just didn't see anything that made me think it's a Jewish memorial."

I had to think how it became fixed in my mind that it was. For one thing, no alternative had occurred, I had seen what I was predisposed to see. Who were the deported of 1945 if not the Juifs, the Israélites? Reflecting on it for a moment, I recalled that tens of thousands of the French Left, and thousands more, shipwrecked on the shores of France by earlier storms in Spain and Central Europe, had also been packed in the trains and sent to the camps.

But the clever girl at the French tourist agency, when she failed to reach the *Ministre à Ancien Combattant*—after conferring with her authority of next resort, hadn't she handed me the address of the *Association Israélite de Paris?* Hadn't the cultural attaché of the French Embassy suggested that I try *Amicale des Déportés Juifs de France?* So not only in my naive supposition but those others who would be presumed to know also believed that, after all was said and done, it was *Juifs, Israélites,* who were sent to the ovens. "And you think that's not the intent of the memorial, Chester?"

"I saw nothing that made me think so."

"You had that confirmed somewhere?"

"I didn't bother. It was a memorial to those who had suffered a terrible fate. It seemed of no importance to refine it."

"That's something only somebody who is neither a Jew nor a Frenchman can say."

"Why do you say that?"

"It isn't a subject on which you have strong feelings. Let me give you a project. Offer to write a brochure for English-speaking visitors. Pro bono."

He put down the fork that had carved into an omelet and used his hands to assemble an idea in the air. His finely barbered head reached toward me, his voice lowered to a strong whisper, not to engage the adjoining tables.

"There will never be a brochure," he said, and dismissing it, "There may be a piece of paper. On the airplane I thought of writing something but couldn't get past the mandatories—where the memorial is sited, what is in it, when it was built and so on. I couldn't find a word to connect a reader to what the memorial was for. How do you write that it is for the man they drowned in a shit wagon? How do you tell people that? How do you say Stop! Think of a man drowning in a shit wagon, the end of a human life! People are on vacation."

In that sense the diners around us also were on vacation. Byerson hunched nearer. "They want to see sights. A memorial is where a notable lays a wreath. How do you tell people that two hundred men, women and children are jammed naked into a shed the size of a one car garage, the doors are closed, and inside in the pitch dark the gas is let in? How do you tell people what the twelve minutes it takes them to die are like? The stronger climb up the weak, trying for better air, trample on their faces. Everybody's bowels and kidneys let go. How do you write about the blood, the shit, the vomit slop? Human beings, made in God's image. Can you get into your head how long twelve minutes is, let alone writing it for somebody else? I didn't even know I knew such things until they came back to me in the vault."

I credited the *New York Times.* All the news that's fit to print.

He ignored levity. A third party, overhearing, would have said Byerson was more serious than I in a matter which to me was terminally serious. He had just had his first real encounter with the Holocaust, while I had it in my inheritance. I am allowed to speak lightly of it, as Claude Prennis is allowed to call another black man a nigger.

He demanded that I tell him how a writer of such a brochure would know he wasn't writing to give voyeurs an erection. "Readers want to get to the rape. It doesn't make a lot of difference whether they're Jewish girls, Polish girls, French girls or Valkyries. From the memorial, visitors are going to dinner and a nightclub."

He declared again, there would never be a brochure. There might be a piece of paper. Spent of argument, he returned to a more upright position and picked up his fork to go on with his omelet. He changed his mind and crushed his napkin on the table. I accepted that his agitation was authentic, not a performance for me, a relative (he wouldn't know *lantsman*) of *déportés*.

"Writers of Holocaust literature have the same experience of frustration with vocabulary, Chester. Still they write. There is film from the camps, but Spielberg made his movie. Art has to think it can find better ways to remember reality. I have a short book, *Writing and the Holocaust*, that may interest you. I'll bring it down tomorrow morning."

"Yes, thank you." He brushed it aside. He had had an experience in the vault. While looking around with other tourists, he had imagined a rough noise of boots on the stone stairs. Uniformed roughnecks crowded in. He leaned toward me again to whisper hoarsely, *"Juifs! Sortez!"*

The question had occurred to him: "If at such a time I looked for somebody to take me in, whom would I ask? You know, that's a hell of a question. Think about it. Of everybody you know, whom would you ask?"

I opened my mouth to claim my copyright. Although the thought may have been original with him, he had not been the first to think it. Nor had I, probably; it came with my inheritance. But Byerson—a Presbyterian from Philadelphia by way of Princeton, a man who said *At this point in time?* I appreciated that he had been moved, that his concern was sincere. Nevertheless, it was of the moment, while mine had been latent in every encounter since childhood.

Then—unbidden—I was given another question, like the one that had come off the text of Anne Frank's diary:

Byerson, my mind turned, was it grandfather Myerson?

It doesn't take even a word, the shift of a single letter can let in light. I examined his face. Wider at the baggy jaw than across his forehead. Complexion somewhat Mediterranean. The same impression of bronze in his small eyes as in the bush of eyebrows. Nose—let me give you my theory of noses: any significant nose regarded steadily becomes Semitic. It is the great case of the observer creating the observed. I read no clue in Byerson's face, except as dwelling on expected evidence notoriously leads to expected conclusions, elsewhere as in medical research.

Talk ebbed. We had appointments. I said again I would bring him the book tomorrow. He said fine, he'd be glad to look at it. He went east and I south.

The question I asked him not aloud has never been answered. I haven't the slightest idea if it has any validity. For all I know, Byerson is a name that goes back to the Norman Invasion, and Chester is merely a man with unexpected sensibilities.

We continue to meet in the elevator and coffee shop. Byerson and I are both men who have escaped ecclesiastical dragnets and do not have occasion for certain conversations. Catholic, Jew, Muslim—these are for us not religious topics but political science or anthropology. Our friendship, which enlarges, still has never gone a foot beyond the edge of the table, and until the police are going around the neighborhood with their lists I won't know how much I can trust him. Or, for that matter, how much he can trust me. How can I vouch for what my behavior will be in the actual inconvenient moment?

Seized by the question on Air France that night, how did Byerson rate me? Good for five minutes? An hour? For the duration, at whatever the cost? I think I would do well, but I just don't know. Sarice Prennis certainly doesn't think of my door as one likely to open for the Prennises on a bad day. Perhaps she will therefore pass it by, and I, observing the street guardedly, will see her glance up toward a window that might be mine, hesitate, and to my shameful relief, walk past.

E.S. Goldman is the author of *Earthly Justice*. This story, his third to appear in *MR*, will be included in a new collection, *The Palmer Method*, due out later in 1995.

SHAH JAHAN IN PRISON / *S. Ben-Tov*

Shah Jahan, who built the
Taj Mahal, had planned an
identical, black shrine; he was
imprisoned, in view of the
Taj Mahal, before beginning it.

Out of the fortress walls, green
parrots flash and dive, to nestle

back in the prisoner's thoughts,
while rising sun swirls silver and copper,

Ganga-Jumna style, on the river water.
A sigh swells to burst anything but stone.

Far off, his Taj appears to float upon
its moorings, an illusion

that awes contemplators like a proof,
the prisoner remembers

a fountain and a garden
where she visited his mind before birth.

But the twin Taj Mahal. The black mirror,
obsidian, onyx . . . wishfulness

at night, when he sees a belt of stars
circling her hips, that she bends to unfasten.

THE LIGHTHOUSE / *S. Ben-Tov*

A land-spit off Northern California,
wedded to fog;

pink five-odd-petalled rose, a rock islet
whiskered with foam, a dirt path to a white-
    washed door,

fog takes them. That is why the many oblongs
of bevelled glass, illusorily green,

compose the lighthouse lens, each side convex
stepped crystal, glowing even on a cloudy day

with the light off. Kindled,
what miniature face in the umbrageous ocean

could the Point Reyes light not rescue?
Unused now;

when I turned around on the dirt path,
the plain tower and whitewashed door were fog,

his blurred figure in an oversize parka
walked into my arms, and we kissed like door
    and frame.

THE ARRIVAL GATE / *S. Ben-Tov*

Your life ended one minute after takeoff.
A flaw branched through an engine casing;
and gray shapeless clouds engulfed
the last seconds you had of yourself.

In free fall, souls slip from brows
like daydreams. Bodies are gently sloughed
in free fall, at higher altitudes,
not at the takeoff, with its moaning boost and tilted
    rows;

stressed metal octaves
sang through pillow-wadded skulls.
Ice rattled in clear cups
abandoned by so many startled hands, at once

everywhere, clinging. Listen! this song's
lines are your instructions. Here
is the red-lined exit, wide as the mouth
of a soprano, prolonging, through the awed hall,
    a miracle.

Out of orange body-bags the exploded jet's passengers
rise, smoke faces becoming flesh;
their personal belongings reattach
handles and shoulder-straps to hands and shoulders;

the crowd surges slowly up the jetway,
spilling into the arrival bay. Monitors show ARRIVED.
We walk the human corridors. You have not changed.
You have not changed, and I ask why you died.

METEOR ELEGY / *S. Ben-Tov*

For Itzhak Bentov ne Imrich Tobias, 1923–79

A star flees space
lightly, in the time
a spark glows in the space
it leaves dark. For an escaped
breath, a free light
dishevels the starred spaces...
Einstein measured space
by point of view. My mind's
doubled over my mind's
wound, a hidden space;
my words are wasted
measuring their waste.

American flight 100 heading west
sheared blue space
that thundered black—his last word was
unknowable—the crash blasted wasteland
a mile wide. Since that time,
through all his wasted
future, my father lives, as far stars waste
away to starlight,
he is daily light.
The hourglass waist,
the stem of falling sand. Love's a determined
loser at the game it masterminds.

The irony of a divided mind
is lively, but on life irony's wasted...
...Czech gene-strands are mine
like strung crystal, reminders
of darkness. A dark and hidden space
of maternal earth minds
our lost family. He kept his mind
a wound never mended in time
to die whole. He fled time
and again into fast planes, reminded

of what made him go lightly—
he still travels light.

Through a library skylight
(dark, rain-scoured, unmindful
of absent gazes) a hollow light
castle manifests, alight
with pure watts
of yearning. The knife-lit
turrets, a hawk delighting,
the crescent spaces
bridges span, the scarp-walled space
lightning
dazzles in transfixed: Time
branching all at one time.

What captures my father? Wartime
bivouacs, tents ruffled with light
hot wind. An English grammar and the *Times*.
Years when military time
was natural rhythm, planting mines
his utmost skill. He had the time
of his life. A cigarette to pass the slow burn time
of the cordite charge that was
his testament to each golden wasteful
Libyan dawn.... He checks the time:
now. Gray mountains space
apart the stars. He feels sound collapse

and hugs ground. Stars pirouette through space.
The flash, timed,
passes over, plumed light.
He's running, never minding
how all around him dreams the sandy waste.

THE GATE OF BABYLON / *S. Ben-Tov*

The Berlin Museum's halls echo more footfalls
than there are visitors.
                              In a skylit room
stands an arch, glazed brick,
of such dimensions that tandem horsemen
can trot through, not lowering their spears:
the Ishtar Gate.
                              How far from Babylon's

brown canals where oarstrokes furrowed
indigo images of walls,
and bronze towers, by palmy steps, zigzagged
    to paradise;
how far from home.
                              The sight of her,
steadying the three-days-distant caravan
gradually disappeared;
                              turned into mound,
trenched excavation, Prussian monument,
cargo aboard an armored train to Moscow;
metamorphosed into this postwar exhibit

                              where the entrance
to the dead Imperiums reassembled:
blistered lapis wall and giant frieze
of fabulous animals, Babylon's memories.

                              Her ancient menagerie
silently paces the restored facade.
The pale bull has eyes alive with kohl,
one indigo tier lower, the serpent
struts, despite Eden, on eagle's claws,
the snarling lion treads a bottom row
of cream rosettes, his ochre musculature
deforming the bricks.

Clouds pass
and the gallery's dim. Visitors adjust
their headphones' multilingual muffs,
like cold children,
                    awaiting sacrifice.

TURTLE BEACH / *S. Ben-Tov*

I will not tell you on what shore
sea-tortoises lie
bleaching,
some thousand basins full of sand and sour light,
that dragged themselves
with strange strength to land.
I walked there, I breathed
stench, rotten footing threw me down—
against my face
like Earth's hard mantle,
the domed carapace contoured with whorls,
over my eyes
a cloud of blackflies.

Ocean sounded all
afternoon, rumbled
the secret
waves too long for the human eardrum.
I cannot tell you
how lonely,
sun and sky
in concentric rings.

S. Ben-Tov's first book was *During Ceasefire*. She has been a poet-in-residence at
Mishkenot Sha'ananim in Jerusalem.

A NIGHT AT THE Y / *Robert Garner McBrearty*

FINISHED WITH HIS DAY JOB, Ralph stops back at his apartment just long enough to change clothes and kiss his wife and baby goodbye before rushing off to his night shift at the Y. He stands behind the front desk, with his left hand picking up phones and with his right dispensing towels and locker keys. With a harried grin, caffeine-inspired energy, and the sinking realization that there is baby spit-up on his blue sweater, he greets the incoming members who are frantic to run, swim, lift, jiggle, jazz, and whirlpool away the jangled nerves of a long day in this fast-paced city just east of the Rocky Mountains. As the members burst through the front doors, stomp snow from their boots, and charge the desk with lowered heads and hunched shoulders, they remind him of truculent bulls, and he is transported by a memory of a day in a mountain town in Mexico twenty years before.

The bulls are poised in the cattle truck, ready for the run. Ralph, twenty-one years old then, full of wild hope and amoebic parasites, dagger-thin and crazed from dysentery and ingestions of medicinal tequila, has taken refuge on the steps of El Patio café.

Nine bulls come down the ramp—motley, scraggly, apathetic bulls to be sure. No monsters of Pamplona in this September fiesta. They clomp into the roped-off square and the crowd lets out a collective half-gasp, half-giggle as it huddles against the barriers and gathers on the steps of the café. Young men prance in the cobblestone streets, whistling and jeering. The bulls come to a standstill, snort, wheeze, roll anxious eyes about. Perhaps in the backs of their dim brains flickers the uneasy suspicion that this bacchanal can only finish with them on the wrong end of a public barbecue.

These humble, pastoral beasts see no cause for confrontation. They show no inclination to trample, hook with their horns or spew foam. They'd like to laugh this off; couldn't it all be resolved peacefully? They stomp on the cobblestones, leaning their heads together, discussing their strategy as their breath rises in white puffs on this crisp, blue Sunday afternoon in late September. They try to back up the ramp into the truck, but four exasperated rancheros swing cowboy hats at their rumps; disconsolately, the bulls come forward into the sunny but bracing afternoon, and the crowd releases another excited cry.

In his memory, Ralph sees himself backing up as high as he can on the café steps, wedging his way behind children and serape-wrapped women. But the other young men, so boldly challenging the bulls, seem to beckon to him: Come down! Run with the bulls! And briefly he yearns to encounter his fate, to die on those dusty cobblestone streets with a horn in his chest, blood in his boots, a wine flask tipped to his lips, while his fingers rise and twitch gracefully, keeping time with the mariachi music as he fades...on brave marvelous soul!

The rank odor of sweat and soggy towels and leather basketballs wafts over the desk, and from the gym comes the reverberation of bouncing balls and the trill of a referee's whistle. Ralph's memory of the fiesta momentarily slips away and he finds himself back at the Y desk, in the present, though he wonders, given the vast and inexplicable discoveries of modern physics, just exactly what *is* the present. His uncertainty about the nature of time makes him suddenly aware that he will never be able to explain modern physics to his son, or even cogently describe the inner workings of a telephone. Thinking of his inadequacies as a father makes his heart flutter as he continues handing out towels and keys.

His rush-hour helper, Maggie Vivigino, the twenty-two-year-old, green-eyed olive-skinned weight room trainer, joins him behind the counter. Her taut body ripples beneath her purple leotard, and Ralph imagines she would have made a wonderful companion for his former self when he was cringing on the steps of El Patio café. But Maggie, he suspects, considers him a loser, working at the Y at his age, though she kindly tries to conceal the feeling.

The evening rush speeds up. The Y members, punchy and frayed from another hectic workday, will brook no delay, resent showing their membership cards.

"Don't you know who I am by *now?*"

"I want a good locker tonight! Last time you stuck me in a drafty corner."

"When are you people going to get your act together?"

Meanwhile the phone lines are ringing urgently, the red buttons pulsating; the callers are desperate with weighty questions. Ralph stabs at buttons, puts people on hold, accidentally disconnects a few.

"Where is my son's soccer game tomorrow?" a caller inquires. "He lost his schedule and I don't have the coach's number."

"How do I sign up for the karate class?"

"Where is the director? I want to speak to the director."

"Have you seen a woman in a green bikini?"

"The Y? I wanted Pete's Pool Hall. How long have you had this number?"

"Who's in charge there? I want to speak to the director!"

"If you see a woman in a green bikini, tell her I want to meet her."

"Are you *sure* this is the Y?"

"If I sign up for the karate class, do I need to know how to kick beforehand?"

"Listen, this is serious. I've got to find out about my kid's soccer game..."

Unfortunately, Ralph has little information to dispense. His job is to answer calls and forward them to the appropriate offices. But it is Friday evening and the director and administrators have fled the building.

"Would you mind if I put you on hold?" Ralph says for the hundredth time.

"Yes, I would mind. I've been on hold twice already. Can't you just tell me where my son's damn soccer game is tomorrow?" By this time, the soccer man's voice has turned thick, hoarse and boozy.

"I'm sorry. I don't have the schedule here. I just answer the phones and forward them to the program desk."

"Then let me have the program desk."

"I'm afraid they're closed. They don't open again until nine in the morning."

"But the game is at *eight!* You people are screwed up, you hear me? Screwed up!"

"Ralph! Help!" Maggie screams from her station behind the desk. Ralph turns from the phone to see a fresh wave of incoming customers.

"I'm afraid I'm going to have to put you on hold, sir. I'll find out what I can."

"Don't you put me—"

He joins the fray and confronts a woman who snarls, "This is the longest I've *ever* had to wait. Can't you make your calls on your *own* time?"

A man flings his key back onto the desk. "This is a *boy's* locker," he hisses in righteous rage.

A tall, bearded man takes a towel from Ralph's trembling hand and inquires cheerfully, "Are we having fun yet?"

Right in front of the customers, Maggie puts her hands to her face and screams, as she screams nearly every day at this time, "I'm quitting! I'm quitting!"

The members meet this pronouncement with a stony indifference, and she continues snatching cards from their hands and hurling their locker keys and towels at them.

Then suddenly the wave dissipates; the customers disappear into the locker rooms and quiet settles over the front desk as another rush hour at the Y comes to a close. Maggie looks at Ralph with a bright mist in her eyes. "This is what I get for not finishing college. I'll always work at crappy jobs."

He takes her aside, draws her back to the tall metal equipment lockers, thinks of holding her steely biceps, but doesn't. He assures her she can still go back and finish college, though inside a subversive voice whispers: Of course you can finish college like *I* did and *still* work at crappy jobs.

As night deepens, only a few people straggle in from the snow. The calls, too, have slackened, though the soccer man keeps phoning, sounding drunker and more abusive each time he calls. Maggie has returned to the weight room to Stairmaster away her blues; her sinewy legs provide inspiration to all the panting after-hours jocks.

Ralph calls his wife and she groans with fatigue. Their six-month-old boy has been crying for hours.

"What did the doctor say?"

"It's probably just teething."

"How long do you think it will last?"

"About ten more years." She sniffles, "I think I'm losing it."

"Courage, love," he whispers, "courage."

He slips away from the quiet desk to take the dirty towels to the laundry room, and his heart twists as the sweet strains of Joni Mitchell drift from the overhead speakers:

I was a free man in Paris
I felt unfettered and alive...

Alive and unfettered indeed, Ralph, on that day twenty years ago, huddles on the café steps as the bulls make rings around the square and feign charges at the young men. The bold ones rush among the bulls, slap rumps and pull horns, and when the bulls are inspired enough to give chase, the young men dive for cover at the last moment.

Robert Garner McBrearty

Ralph remains on his perch, cautiously watching the action. He detects about him, in subtle glances and stiffened shoulders, the faint signs of disgust: Oh, cowardly American, go down with the other young men and do battle with these ferocious bulls!

Out of nowhere, a boy of about four has wandered into the middle of the street in front of the café. Too late, the crowd on the café steps spots him. In the same moment a bull, ten yards away, lowers its horns and charges.

The crowd is paralyzed, deathly still, as if by holding its breath it can make the bull turn aside. Then its silence gives way to a panicked roar. Ralph is not certain, but later he thinks that he felt a push on his back—a palpable, yet unearthly touch. Barely conscious of what he is doing he rushes through the crowd—a fish gliding past boulders that give way to him—and leaps off the steps. Too late to sweep the boy aside, he runs directly in front of the bull. He feels a bone-jarring impact in his side; his shoes seem stuck to the pavement while the rest of his body flies upwards. He is totally breathless, yet at the same time trying to puke. He's vaguely aware of sailing beneath a blue sky before he loses consciousness.

As he awakens, a wooden ceiling fan is twirling slowly overhead. His eyes flicker open and shut, open and shut. The examining table is hard, and the scent of alcohol is familiar and comforting. The doctor and his nurse are marvelously efficient and reassuring as they smile down on him and tape his ribs. The young doctor is dashing in his street clothes; called away from the fiesta, he smells of beer and his eyes glitter. The nurse wears a low-cut flowery dress, and she leans over him and caresses his brow with a moist palm.

"How are you feeling now, my hero friend?" the doctor says, with only a slightly Spanish accent.

Ralph blinks. "Is the boy okay?"

The doctor and his nurse grin at one another, and their eyes shine. "The boy is fantastic," the doctor says. "And you will be okay. It's the bull we are worried about now."

The doctor and his nurse fall against each other in a paroxysm of laughter and then topple lightly onto Ralph, who puts his arms around their quaking backs.

"'Kay wise guy, where's the soccer game? Tell me where my son's soccer game is. I'm not dropping this."

"Look, I've done everything I can. I even tried to call the program director at home, but there was no answer. I don't know what else I can do."

"That won't do, my friend. That won't do. I only see my kid every fourth weekend. You're not screwing this up for him. Somebody knows. Somebody there knows." His voice rises, takes on a chanting quality: "Somebody knows, somebody there knows, somebody knows . . ."

"Look, I'm really sorry. But I've got to get off now."

"Don't you cut me off, you son of a bitch. Don't you—"

Ralph stares at the phone, but it doesn't ring again. He almost regrets it because there is a sadness at the Y now as the hour grows late. Most of the members and all the other attendants have come and gone, and there are no distractions from his worries. He wonders if his family will make it in this new part of the country they have moved to. Will he find a better job? Will his son be happy growing up here, in this town hard-pressed against the Rockies? Will his wife's health, already fragile, hold through the fitful nights as they get up again and again to comfort the baby?

Out of the dark comes a family—a father, a mother, and a boy of about four. As they come through the front doors, they pause, half inside and half out. Behind them, the night pours snow; a gust of frigid air rushes all the way to Ralph at the front desk. They hesitate in the doorway. Then the man gives the boy a gentle nudge, and they all come forward anxiously toward the desk.

The man, about Ralph's age, is short, thick, bearded, with a burly chest and wide hunched shoulders; he looks as if he has seen a lot of rough weather, done a lot of hard labor, yet there is something weak about him. His smile is tremulous. The woman is Hispanic, with dark somber eyes. When they reach the desk, the man keeps his family huddled close, one hand resting on the boy's black hair, the other holding his wife's elbow through her old flannel coat. In a quavering Texas accent, his voice coming out high at first before it finds its range, he says, "Hi. Think you can rent us a room?" He shrugs apologetically. "We can't pay motel prices."

The one word Ralph doesn't want to say to the worn-out looking family is *no*, but this is what he must tell them.

"I'm sorry, but I'm afraid we don't rent overnight rooms here. We're mainly a gym. The Y in Denver rents some rooms."

The man's shoulders slump another notch. The woman's eyes explore Ralph's face, searching for lies. "Damn. We came through there an hour ago," the man says mournfully. "We're headed for

Seattle... from Houston," he adds, as if that explains their plight. He shakes his head and mutters, almost as if repeating a mantra, "Got good jobs in Seattle. Houston ain't nothing but a bust." The woman nods grimly, agreeing with him about Houston. Ralph wonders if she believes in the good jobs ahead.

Ralph sees that they are all dead tired. The man and woman glance sidelong at one another, calculating the time back to Denver, this late at night, in the bad weather, the lost time on their journey; the decision is coming down against it.

He is tempted to offer them lodging in his cramped little apartment for the night. But what would his wife say? Too dangerous to bring strangers in. Even though she is kind-hearted, her fears for their son would make her say no. He knows he is only using her as an excuse, though. Even if he lived alone he wouldn't offer, wouldn't want to be drawn into their troubles. But the dark, round, staring eyes of the little boy remind him of what his own family might come to under different circumstances, adrift in a strange city, no money for a motel.

"There is a hostel by the campus," he says slowly.

The man blinks. "A hostel?"

"It's kind of like a dorm, but you don't have to be students. It's only a few dollars to stay there."

The man glances at his wife, still clutching her elbow. She looks at him, and then down at her son. She puts her hand on the boy's head and draws him tighter against her leg. She angles her thin face away from the man and her jaw stiffens, a shift which seems to freeze the man. There is something about the word *hostel*, Ralph sees, which has stopped her, become a stumbling block.

The man sighs and turns back to Ralph. "We'll go on and look for a motel, I guess. You know anything cheap? It don't have to be nothing fancy."

"I haven't lived here too long myself, but we can look through the Yellow Pages. Most things are kind of expensive in this town, though."

As he reaches under the desk for a phone book, a sheet of pink, lined paper flutters out; he glances idly at it for a moment, and then stares in amazement at the columns of writing. He slips the sheet of paper under his sweater into the top pocket of his shirt and pats it to secure its position, as if the paper is some treasure of great worth.

The man stands at the front desk, thumbing through the Yellow Pages and making his calls from the desk phone. He stumbles over his questions, his brow furrowing as if he can't quite figure out what people are telling him. With each call, his voice quavers more; sweat springs out on his forehead and his blunt stubby finger makes mistakes dialing. Ralph eases the phone away from him and makes a few calls himself, but it is a football weekend and the motels are either full or too expensive.

Because he can't bring himself to offer his apartment, he says instead, knowing the inadequacy of the offer, "May I buy you all a cup of coffee? And a hot chocolate for your son?"

The man, who has gone back to calling himself, holds the phone to his chest, momentarily stunned by the offer. The boy's eyes brighten as he looks over at the coffee machine against the wall. The woman moves away from the man's side. As if it's a way of saying yes, she wraps her arms around herself, gives an exaggerated, friendly sort of shiver, and says, "It's cold here."

Ralph makes change in the register and goes around the desk into the lobby. The boy follows him to the machine. He takes hold of Ralph's pant leg and stares silently as the cup drops down and fills. The woman wanders over to the green vinyl chairs, set in a circle around a worn coffee table, and sits down. She lifts a magazine and crosses one slim leg over the other, frowning at the no smoking sign on the wall. Ralph distributes the coffees and hot chocolate. As the few remaining members drift out from the locker rooms, the woman, unlit cigarette in mouth, stares at them with narrowed eyes. The boy follows Ralph as he makes a quick tour of the offices in back, making sure doors and windows are locked. The boy slips his hand into Ralph's and as he holds the tiny, cool little hand, he wishes he could do some finer thing.

With his ribs taped tightly, Ralph rises stiffly from the examining table. The doctor and nurse help him back into his shirt, and the nurse kisses him on the cheek and ushers him into the waiting room where a small entourage rises and cheers him as he wobbles forward. They offer to see him home, but what he really wants is tequila, he tells them. His request is greeted with a chorus of approval and he is taken up by his new friends and escorted to a cantina near the square, where he drinks icy Tecate beer and shots of José Cuervo, and his newfound best friends embrace him again and again.

Later, he will dimly recall making fervid offers to take his friends to a ranch in Montana where they would live off the land and practice medieval chivalry. "You will need English lessons, Juan," he recalls himself saying to one particularly affectionate but incoherent man who kept putting him in headlocks and lowering his nose to the bar.

A bloody sunset glows over the ancient mountain town as he stumbles out the swinging cantina doors; he is on the march again with his entourage, this time slipping through the barricades back into the square where the bulls, at last thoroughly pissed off, have gone into higher gear and are managing to hook a few overconfident young campesinos in the seats of their jeans.

For what seems like hours then, but what must have been, in reality, only a few glorious minutes, he experiences what feels like saintliness. The bulls cannot hurt him. They charge at him and he stands motionless; at the last moment, he gives a sweep of his hands and sends them veering away. When he sees anyone in trouble, a bull moving in, he glides over and with a light touch on the rump turns the bull aside. The townsfolk scream his glory, a great roar rising from behind the barricades. They scream the only name they know for him: "GRINGO! EL GRINGO!" Sombreros fly his way, coins, roses; a beer can bounces off the side of his head.

But back at the Y, saintliness is in short supply. The man is running out of motels to call and it is nearing midnight. The Y will close in ten minutes. Only a diehard weightlifter or two remain somewhere in the dank bowels of the building.

It is time for the nightly closing announcement, which Ralph amends from night to night. Over the intercom system, his voice echoes back at him, "Another night at the Y is fast drawing to a close. Prepare to go forth, repaired of body, mind, and spirit...."

The man pauses with his finger on the Yellow Pages and gives him a pained smile. Turning, the man signals to his wife, who rises wearily from her chair and joins him. The boy, who has been staring mesmerized through the plate glass doors at the silent blue swimming pool, comes over and leans his sleepy head against his mother's legs. The man closes the phone book and says to his family, "Looks like we'll rest up in the truck tonight." His voice is a dry whisper, "We can run the engine enough to keep warm."

The woman nods, her lips forming a tight line, and Ralph notes that she is not blaming the man, or trying to make him feel worse, which somehow makes him feel sorrier for them. He thinks again of inviting them to his home for the night, but is silent. The boy presses himself tighter against his mother's legs. The man shuts his eyes for a long moment, rubbing the back of his neck and swinging his head like a tired old bull. When he opens his eyes and stares across the front desk at Ralph, he looks amazed to discover himself here, at this moment in time. Slowly, he sticks his hand out across the counter and Ralph grasps it. The man's hand is dry and rough. He shakes without force. "Thank you, sir. You were real helpful. We thank you."

"I wish I could help, but—"

"We'll be okay." The woman's blunt tone silences him. She kneels, pulls her son's hood up and ties the drawstring. Though he is old enough to walk alone, she cradles him and hoists him to her chest.

Ralph comes around the desk and follows them toward the front door. They are halfway through the lobby when a tall shape appears on the other side of the glass doors; a man, clutching his jacket to guard his neck from the cold, lurches in from the snowy night, followed by a stream of frigid air. He shivers, stamps snow from his shoes, and glares wild-eyed at Ralph and the little family. He charges forward menacingly.

Instinctively, Ralph moves in front of the family. "May I help you?"

"You work here? You're the one I've been talking to?" His head bobs on a long neck. He glowers. His face is flushed, and his breath reeks of whiskey.

The family shrinks back behind Ralph as the stranger points his car keys at Ralph's chest. "I drove all the way through the fucking snow and ice, pal, to personally chew out your ass, and I'd better get some straight answers this time. Where is my son's soccer game? Where, dammit?"

Ralph stares at the man. Then he reaches under his sweater and whips out a pink sheet of paper. "Which team?"

"What's that?" The man blinks. "The . . . Rockets. Yeah, the Rockets." He looks profoundly confused by the schedule Ralph is holding.

"El Centro Elementary. Folsom Street. 8 A.M."

The man rocks back on his heels as if someone struck him, then tips forward, pressing the points of his keys to Ralph's chest. The astonishment in his face turns to rage, "Why did you make me go through hell to—"

"Easy," Ralph says. "Easy," and he takes the man by the arms. Gently and gracefully Ralph walks, almost waltzes him the few steps to the coffee table. He pushes the man down in a chair, and takes his car keys. "I'll call you a cab."

The man tries to rise, but Ralph puts a hand on his chest. The calmness of his own voice startles him. "It's that or I can call the police."

The man stares up at him drunkenly. He stiffens as if to fight, and then collapses. He sinks back in the chair and with a defeated expression he looks about the lobby for someone to make his case to; finally, his eyes light on the wall photos of the Y board members, and to their smiling, broad faces he protests, "What a fucked up place this is." But he stays put, shivering, letting out disgruntled sighs and groans as a puddle of melted snow forms around his shoes.

Meanwhile, Ralph sees that the family has slipped away. He rushes into the night and sees them trudging across the parking lot in the snow, the boy over his mother's shoulder. "Hey!" he calls, running after them. "Wait!" They glance back, but hurry on for their truck.

Catching up with them, lightly touching the man's elbow, he talks quickly, getting the offer out before he can stop himself. "You can spend the night with us if you like. It's not much. We'll have to put out sleeping bags on the floor. And we have a baby who's been crying a lot. But it's warm. You can stretch out. Have a shower in the morning. Breakfast..."

The man's eyes widen and he looks in consternation from Ralph to his wife. She holds her boy tighter to her breasts, and Ralph speaks to her now. "It's all right. Really. It's no problem. I want you to stay with us."

Her face hardens, and for a scary moment he thinks she is going to tell him to shove his offer; then, in an instant, her face softens and he sees something more frightening: he believes she is going to cry. She gives his hand a light squeeze, and nods faintly.

"Okay," Ralph says. "Okay. Great."

His shoulders relax and drop, his chest expands; an adrenalin-like thrill rushes through him. Turning, he lifts his face to the wet white shower of snow and starts back for the Y. The family follows close behind him, as if they are afraid to lose him.

And twenty years in the past (though, given the vast and inexplicable discoveries of modern physics, who can say just what the past is) he is seized by two policemen. One of them screams in his face, "Out of the street, cabrón! You want to get keeled?!"

They give him the bum's rush out of the square. Then he is weaving home through the cobblestone streets, followed by his loyal entourage and a ragged mariachi band...weaving his way home through the last bloody rays of the sunset, weaving below the flowered balconies, a beautiful woman waving from a window...the bugles serenading a young man home as he takes a glorious walk toward the future, toward a long wintry night at the Y.

Robert McBrearty has published in numerous literary magazines and earned a Pushcart Prize. This is his second appearance in MR.

THE ORDER OF THINGS / *Ranbir Sidhu*

IT'S ONLY A GAME, his voice fading on the wind. That's what he said. I could still feel the grip of his fingers where he had held my child's arm, his hand, large, engulfing it, fingers touching at the tips. There was already a line of grey in his beard, though he was a young man, even then, already retired, a national name. His beard tied back into a second, scruffy chin, a pink turban, his eyes on me, Watch the ball, not me, and again his voice, Watch the ball! But I always looked back into his eyes. Why was he here, why wasn't he out there, where the newspapermen attacked each other for his photograph, where the radio sang his praises, where all India looked to the holy dirt his feet walked on? It's only a game, he shouted. They said he had walked with Gandhiji to the sea. They said that he never, not even as a baby, wore anything but homespun. They said that on every corner he passed, an assassin waited—why?—but that divine forces always protected him. I launched the cricket ball into the air, but it fell thudding in the hot dirt only a few feet away, a red, undistinguished ball, and he looked at me as though I, personally, had lost Pakistan.

Over thirty years later they found his body in one of the small alleys suffocating the dark streets around the Golden Temple of the Sikhs, the shops crowding into it, the hands of beggars having stripped most possessions from his body, a *kirpan*, a holy knife in his gut. I heard this on the BBC World Service, sitting alone—my wife had taken our daughter shopping for a prom dress—in our Berkeley home with its false English countryside facade. Outside, the automated sprinklers silent—there was a drought and the lawn slowly died as summer aged. Three days ago and only now had the news squeezed out of a Punjab under martial law. A month before, Indira Gandhi's own Sikh bodyguards had murdered her, claiming it as vengeance for the attack she had ordered some months previous on the Golden Temple. Thousands had been killed in that original attack, and thousands more died after the assassination. Anil was Kirpal's son and my business partner and he celebrated both events, because both, he said, would show the Sikhs how important it was to have a separate country, to finally rise up and forge Khalistan from the alloys of the Punjab.

But why hadn't Anil told me of his father's death? I had spoken to him two days before and he had said nothing. I pressed the button on my phone with his name on it. Anil? Anil, I heard, I...I don't know what to say.... His voice, clear, strong, Yes, yes, I know, the falling sari prices in Pakistan. Have you seen *The Wall Street Journal?* What? I said, confused. No, Anil *bhai,* I heard about your father. Kirpalji. Your father. It is terrible news. I am so sorry. And then, my voice revealing a strained but rising frustration, Why didn't you call and tell me, why did I have to hear this on the radio? Anil was silent, and I could imagine him looking into the telephone, annoyed. He was never one to talk about things like this, never one to give reasons, root out explanations. Finally he said, The funeral was yesterday. They took his ashes and they dumped them in the Ganges. His wish, and not the Sutlej as we wanted. For all he did, he was at least a hero of the Punjab, and not one of India. They should have thrown his ashes in the Sutlej. Then he added, his voice crisp unaffected, We are still on for the auction tomorrow? It is important with all that has happened. But I protested, Anil, we don't have to do this, we don't you know. But he insisted, adding, You know Papaji and I, we had our differences. The dead lawn, fading into dusk, and I thought of my father's house in India, in the Punjab, standing next to Kirpal's with its constant guards, and our small, cramped rooms leaking out onto roads of dust, fields of dirt, and thought how far we had come in so few years.

Both houses looked out onto a large square of dirt, where every now and then, tents blossomed overnight like mushrooms, heralding the sudden animation, the music, the air of license and possibility of a wedding celebration. At other times, we kids played in the square, kicking up dirt, running, a kite string threading through my fingers, the paper kite behind me, rising until it was almost gone, smaller than the sun, and I would pull it in, down, afraid it might disappear. Anil, eyeing the dead kite, a lazing bird, feathers ruffled by the breeze, would shout at me, Why did you stop? Why did you pull it down? His face angry, as though my fear had lost him that world up in the sky where he could look down and see his father only as a dot, getting smaller and smaller.

Those days, hot, my legs stuffed into trousers, a white cricketer's shirt, and Anil the same, his fingers pulling at the collar, Papaji, it's so hot, and Kirpal saying, This is how real cricketers play. And on the far edge of the field, the kids we always played with, dressed in torn shirts, no shoes, we envious of their freedom, and they awed by the shadow of the great man, too timid to approach. They said he argued with Nehru over Partition. They said his voice rang out in fury when Jinnah announced, a day early, the formation of Pakistan, casting the shadow of a split land onto the fireworks, the celebrations of India's birth, because, they said, Kirpal didn't care whether the British stayed or left, all he wanted was India whole. Nehru's ears rang with his abuse, Why do you let Jinnah split up the land? Why do you let them take a knife to our Punjab? But to us he was the memory of fame, that arc of muscled arm, that streak of red through the sky, toppled wickets, victory.

Kirpal's thick fingers enclosed my arm, holding it just right, forcing my hand around the red ball, hard enough to kill a man. Like this, no, like this, he said, his fingers pushing my hand into impossible positions. Cricket is a ballet of the hand, and, You must learn the moves precisely, that's it, yes, that's right. I would throw the ball, watching it skid far off in a momentary breath of dirt pulsing up from the ground. His shout, Anil, get the ball! And Anil would run, faltering, his father's voice, Quickly, quickly, my arm still hurting from where he had gripped it, where his fingers pressed into the soft flesh. And Anil, standing, his eyes on the ground, in the distance the kids watching, a kite on the ground, unmoving, Come on, boy, that's it, hold the ball, just so, no, not like that, here, put your arm like this, here, bend your elbow when you bring it back up, keep the wrist loose, no, Anil, not like that at all, you're holding the ball like a girl, hold it like a man, you can't always throw underarm, a man, Anil, do you know what a man is? do you know what a Sikh man is? Come on, hold it properly, who formed the Khalsa? do you know why? Anil! hold the ball like a man, properly, no, I'm not hurting you, I'm only showing you how to, Anil! okay, go inside, go sulk, be a girl! And the great man watched his son kick dirt up, Anil's hands on the tight collar, his eyes to the ground. Now, Raj, again, but keep your wrist more loose when you run, yes, that's it, great! I threw the ball as hard and fast and straight as I could and watched it bounce some distance off, the red of it fading. I knew, even then, that if I were a real friend to Anil, I would have dropped that ball at Kirpal's feet, I would have walked away, my hand fingering my collar, my feet kicking at the dirt. But this was Kirpal, the dying sun behind him, and even so young we had our gods.

Anil double parked his orange Mercedes outside my store in Berkeley, one hand pressing on the horn, the other waving at me, his lips moving, Hurry up! hurry up! It was a busy morning, the students filling the sidewalks with their bodies, their nervous, urgent energy, and I, not even finished with my first cup of tea and already in the middle of a big sale, and then Anil, the horn blaring, the arm waving. Neema! I called out to my wife. Neema, Anil *bhai* is waiting, and I still haven't finished with Mr. Sheik. I smiled at Mr. Sheik. Neema, please finish with Mr. Sheik, and to Mr. Sheik, thin, balding, though young, eyes alive, I said, My dear wife will conclude the sale if you do not mind. My business partner is impatient this morning. Mr. Sheik nodded, Yes, he said, Please to tell we are all sorry for his loss. Yes, yes, of course, gathering up my briefcase, the horn blaring, and Neema, Don't forget your jacket. Of course, I get it, but she is frowning, her eyes not on Mr. Sheik, an important customer, but on the orange Mercedes, orange, the national color of Khalistan, her tongue nervous, Give him my best, and say I will call Anita this evening. I nod. The street, treacherous with students. Why the hurry? But the car is already swerving onto University Avenue, and Anil, his face dense, illuminating nothing, says only, These bloody hippies, If I could kill one. . . .

Anil is a short man, strong, broad-shouldered and muscular, hair creeping up the sides of his neck. Ever since those days of playing cricket, he has grown to the sides and not up, building up layer upon layer of muscle, fat, as though almost preserving that self he was then, kicking up the dirt, his eyes down, the cricket sweater tight, hot, the collar annoying. Before he started wearing a turban, his hair was already thinning, greying, and his hands, when we would sit together some evenings, a bottle of Johnnie Walker between us on the table, his hands would find his head, straightening, covering up those first signs, not wanting to admit that one day his own hair would be like his father's.

I didn't know what to say, so I said, quietly, Anil *bhai*, searching for traces of grief in the profile of his face, but all I found was the hard shell of something else. Anil *bhai*, I am so sorry. Neema too. Mr. Sheik even. He shook his head. At a light, he pressed his hand on my arm, and briefly, he glanced over at me. Do not say anything. I know. It is not easy, but work must go on. I said to Anita this morning. Anita, I need to work, without work, what am I? And she still crying. Did I cry? No, he was an old man, and old men die. The car lurched forward, his hand on the stick again, and then he burst out, Bloody hippies! because a young woman dressed in tie-dye and her long hair flowing was walking in the street, casually, and Anil had to swerve to miss her. That was why I was late this morning, he shouted, because of *gora* hippies like that one. They parked me in, some VW with stickers all over it. The Grateful Dead, and all that whatnot your daughter listens to. Next time.... But he broke off here. We were on the freeway, and his foot went to the floor as the car menaced across four lanes, the horn suddenly blaring at someone who tried to cut us off. I had never seen him drive like this, overtaking without giving cars a chance to get out of the way, or if this was impossible, flashing the lights, pressing the horn, Come on! Come on! What are you doing you stupid woman! Go back to Mexico! Berkeley became Oakland, its long stretches, dead tires rolling between lanes, sixty, seventy, eighty....

Over twenty years ago, our parents waved to us from the dock, their small figures submerged in the crowd, until eventually, we couldn't tell whose parents were ours, and the whole dock, those thousands of faces, merged into the grey horizon that kept us looking back to India, enchanting us with its memory of stillness. When we approached the United States, for some minutes we had the illusion of returning, but this was gone when we saw the hubbub on the dock, the skyscrapers behind it, and no one there, waving to us. We started a business in Berkeley, and in a few years, our small import-export storefront had expanded so fast that soon we controlled much of the sari trade on the West Coast, and even parts of Canada. Our parents found us wives, and we flew back for the weddings, nervous, laughing, smuggling Johnnie Walker in our luggage, all the time talking boldly of what we would do that first night as men.

Anil, come here, son, he said. I stood watching, the hours after the wedding. He looked so much older, the grey in his beard having expanded like a fungus, eyes tired. He hugged Anil, his broad chest pressing his son close. Now you are married, and Anita such a fine girl, with a degree and everything, just like you wanted. The old man smiled, beaming. Anil, his body limp in his father's arms, already strong, stocky, no turban yet, pushed Kirpal away, though gently, without force. Thank you, he said formally.

And Kirpal again, Now I am in the government, you know, I hope you do well to my name abroad. I am more important than ever. I have meetings with our dear Indira almost every day. Indira! snorted Anil. She is a. . . . But he stopped himself, and I could see the red rise to his face. Sorry, but I don't share your politics, father. And Anil moved back, turned, and quickly pushed out through the tent which stood on that old field where we had practised cricket until our arms hurt and our knees ached. I thought I saw in his retreating figure something of the boy pacing away, angry. But he was a man now, and there was nothing Kirpal could shout at him. Kirpal stood alone, suddenly ancient, his shoulders slumped, his eyes looking down at the dirt, one foot etching a circle. If there had been a cricket ball in sight, I would have picked it up, running, my arms and hands perfect, the arc of that ball, just to show that after all these years I had not forgotten who he once was. But there wasn't, and so I said, *Sat sri akal,* bowing slightly, and followed Anil, nervous, thinking, Neema is more beautiful than in the photographs, but I hope she doesn't want too many babies.

The 1980s closed around his neck like a noose, those years before his murder, when the rumors began to surface. Slowly at first, like the dead bodies on the side of the road, those rare births of night, first a Hindu, an old man, then two nights later, a pair of Sikh brothers, then a Hindu family in a neighboring village, then. . . . The rumors were like this, expanding in the heat of the worsening trouble, when, so many years had gone by, and all Kirpal wanted was the mantle of the old statesman, the dignified aspect of his beard, one shake of the hand and the deal done. He felt forced to give a speech against the separatists, against the widening cycles of violence. The Punjab must never become Khalistan, thumping his fist on the armrest of the chair, his face on every television. India must remain whole, though wounded, having already lost its pound of flesh in 1947. The radicals were murderers, arsonists, nothing more than petty criminals and terrorists. The police must be given full authority to quell these troublemakers. I did not walk with the Mahatma to see our country come to this. His face lost in nostalgia. I watched the videotape he sent Anil of the speech, specially copied to play on an American VCR, only to sit as Anil frowned, grinding his teeth, The old fool, he doesn't know history when he sees it, Khalistan will overrun him. But watching Kirpal's face on the television filled me with an old feeling, and I remembered I had always thought of him as my father, the one who made it possible for me to come to the States. But to Anil I said, You're right, the old fool. And it felt right.

It was only a month after this speech that she ordered the attack on the temple, and it was Kirpal, so rumor had it, that pressed her to rout the terrorists and separatist from our holy shrine.

But other rumors were already being passed by whispers and after the attack burst open to bring the old man down. They said the reporters started them, always pushing their noses in, but others that someone in the government, in his ministry itself, an internal power struggle after the attack on the temple, a hand that forged originals, changed the past, but others that the CIA was involved, or even the KGB—they all knew his hatred for Communists—but no-one could prove anything. They said, wasn't it strange he retired from cricket in 1947, the height of his career? They said, but this was only a rumor of a rumor, that he refused to play for a free India, that he only ever played for the glory of the Raj. They said, laughing, the old man wants the British back. Why not send him over there, retire him with an O.B.E.? There were old photographs from the forties—him, no turban, on his knees to some white sahib, his lips approaching the feet and this on the front pages of all the rags. And then they said he never marched with Gandhiji at all—he was playing a match in Trinidad. Where were his loyalties in 1947? Was his argument with Nehru only a speech he gave attacking Nehru, attacking the bloody passage of independence? And where were his loyalties now? Why did he attack the separatists when all knew what his son was up to? The old man's hand in every pot, his fingers dirty.

They made him resign, made him leave the humiliations of Delhi and return to his Punjab under martial law. Arthritis in his joints, feet shuffling from the house, across that old square field, barely the strength to kick up any dirt, walking to the bomb-scarred and shattered walls of the temple. They said he sat for hours in prayer, sometimes overnight on the cold stone of the Golden Temple, his eyes on the water of the temple pool. Anil said it was better this way, better he was out of politics, even though he still gave speeches, still attacked the separatists. It gives me a free hand, no more of his damn meddling, always messing things up, Do you know, but.... But I stopped listening. I felt that this was not the way it should be. I can't explain that. I felt that an old world, an old nostalgia had been laid bare, battered, dead. Those ancient gods had vanished, when all I wanted, middle-aged, was an order that would assure me, tell me who I was, now, so far away.

It was during these years that Anil started wearing a turban, attending *gurdwara*, the temple, regularly, a *kara* on his wrist, a painting of Guru Govind Singh garlanded in the living room, and a *kirpan*, the sheath studded with jewels, hanging over his desk. Often, when I needed him, he was gone, his secretary smiling, *Sat sri akal*, Mr. Gill Singh, she nodding, But Anil Singh is at the *gurdwara* so please to wait because he will be back soon. At the *gurdwara* at two in the afternoon? I would ask sometimes, and she would smile, nod happily, Yes, of course, Mr. Gill Singh, your partner is very devoted these days, and her secure voice would intone, *Wah Guruji*. On the wall a calendar showed Hindu atrocities against the Sikhs. This month a man lay in a pool of blood, an old man, his body riddled with bullets, and somewhere in the shadows, where the camera lens could barely focus, a woman caught in her sudden grief.

At the sari auction all deals went to us. It was a large cold hall, with makeshift chairs and tables set up informally, everything hopelessly confused. Bidders wandered for minutes unable to find where to sign in, and Anil watched smiling, his eyes on the eyes of others, searching for what they were looking for. He was a master at these auctions, his instincts exact, knowing when to let off bidding, certain always when no one would challenge his last bid, when to give in and allow something to go to another determined hand. But this day he never gave in. Everything he wanted he got. I don't know if it was out of respect for his father, or just that Anil looked fierce, looked unstoppable, something burning inside him, but no one challenged him for long, their hands fading from exhaustion. That day, Anil made for us the greatest deals of our lives. It was something to watch.

Hands slapped Anil on the back, others shook him, hugged him nervously. *Sat sri akal*, we are all so sorry to hear, Parvati, she says, Oh, what a great man Kirpalji was, oh, what a great man. And others, *Wah Guruji*, So terrible, not only a personal loss, but loss to the country, and the way he died, oh, oh, oh. Such a pity. But Anil backed away from the hands and the long lines of condolences, many mixed with a look of awed respect at how much he had made in a single day. His eyes no longer searched through the room, guessing at tactics, but drew into themselves, in what seemed like a proper remorse, almost a grief. But there were other voices, ones I heard but I doubt Anil did, Shhh, not here, the ashes still warm, and, All his money goes to them to buy—and I caught the conspiratorial nod that ended the sentence. And others, voices lowered, my own hearing heightened, They say it was him that gave the stories to the papers, those stories that brought him down, The disgrace, the shame of him. I told Anil that we should be leaving now, that Neema was probably swamped back at the store, and there was no one else to help today. As we walked out, eyes on us, I felt uncomfortable, even though I was among so many familiar faces, as though I too had played a part in Kirpal's death.

My father was a communist. Not the modern type, the failed type now eulogized on CNN, but he was a successful communist, as far as one can exist. He was the old sort, the intellectual, who read Marx and Engels, had in his youth modeled himself after Trotsky, and even with Stalin's betrayal, could find no stain on the body of the Soviet Union. His world was one of ideals, of possibilities, but also one of a genial pragmatism. It was not my world. I never saw any sense in equality. What could equal Kirpal's arm as it bowled one of its famous fastballs? Why did the neighborhood kids always stand in awe of Kirpal, afraid to approach? These were elemental questions my father's politics could never solve. When Kirpal was elected to the National Assembly on the Congress ticket, my father saw no contradiction in walking across to his neighbor's house with a plate full of freshly made *ludoos* to celebrate the victory. I never forgave him for that, to bring Kirpal down, to make him an equal.

But still, he was a communist, and with that went almost monthly raids, occasional imprisonments, sometimes even of guests, his papers searched through, and once, Neema's letters, the letters of his new daughter-in-law were confiscated, examined for potential subversion, and to this day rot in some file in Delhi. When my father died, he died broken-hearted, recently returned from jail and countless rounds of humiliating questions, and even some beatings I have heard. Kirpal wrote to tell me how sorry he was for my father's death, and that, and here the pen wavered slightly on the paper, it was he as Minister for Internal Security who had ordered the raids, the persecutions that had slowly withered my father's heart, finally eroding his faith in all politics, until, in his last days, all I am told he did was watch the occasional test match, the red ball arcing through the air, the wickets flying, a place finally where he could find grace and justice. I didn't feel any resentment or anger against Kirpal when he wrote to tell me this. I don't even know if I still have the letter. Of course it was necessary. In those days, everything seemed necessary, reasonable. It made sense to me, and strangely, it revived my faith in my father, restoring him to an order he had always sought to break, and I sympathized with Kirpal's anguish. I was shocked to find Neema so angry, almost screaming, when I showed her the letter. He was a communist after all.

We sped away from the auction, Anil driving faster now than before, as though possessed of some need to get away as quickly as possible, to escape from those voices offering condolences and congratulations in the same breath. On the freeway, he pressed the horn at the slightest provocation, at people fifty meters ahead changing into our lane or at a car going seventy-five in the fast lane. I was nervous now, though not about an accident, because I began to sense something else in Anil's face, in his almost maniacal driving. I felt, strangely, that there could be no accident. The accident had already occurred, and this is what gave Anil the courage to drive like this. My nervousness grew, ballooning, almost reliving the accident that hadn't happened, spinning, tumbling over and over. Soon I saw that we were already on the streets of Berkeley and Anil's driving was no better. Ahead of us, an old black woman crossed against our green light, and I was jolted by the car horn, somehow more insistent than before. Anil didn't slow down, though now the woman was out of our lane. The horn blared on, Anil shifted the wheel, pointing the car at the woman, and we headed for her, though she refused to acknowledge the screaming horn, the screeching brakes. The car spun out of control in the intersection. The seat belt ripped into my chest as my body rushed forward, Anil swearing beside me. We came to a stop, all turned around, facing the oncoming traffic, horns blaring around us, the old woman still ambling away, ignoring the commotion, Anil's yells, You bitch, you bloody bitch!

In those years of Kirpal's waning influence, as the rumors gathered around him like a mist that no power seemed able to dissipate, that led him, blind, to his murder, Anil, they said, was seen in the company of certain men. I never asked him about this. It was none of my business whether his share of the profits went to help finance the separatists, to lay the foundations of a civil war. Even before the rumors began to strangle Kirpal, before the separatists became a threat to the fabric of India, Anil, they said, was sending them money. And later when the temple was attacked and those thousands killed, and Anil stormed into my shop, I could read on his face a mood caught between the poles of emotion, a grand anger against Gandhi for what she had done, yet a joy also, for he carried a newspaper which he waved like a flag and shouted, The war is here, clapping his hands together like some magician. I looked at him. Neema stood behind the counter and I caught her shaking her head. I knew she was going to shout at him, and so I had to stop her. Anil, I said, what are you talking about? This is the temple they attacked, what is there to celebrate? But he laughed, Come with me, we should go meet some men I know, and I was already following him when I glanced back to Neema and saw anger and reproach in her eyes rising like dust on an old field. Neema said nothing, and I stood there, unable to move, and prayed for someone to tell me what to do, because all I wanted was to know who I was in this world and where my place ought to be. I stood paralyzed waiting for something to happen, for someone to do something. Perhaps for an assassin's bullet. But nothing happened. Anil only laughed again and walked out as though there was no question in his eyes where I stood, and it was some months later that I heard on the radio of Kirpal's death, and I thought again of Anil's laugh that day and of myself, standing, as though I was a child waiting for Kirpal to throw me a ball. When Anil left that day, he no longer walked with a child's self-conscious gait, and I remember this because I searched for something familiar in his retreating form and I found nothing that I knew.

Many people sent them money. We all knew that. Many were proud of it, and I wouldn't take anything from that pride, well deserved if they were doing something for what they believed in. I did not finance the separatists, and neither did I speak out against Khalistan. I still remember that look of anger on Kirpal's face, that look of defeat when I would throw the ball and it would land only a few feet away, a look which said that it was this sort of failure, this specific lack of effort, that had allowed India to be split up. I don't know if this is true. All I know is that all those around me, my father, Kirpal, Anil, they all seemed reasonable and honest men.

The car wasn't seriously damaged and we were able to drive away before the police arrived. Anil was silent, no more swearing, and when he dropped me off at the store he told me not to worry, With all we did today, the Punjab will soon be free, a Sikh state. I placed my hand lightly on his lap and stepped out of the car feeling empty and exhausted. My heart was beating fast. The street was less crowded now, though a young man in torn jeans, no shirt, long blond and knotted hair took a meandering path toward me. I stopped. I don't know why. I thought for some strange reason he was going to hit me, and that if he does, it will be right because that is the order of things. But he just passed me by.

Ranbir Sidhu is a student at the University of Arizona writing program. This is his first published story.

Reviews

Without a Hero and Other Stories
by T. Coraghessan Boyle
Viking, 1994, 237 pp., $21.95

With a few brilliant exceptions, the bulk of the stories in T. Coraghessan Boyle's uneven collection rely on clunky irony and a smug detachment to pack their tiny punch. The first story, "Big Game," about a real estate magnate's hunt on an exotic game ranch outside L.A., ends with him blowing away a one-tusked former circus elephant. The point, in case we didn't get it, is that big game hunting is a "big game." In "Carnal Knowledge," a horny man with a dead-end job follows a beautiful woman animal-rights activist to a raid on a turkey farm, only to see the newly freed birds get squashed by a semi. Other stories depend on similarly contrived situations: a football player who has never won a game, a father lying to his son about his past drug use.

Without a Hero is not a total loss, however. When Boyle focuses on people, not the self-consciously fabricated circumstances in which he puts them, his fiction is delightful. In the title story, the protagonist loves and loses a beautiful vinyl-boot-clad Russian immigrant, and in "Little America," a homeless man shanghais William Byrd III, son of the great Arctic explorer, who is suffering from Alzheimer's. The odd circumstances of these stories are vintage Boyle, but unlike the rest of the collection, they are compassionate toward their characters.

The Alienist
by Caleb Carr
Random House, 1994, 496 pp., $22

It is 1896, and in New York City, young immigrant boy prostitutes have become the prey of a seemingly unstoppable serial killer. The press will not cover "the boy-whore murders," and the police, little better than criminals themselves, refuse to acknowledge homosexual prostitution, or to go after an assailant who works with Jack-the-Ripper-like savagery.

In Caleb Carr's historical detective novel *The Alienist*, an unlikely group of people assembled by police commissioner Theodore Roosevelt, join forces to covertly investigate the grisly mutilations. Headed by renowned psychologist, or "alienist," Dr. Laszlo Kreizler, the team also includes John Schuyler Moore, a *New York Times* journalist with knowledge of the criminal underworld, and Sara Howard, a police department secretary with a thirst for serious investigative work. The novice detectives use the work of philosophers and evolutionists, from Hume and Locke to Spencer and Schopenhauer, to rid themselves of preconceptions about human behavior. They operate according to the unconventional premise that killers are not born, but made. Thus by recreating the context of the perpetrator's life, they hope to find the murderer. Despite their intensive efforts, they remain one step behind the shrewd killer, leading them to believe that they are being manipulated every step of the way. Frustrating their investigation even further are the "guardians of the social order," the Episcopal church, American financier J.P. Morgan and anti-union politicians, all of whom view the murders as a way of keeping the immigrants scared and in their place.

In straightforward, unfussy prose, Carr recreates the seaminess of the New York underworld in the 1890s, and juxtaposes it with the lush lifestyles of business tycoons and the Four Hundred top families. Though excessive details from Carr's research occasionally slow the pace, *The Alienist* is a gripping historical mystery.

A Handbook of Tibetan Culture
Compiled by the Orient
Foundation
Edited by Graham Coleman
Shambhala, 1993, 430 pp., $18

The Encyclopedia of Eastern Philosophy and Religion—Buddhism, Hinduism, Taoism, Zen
Edited by Ingrid Fischer-Schreiber, Franz-Karl Erhard, Kurt Fredrichs, and Michael S. Diener
Shambhala, 1989, 468 pp., $22.50

Books about spiritual practice have been reaching general popularity again, so much so that *Publisher's Weekly* recently ran an article about the astounding sales success of books that purport to answer the soul's deep longings. Both authors and presses are falling all over themselves trying to catch the wave of popularity. Unfortunately, works that promise to quench spiritual thirst often deliver, instead, a boring set of platitudes sunk in a mire of psychological oatmeal. Worse are the New Age novels that pretend to discover a revelation or "Way" and are instead just sound bytes of ancient truths.

One press that has consistently avoided such spiritual materialism is Shambhala from Boston. With an editorial policy that steers away from tripe (even if it sells) they have maintained a standard that appeals to the authentic side of the spiritual market.

And Shambhala has brought out two genuinely helpful books. The first, *The Encyclopedia of Eastern Philosophy and Religion*, takes on the formidable task of presenting the basic terminology and doctrinal systems of Buddhism, Hinduism, Taoism, and Zen. The encyclopedia is set up in dictionary format to "help general readers find their way through a thicket of unfamiliar terms and concepts that are frequently encountered today in widely varied fields of interest." The book accomplishes this purpose without excess didacticism, and is well worth its price. The editors have included detailed primary source bibliographies of the four systems of thought, as well as a Ch'an/Zen lineage chart.

The second text, *A Handbook of Tibetan Culture*, brings the poignant fact of Chinese occupation of Tibet into focus. In the forty years since the Chinese takeover, Tibetan people, art, beliefs, and social ideology have made their way into both hemispheres. Many artifacts and priceless *thanka* paintings had to be smuggled from Tibet over treacherous Himalayan paths, so only a small portion of texts from a 2,500-year-old cultural inheritance could be saved. The rest were looted and destroyed by the occupation army. Since the world has suddenly become home for so many diverse forms of Tibetan culture, it is prudent to catalogue their whereabouts. The *Handbook* not only accomplishes this task by including an international Tibetan resources directory that provides locations of and information about Tibetan centers throughout the world; it also informs the reader of the locations of the world's largest collections of Tibetan art. Other sections include biographical data about contemporary Lamas and scholars, and a glossary of Tibetan, Buddhist, and Sanskrit terms.

Moses Supposes
by Ellen Currie
Simon & Schuster, 1994, 219 pp., $20

Ellen Currie is an anatomist of narcissism. From a self-centered adolescent schoolgirl to an insufferably self-righteous housewife, *Moses Supposes* offers incisive portrayals of egocentrism. In these twelve short stories, Currie uncovers the selfish motives behind everyday behavior. A woman's seemingly innocuous habit of coloring her gray, for example, is revealed by her son to be a smug act of narcissism: she dyes only the area she can see herself and leaves a frowsy white shock in the back, as if to moon people.

By exposing people's pretensions, Currie also unveils the comedy inherent in disastrous situations. Her omniscient and unabashedly frank narrative voice tells how the characters create their own mayhem; thus, a botched suicide attempt, an unplanned pregnancy and a devastated marriage are portrayed as poetically just and inevitably comic outcomes to selfish pursuits.

For the most part, *Moses Supposes* is mordantly realistic; however, Currie occasionally throws in an absurdly contrived character, like the middle-aged housewife who wears old finery for household chores, wringing, in her view, the last drop of use from it. But these caricatures are forgivable because they force us to examine our own foibles. Currie's deliciously sick sense of humor magnifies the small but telling ways in which people reveal their own vanities.

Paddy Clarke Ha Ha Ha
by Roddy Doyle
Viking, 1994, 282 pp., $20.95

At first glance Paddy Clarke, the ten-year-old narrator of Roddy Doyle's fourth novel, seems precocious. But though he is as witty, perceptive, sensitive and cruel as many adults, his desires are those of an average ten-year-old. That Paddy seems wiser and funnier and crueler than his years is part of the magic of this novel, which renders the mind of a child with precision and insight.

Doyle's story describes the disintegrating marriage of Paddy's parents, and the gradual changes in his working-class Irish town, as new subdivisions replace the woods and fields. However, the real energy and concern of the book is neither Paddy's home nor his family, but his own voice and vision as he tries to make sense of the complexities of the world. How can he love and hate his father at the same time? How can he tease his younger brother heartlessly and yet want him around more than anyone? Paddy is funny and honest. He does not flinch when speaking about the brutality he witnesses, whether it's his father hitting his mother, his teacher humiliating students, or his friends sadistically teasing each other.

Such painful events, and Paddy's own complex questions about them, could have easily turned the book into a maudlin tract on the loss of innocence. Instead, Doyle's stunning novel, the winner of Britain's 1993 Booker Prize, reveals that we never have any innocence to lose.

Firefall
by Mona Van Duyn
Knopf, 1994, 83 pp., $11

Van Duyn's ninth book of poems is evidence of how a poet can practice what Wallace Stevens wrote that all people should do: see with "the hottest fire of sight." The former Poet Laureate illuminates every part of her past and present worlds, presenting us with images of marriage, mother love, politicians—and even dogs, in her series of new sonnets and praise poems, full of the poet's love of the things of the world. Van Duyn's work is alternately funny and serious, yet her ordinary subject matter reminds us that we are reading the work of an artist who lives in the same world we do.

Firefall, divided into three sections, gives Van Duyn a chance to experiment with the kind of "translation" of literary classics that Anne Sexton did in *Transformations* (those amazing revisions of Grimm's Fairy Tales). Van Duyn adapts, or "trans-

lates" Eliot's *Prufrock*, and Yeats' "The Circus Animals' Desertion" and "A Prayer for My Daughter." The poet maintains her familiar conversational tone throughout, and refers, as she always has in her books, to close friends and fellow poets. The title poem is autobiographical, taking its reader back to the poet's home in Iowa, to her education at a teachers' college, and to her discovery of her "own truth in [a] waterfall" of "—Words. Words." These are tender, sometimes sad, sometimes amusing poems written by a poet who continues to see "blazing bright" the firefall that is "a self . . . being born."

Looking at the Sun
by James Fallows
Pantheon, 1994, 517 pp., $25

Based on a series of essays about East Asia that first appeared in *Atlantic Monthly*, Fallows' excellent book is hard to classify. It's not a typical travelogue, since the usual descriptions of getting from place to place are missing. Except for its more dispassionate tone, it could be considered another wake-up call about the decline of the West and the rise of the East. But the book is probably best described as a long essay by an amateur economist that introduces the American reader to contemporary East Asia.

The first half, dealing mainly with Japan, discusses the differences between the Japanese economic system and ours. Fallows' main point is that Japan believes not in making its citizens better consumers, but in making the nation as a whole capable of producing or easily obtaining whatever it needs—a very different philosophy from the West's free-market theory.

Fallows argues that Japan

is obsessed with self-sufficiency because of its profound embarrassment at having awakened during the last century to find itself at the mercy of the West. Japanese leaders judged the source of the West's power to be science and technology; other cultural inventions like democracy haven't interested them, despite their having erected, after World War II, a facade of democracy to satisfy the victors.

The second half of the book deals with other East Asian countries: those that have a chance of enjoying an economic success like Japan's, those that are presently being exploited by Japan, and those that are likely to miss the boat.

Fallows does not harangue, although he is long-winded on occasion. A true democrat, he leaves the final judgments and prescriptions to us.

Paul Revere's Ride
by David Hackett Fischer
Oxford Univ. Press, 1994, 445 pp., $27.50

On the night of April 18, 1775, General Thomas Gage, commander of the British forces stationed at Boston Harbor, sent seven hundred troops to seize the supply depot of Concord's rebel militia. At the risk of conflict, he gave orders to disarm the rebels and conduct a dragnet to catch rebel leaders like Samuel Adams and John Hancock, whom he knew to be in the area. Through Gage's American-born wife, patriots got wind of the plan, and Boston's revolutionary Committee of Safety sent Paul Revere and William Dawes by separate routes on their famous rides to alarm local officials from Boston to Lexington and Concord. After a bloody skirmish at dawn on Lexington Green, with outnum-

bered but spirited revolutionaries, Gage's redcoats were later routed by well-prepared minutemen at Concord, and forced to retreat twenty miles to Charlestown Harbor, as embattled locals sniped at them from behind trees, houses, barns and stone walls.

In *Paul Revere's Ride*, David Hackett Fischer paints vivid portraits of the key events and protagonists at the beginning of the American War for Independence. Despite the recent vogue among historians for studying larger historical processes and downplaying the significance of individual events and people, Fischer finds that the casual decisions of the figures he writes about *did* make a difference in American history.

Drawing on extensive archives, Fischer makes a major historical contribution to our understanding of the period; the known details of the confrontation at Lexington, for example, were previously sketchy. He is also a fine storyteller. His skillful narrative makes fascinating reading for both experts and laypeople.

Materialism
by Jorie Graham
Ecco Press, 1993, 160 pp., $22

At her best, Jorie Graham is capable of writing poems as musical as they are intellectually complex. *Materialism*, sad to say, is far from her best. Many of the poems are forced and flat, lacking the sophisticated layering of image and allusion that we expect from Graham.

Her ambitious purpose is to explore the place of the self within the Western intellectual tradition. In an attempt to achieve it, she draws heavily on the works of some of the most renowned philosophers and artists, from Plato and da Vinci to Whitman and Wittgenstein. The problem is that these borrowings are often more interesting than her poems. While there are some exquisite moments—her translation of Dante's Canto XI, for instance—the collection as a whole seems slight in comparison to the great works that inform it.

The Chamber
by John Grisham
Doubleday, 1994, 486 pp., $24.95

Here's a great idea for a novel. A Mississippi lawyer, tired of the earnestness and tedium of his practice, decides to become a novelist. His first book, a potboiler about a black man who shoots the redneck who raped his daughter, is a huge best-seller, and the lawyer signs a big contract to write several more novels. He writes three increasingly commercial thrillers, with characters flattened by the speeding plot, and even his fans begin to wonder whether he hasn't burned out in the usual American way. So he returns, for his inspiration, to Mississippi (physically he has been there all along), and writes a new book about race relations, the Ku Klux Klan, and the death penalty.

This is a rough synopsis of John Grisham's publishing history, and the story behind *The Chamber*. In Grisham's latest novel, Sam Cayhall, Klan member and terrorist, is on death row in Parchman, Mississippi. The elderly *pro bono* wing of an elite Chicago law firm is ploddingly handling his appeals, until Adam Hall, a recently hired lawyer, begs to take over the case. Adam turns out to be the grandson Sam had never met.

Grisham's novel isn't a story of innocence wronged, or of legal heroism. Sam does not seem to have been falsely convicted, nor is he even a good man trapped by circumstance. He is admirable only for a certain impassive fatherliness he shows the other death row prisoners. And Adam is no master of legerdemain—we are not even sure that we want him to win. The appeal of this novel, rather, is in the exploration of a family that encompasses two eras and two poles of morality; and the appeal is considerable.

Summer of the Redeemers
by Carolyn Haines
Dutton, 1994, 391 pp., $22.95

Carolyn Haines' suspenseful coming-of-age novel is set in rural Mississippi of the 1960s. For young Bekkah Rich, the summer of 1963 appears at first to hold only the usual prospects of long swims in the creek and bike rides with her best friend. But things are changing on Kali Oka Road, where she lives. A religious cult, calling themselves the Blood of the Redeemers, has taken over the abandoned church at the end of the road. Their secretive ways, and the rumors she's heard of their occult rituals, baby-selling and snake-handling, awaken Bekkah's curiosity and start her snooping on Redeemer property.

The Redeemers aren't the only strangers who have invaded the formerly dull world of Kali Oka. When Nadine Andrews and her nine show horses move into the old McInnis place, her bleached hair, brazen attitude and bachelorette status are a cause for more gossip— and yet another source of intrigue for Bekkah, who goes to work for Nadine in her stables. Bekkah meets

Greg, a teen from the Redeemer clan who also works for Nadine, and is dragged along by Nadine on a reckless trip to the Redeemer church. Through her naive but increasingly enlightened perspective, we gradually learn the truth about the shocking events along the Kali Oka Road.

The Deep South lives and breathes in this novel, in the portrait of a peaceful rural countryside replete with lemonade, magnolias and rocking chairs. But it's an idyll marred by evil, and Haines never lets us forget it. The aura of danger hovers over every page, like the threat of a summer thunderstorm.

A Map of the World
by Jane Hamilton
Doubleday, 1994, 390 pp., $22

Living in the world after tragedy strikes is the dark landscape explored in Jane Hamilton's second novel, *A Map of the World*. Alice Goodwin must pick up the pieces after a single mistake changes her life completely. When she stumbles upon a map she drew as a child, it distracts her attention from her own children and the two she is babysitting. A few minutes are time enough for her best friend's two-year-old daughter, Lizzy, to wander off and drown in the family's shallow pond.

Everyone touched by the tragedy has their own remedy for the anguish it causes them: Lizzy's mother fervently rediscovers Catholicism, and her father throws himself into his work. Alice's husband, Howard, tells her to keep in motion, but all-out grief is her response to Lizzy's death. She goes to bed, where nothing can harm her. In the middle of her mourning, a seemingly minor past mistake

comes back to haunt her and further shatter her life. As a part-time school nurse in her small community of Prairie Center, Wisconsin, she once lost control and slapped a violent student. The incident resurfaces as an accusation of child molestation. Alice's worse crime, though, was being a slightly off-balance hippie-farmwife in conservative Prairie Center. She soon learns the danger of small-town rumor mongers, whose talk is lethal.

Told from the alternating viewpoints of Alice and Howard, Hamilton's novel shows the couple struggling to find ways to deal with the disturbing realization that the world is a sorrowful place where we are all expendable. The young married couple must also discover how a relationship can survive calamities they could never imagine or prepare for. Patience and forgiveness are the only answers.

Selected Poems
by Daniel Halpern
Knopf, 1994, 220 pp., $23

As editor of *Antaeus* and Ecco Press, professor at Columbia University and instigator of projects like the recent group translation of Dante's *Inferno* by some of America's top poets, Halpern is a long-time promoter of good writing. He has also written seven volumes of poetry himself. This selected edition is a substantial introduction to his work, and a fascinating record of his artistic progress. The first line of the first poem, "I've been after the exotic for years," is characteristic of Halpern: swift and transient, with a dark energy. Later poems show us Halpern the husband and father-to-be, reflecting on his "life at the midpoint" and remembering dead boyhood friends and the great poets that came before him.

Finishing the book, one is struck with the consistency of Halpern's creations. All show an impressive verbal economy and starkness of form. If some poems unfold too smoothly and seem too restrained, as if the poet were merely a clever observer, there are still plenty of sparks. The really good poems in this selection leave the reader with an admiring surprise, at times even a disbelief of the very best kind.

Life Estates

by Shelby Hearon

Knopf, 1994, 231 pp., $22

At the heart of Shelby Hearon's latest novel is the deep friendship of Sarah Cooper and Harriet Sloane Calhoun, formed in boarding school over thirty years ago. Since then, both women have married, had children, relocated to separate bedrooms and ultimately lost their husbands at roughly the same time. While Harriet struggles to construct a new identity for herself as a widow, Sarah settles into her new, single life more easily, content with her wallpaper business, her South Carolina home, and the affections of her late husband's doctor.

Not surprisingly, the two women soon find that their lives aren't as parallel as they once believed them to be, but it's Harriet's discovery that in boarding school Sarah had a secret lover that brings all of their submerged conflict to a head in the climactic scene.

In this graceful, loosely plotted book, Shelby Hearon gives us a realistic account of how old secrets and new circumstances can threaten even the best friendships.

The Glass Hammer

by Andrew Hudgins

Houghton Mifflin, 1994, 97 pp., $18.95

In *The Glass Hammer*, Hudgins offers 65 spare stories in verse from his childhood, told by a narrator fascinated with the fault and paradox within his family, his region and himself. In the past, that fascination has helped make Hudgins winner of the Poets Prize for *After the Lost War*.

This volume returns to his old stomping grounds of Montgomery, Alabama—self-proclaimed cradle of the Confederacy, birthplace of the Civil Rights Movement, home of the Sidney Lanier High School "Fighting Poets." Hudgins' humor is evident in poems such as "James Bond Considers a Career in Library Science," or "Huge," a long poem about sexual awakenings, in which he observes: " . . . To think/ of doing something was the same/ as doing it, the Bible says,/ though many theologians wish Saint Paul/ had only thought that verse." Wit combines with social consciousness in poems like "TeeVee with Grandmomma." Confronted with her grandson's statement that "colored people are just like us," an old woman responds, "Well, maybe they're just like you." The grandson replies, "Then I,/ to make her angrier, agreed."

Hudgins' narrative power and the progression of the collection from poems about childhood to poems about adulthood make it almost a novel in verse. The closing poem, "Afterword," employs the metaphor of family house-cleanings to illustrate the paradox of familial love: "And if, despite our scrubbing, dirt remained/ Mom said, 'It's our dirt now. It's clean.' "

The Girls
by Elaine Kagan
Knopf, 1994, 307 pp., $23

Elaine Kagan's first novel begins and ends with the death of Pete Chickery, a blouse salesman so vain he wears shirts to match his eyes. When Pete is shot and killed by his ethereal blonde wife Jessie, "the girls" (Jessie's, and to a lesser extent Pete's old school friends from Kansas City) all attend the funeral.

The first part of the novel is a series of monologues by "the girls." Through their voices, a multifaceted picture emerges of Pete: a man who is both a manipulative womanizer and a supportive friend to women, even a savior. The central question of the novel is, "Who was Pete Chickery?"

Each of the five women has a different answer. To Ellen, Pete is the childhood friend who later took her to the prom; he is also the man who was cheating on, and disgracing, Jessie. Tee, the unstable one, recalls Pete as both a lover and a counselor. Jessie's older sister, Anne, remembers him telling her that not being able to have children was all right, and encouraging her in her career ambitions. Yet Pete's younger sister, Anita, refuses to cry at his funeral. To her, Pete was a grotesque figure who preyed on women. Frances, a Broadway actress who has undergone a mastectomy, recalls him as a long time lover who made her feel whole.

The second part of the book seems gratuitous after the women's monologues. The focus moves to the funeral, and then to the wake. Only in the final two sections, told from Jessie's and Pete's perspectives, do we learn the actual details of the altercation that precipitated the murder. But "the girls'" collective portrait of the living Pete Chickery is enough to sustain this novel; we don't need to see the gun that kills him.

The Harafish
by Naguib Mahfouz
Doubleday, 1994, 406 pp., $22.95

In this fabular epic spanning well over twenty generations, Mahfouz, winner of the 1988 Nobel Prize for Literature, chronicles one working-class Egyptian family's struggle to live up to the glory of its founding ancestor, Ashur al-Nagi. Ashur was one of the wretchedly poor Harafish, who lived in a decaying Cairo back alley and fought to survive by selling fruit or cleaning stables. From this squalor, he rose to challenge the head of the gang that terrorized the alley. Part philosopher, part mobster, Ashur reversed the old ways of bleeding the poor and instead demanded tribute from the formerly untouchable merchants who had exploited them. Under his protection the Harafish regained their self-respect, and their alley was the envy of all the others. At the height of his power Ashur wandered out into the desert and disappeared, becoming a legend.

Mahfouz's classic lessons are that power corrupts, privilege breeds cruelty and arrogance, and only suffering purifies the soul. Ashur's descendants who people the novel enjoy the material benefits of his legacy, but they lack the humility, courage, and principles he acquired through hardship. The generations succeeding him try to regain his glory and power. Some struggle to rule justly, as he did, but are overcome by their own greed. Others mock their ancestor's protection of the poor and grow even more violent and corrupt than the clan bosses Ashur himself fought against. Over the course of the novel, the al-Nagi family produces prostitutes, parricides, merchants, sages, saints, and devil-worshippers, but never another Ashur.

School for the Blind
by Dennis McFarland
Houghton Mifflin, 1994, 287 pp., $21.95

The main characters of McFarland's second novel are an elderly brother and sister, but the real subject is child abuse. When Francis Brimm, a retired newspaper photographer in his seventies, returns to his childhood home in the coastal Florida town of Pines, he stumbles upon some bones that have been dug up by dogs, evidence of a recent pair of gruesome murders. The victims turn out to be two female students from a local school for the blind, where his older sister, Muriel, once worked. After the first newspaper accounts of the murder are published, Brimm and Muriel receive threatening, anonymous phone calls, warning them that "what's buried ought to stay buried."

But letting things "stay buried" proves impossible for the pair. They have never been close, but now their distress over the murders unites them and causes them to dredge up several puzzling incidents from their childhood. Then the murderer writes an anonymous letter which is published in the newspaper, describing the horrific abuse he endured as a child. Suddenly, Muriel recalls their abuse by an alcoholic father, and begins to understand why neither of them ever married or formed intimate friendships.

McFarland's narrative skill, and the intelligence of this book, turn what might otherwise seem like a fictional rehash of pop-psychology theories into a real and moving story. The one flaw of the novel is that the mystery of the blind-girl murders is sidetracked, as the Brimms delve into the older mystery of their past. But while McFarland fails to orchestrate the plot as well as he might, the depth of his characters, and the sheer beauty of his prose make up for it.

Silk Hope, NC
by Lawrence Naumoff
Harcourt-Brace, 1994, 352 pp., $21.95

Lawrence Naumoff's fourth novel is about female independence. It's the story of Frannie and Natalie, two small-town sisters whose mother's family, since the time of their great-great-grandmother, has passed the family home from mother to daughter so the women of the family would always have a refuge. When Frannie and Natalie inherit the house they immediately begin to argue over what should be done with the property. Frannie, the wild younger sister, has trouble coming to terms with her mother's death, and desperately wants to keep it for the family traditions it represents. Natalie, the older, more pragmatic sister, aspires to yuppiehood. She and her banker fiancé want to sell the property and move to the city.

The story is propelled by the sisters' different attitudes about the past, especially about the father who abandoned their family when Frannie was eight. Frannie becomes obsessed with finding him, and is determined to keep the house, in part because of her memories of the time when he lived there. Natalie knows the truth about his disappearance and never wants to see him again.

Naumoff's book is by turns thoughtful, funny, and sentimental as it shows the reader the struggles of two modern women trying to understand their past and dealing with their uncertain future.

The Longings of Women
by Marge Piercy
Fawce. Columbine, 1994, 464 pp., $22

Once again Piercy explores the inner lives of women. In this novel she deftly juxtaposes the experience of three very real female protagonists: Leila, Becky and Mary. While Leila treads water in a doomed relationship with her promiscuous theater-director husband, Becky strives to free herself from the class limitations imposed on her as the daughter of a Portuguese fisherman, and Mary lives the shadowy life of a homeless person, trying to stay respectable by cleaning houses. As the story progresses, the three women's lives overlap. Leila hires Mary to clean her house and does research for a book about Becky, who is under suspicion for murdering her husband.

The book's weakness is that all three women are introspective planners to excess. Every possible move is analyzed, often in the language of pop psychology. At times this mental cud-chewing detracts from the believability of the characters, and it definitely slows the action. Fortunately, toward its ending the story gains momentum, as the characters' lives become more closely intertwined in unexpected ways.

True to its title, The Longings of Women is about what the three women—whom Piercy clearly means to represent all women—desire. All three want to forge and maintain their own identities in situations that enforce their dependency on others. As usual, Piercy has a mission: to educate her readers about the evils of class and gender inequality.

Blacker than a Thousand Midnights
by Susan Straight
Hyperion, 1994, 388 pp., $21.95

Susan Straight's second novel, I Been in Sorrow's Kitchen and Licked Out All the Pots, was enthusiastically acclaimed for its convincing portrayal of a black woman struggling to overcome racism, poverty and low self-esteem. Together with her first book, Aquaboogie, it established Straight, a white woman married to a black man and a longtime resident of a predominantly black community, as a legitimate chronicler of African-American culture. In her third book, Blacker than a Thousand Midnights, Straight reaches even further beyond her own experience. With insight and empathy, she captures the essence of "brotha-man-hood," or what it means to be a working-class black male.

The story concerns Darnell Tucker, a firefighter who, as the book opens, must decide whether to marry his pregnant high-school girlfriend. Darnell has grown up in a culture with two opposing definitions of manhood: his friends define it as fierce independence, while his father insists that a real man is a provider. Darnell ends up "doing the right thing" and gets married, but conflicting notions of manhood continue to plague him throughout the story.

The central conflict, however, is Darnell's struggle to support his new family in a neighborhood terrorized by gangs, pushers and brutal cops. In this grim setting Darnell makes a modest living mowing lawns and doing odd jobs; meanwhile, frequent wildfires during a prolonged drought remind him of how family responsibilities forced him to give up his seasonal firefighting job for year-round work.

Straight's portrayal of a working-class black neighborhood is convincing and poignant, though a few readers may feel that her novel perpetuates negative stereotypes (for example, while out of work, Darnell convinces his wife, Brenda, to come home on her lunch breaks to satisfy his insatiable sexual appetite). Ultimately, however, *Blacker than a Thousand Midnights* celebrates the strength and vitality of "brotha-manhood" in language that is plain and compelling.

Brazil
by John Updike
Knopf, 1994, 260 pp., $23

In his latest novel, John Updike rewrites the medieval legend of Tristan and Isolde as a story of two star-crossed lovers in modern South America. Tristao, the poor son of a black prostitute, falls in love with Isabel, the spoiled and virginal daughter of a wealthy Brazilian government bureaucrat. Because their families, especially Isabel's father, disapprove of their love, as does their racist society, the two flee deep into the Brazilian interior. As they endure unbelievable hardships, they magically switch races before they at last decide to return to the city to confront Isabel's powerful father.

Readers familiar with Updike's suburban American fiction may be disappointed by this sojourn to the tropics, as many were with *The Coup*, his African novel of 1978. Both novels are a little bookish in their research and background details. Such tactics as the extensive description of flora and the use of Portuguese obscure the story rather than enhance it. And at times it's difficult to know whether the dialogue is supposed to be serious, or a parody of the rituals of courtly love ("'I like you,'" Tristao says to a prostitute he has just met, "'but my heart is pledged to another, whom I am on my way to rescue'").

Still, Updike is Updike. Even on off days he's a master. In the best parts of *Brazil*, his trademark style shines through, startling and fresh as ever. By the end of the novel, few will not find themselves swept up by this magical and ultimately tragic love story.

Book reviews by: Willoughby Johnson, Kris Somerville, Chris Michener, Mike Land, Julie Gochenour, Jim Steck, Brett Rogers, Pam McClure, Jeff Thomson, Virginia Jones, Evelyn Somers, Ginny Morgan, Brett Foster, Dawn Klingensmith, Mary Creger, Elizabeth Lenz, Stefani Kronk, Kenneth Soucy.

STORIES WORTHY
OF THE TELLING

New Nonfiction

THE DROWNT BOY

An Ozark Tale

ART HOMER

"Art Homer's *The Drownt Boy* is a complex and magical evocation of place. Its Ozarks are made of the deep stuff of boyhood memory and family life and of a carefully described, present-day canoe trip down the Current River, taken at flood-stage, by Homer and his stepson. Both journeys—past and present—require an immersion in the language and lore of the place, combined with a disciplined attention to detail, as it is encountered or recollected."
—Michael Anania. 168 pages, **$19.95**

THE *GAZETTE* GIRLS OF GRUNDY COUNTY

Horse Trading, Hot Lead, and High Heels

GWEN HAMILTON THOGMARTIN & ARDIS HAMILTON ANDERSON

"In alternating chapters, perfectionist, no-nonsense Ardis and her more gregarious, enthusiastic sister (one spelled, the other didn't) recall the days when type and women were hot. . . . A thoroughly charming little memoir."
—*Los Angeles Times Book Review.* 176 pages, illus., **$19.95**

At bookstores or from
MISSOURI
University of Missouri Press
2910 LeMone Blvd., Columbia 65201
1–800–828–1894

New Fiction

KNEELING ON RICE
STORIES BY ELIZABETH DENTON

"Combining the powerful characters of Margaret Atwood and the darkly comic situations of John Irving, Denton's stories deserve a niche of their own. . . . Hers is a name worth remembering."—*Publishers Weekly.* 184 pages, **$14.95** paper

MISSISSIPPI HISTORY
STORIES BY STEVE YARBROUGH

"*Mississippi History* is a pungent and memorable book. His characters may sometimes be losers, but they are never wimps. In their struggles we see what large truths they create."—Fred Chappell. 168 pages, **$14.95** paper

A GREAT WAY
TO WAKE UP ON SUNDAY

ACOUSTIC SUNRISE
on
106.1 FM KBXR

Try **106.1 BXR's Acoustic Sunrise.** You'll hear great music you've never heard on the radio.

You'll get to know artists like Pierce Pettis, Lucinda Williams, John Gorka and Jerry Douglas.

You'll also hear tracks from Linda Ronstadt, James Taylor, Michelle Shocked and Dan Fogelberg.

You're looking at just the tip of the CD mountain containing today's best acoustic music ... and **Acoustic Sunrise** will present this music with the same variety and creativity that you hear every day on **106.1 BXR.**

Join Terry and Naomi for what they love to do on the weekend. **Acoustic Sunrise** ... Sunday mornings from 6 to 10am... only on **106.1 BXR.**

106.1 **BXR**
RADIO
Where The Music Comes First

The Southern Review

Sixtieth Anniversary Year: 1995

Fall 1994
CONTEMPORARY SOUTHERN POETRY: A Special Issue
Is there still a poetry of the American South that is recognizably in
the tradition of Ransom, Warren, and Tate?
A. R. Ammons, James Dickey, Margaret Gibson, Andrew Hudgins,
Donald Justice, Yusef Komunyakaa, Elizabeth Seydel Morgan,
Ernest Suarez, and others.

Winter 1995
CONTEMPORARY SOUTHERN WRITING: A Special Issue
Poems, memoirs, essays, stories by James Applewhite,
Reginald Gibbons, Robert Morgan, Elizabeth Spencer, and others.

Spring 1995
A TRIBUTE TO CLEANTH BROOKS: A Special Issue
Essays by various hands and correspondence between
Cleanth Brooks and Robert Penn Warren.

Summer 1995
CONTEMPORARY IRISH POETRY: A Special Issue
Poetry and criticism by Michael Allen, Guinn Batten, Eavan Boland,
Pat Boran, Ciaran Carson, Katie Donovan, Paul Durcan,
Seamus Heaney, Biddy Jenkinson, Brendan Kennelly, Thomas Kinsella,
Edna Longley, Michael Longley, Derek Mahon, Medbh McGuckian,
Máire Mhac an tSaoi, John Montague, Paul Muldoon,
Eiléan Ní Chuilleanáin, Nuala Ní Dhomhnaill, Dennis O'Driscoll,
M. L. Rosenthal, Peter Sirr, Matthew Sweeney, and others.

The Southern Review Order Form

Special Offers:

____ Order now to   ____ After Jan. 1,
receive all 4 special   1995 all 4 special
issues: $18.00   issues: $20.00

Order as single copies:

____ Fall 1994   @$5.00 each
____ Winter 1995   @$6.00 each
____ Spring 1995   @$6.00 each
____ Summer 1995   @$10.00 each

Order total: _____   ____ I enclose my check.

____ Charge my VISA/MC (Acct. No.)_____ Exp.date ____

(Name)_____

(Address)_____

(City/State/Zip)_____ (Country) _____ (mr)

Return this coupon with payment to: Managing Editor, The Southern Review,
43 Allen Hall, Louisiana State University, Baton Rouge, LA 70803-5005 (USA)

the minnesota review
(a journal of committed writing)

back issues

"PC Wars"
ns 39, Fall / Winter 1992/3

"The Politics of AIDS"
ns 40, Spring / Summer 1993

current issues

"The Institution of Literature"

i. Reconfiguring Fields and Theories c.1994
ns. 41-42, Fall 1993-Spring 1994

ii. Institutional Structures and Stories
ns 43, Fall 1994 (deadline 1 May 1994)

iii. The Politics of Publishing
ns 44, Spring 1995 (deadline 1 Nov. 1994)

with work by Crystal Bartolovich, Michael Berube, Terry Caesar, Don Bialostosky, Ross Chambers, Tom Cohen, Jennifer Cotter, Lennard Davis, Ortwin de Graef, Cora Kaplan, Amitara Kumar, Devoney Looser, Julian Markels, Louise Mowder, Mark Redfield, Bruce Robbins, Veronica Stewart, Paul Trembath, Alan Wald, Evan Watkins, Mas'ud Zavarzadeh, and many others

in planning

"The White Issue"
ns 45, Fall 1995 (deadline 1 May 1995)

Subscriptions are $12 a year (two issues), $24 institutions (+$5 foreign, $10 air) *minnesota review* is published biannually and originates from East Carolina

Please send all queries, comments, submissions, and subscriptions to: Jeffrey Williams, Editor, *minnesota review*, Department of English, East Carolina University, Greenville, NC 27858-4353

The Missouri Review would like to express its deep appreciation to the Board Members of *The Missouri Review Trust Fund* for their support and dedication:

Curtis Bourgeois	Valerie Lawlor	Peggy Poe
Jeff Viles	Melissa Williams	Mary Windmiller

The Board members join us in our thanks to the following original donors who made the *Trust Fund* possible:

FOUNDERS

Boone County Community Trust   First National Bank of Columbia

BENEFACTORS

Charles & Pattye Barbee	Karlene Gentile	Dr. & Mrs. David Payne
J. Robert Barth, S.J.	David Woods Kemper	Margaret S. Peden
John Blakemore	David Knight	Peggy Poe
Dr. & Mrs. W.R. Bynum	Leo & Charlotte Landhuis	Gil & Georgeanne Porter
Canterbury Travel	Mrs. Lezlie Laws-Couch	Betty Proctor
Commerce Bank of	Mrs. Jeanie McAfee	Martha Proctor
Kansas City	Thomas McAfee	Shelter Insurance Foundation
Dr. Thomas Cooke	Greg & Gena Michalson	Jo & David Sapp
Dr. Walter Daniel	Mid-America Petroleum, Inc.	William & Eva Trumbower
Larry Epps	Midland Oil Company, Inc.	Mr. & Mrs. Jeff Viles
Kansas City Life	Mobil Foundation	Dean Richard Wallace
Insurance Foundation		Dr. Sam Werner

The Trust Fund Board and Editors invite you to become a Missouri Review Patron. Your gift now as a Litterateur ($250), Scribe ($100), or Muse ($50) will be recognized in the magazine and will bring you a free one-year subscription and one for a friend of your choice. Your gift as a Founder ($10,000), Angel ($5,000), Publisher ($1,000), or Benefactor ($500) will be recognized in each issue and entitle you to a free lifetime subscription. We want to thank all the contributors to our annual giving campaign to date.

1994 BENEFACTORS

Valerie Lawlor	Les Bourgeois Winery	Murry's Restaurant	Steve Weinberg

LITTERATEUR

Kathryn Allen

SCRIBES

Barbara Carr	Dr. & Mrs. Charles Cheek	Robert Engleman	William & Margaret Peden
Victor M. Cassidy	Diane P. DeWall	Eric & Ruth Kincanon	Melissa Williams

MUSES

Priscilla Belden	Mary C. Hershey	Osmund Overby	Mark Sickman
William L. Blizek	Alice Landrum	Doyle Patterson	Marianne Thomas
Michael H. Finkelstein	Robert M. Lewis	Loren & Augusta Reid	Richard C. Thompson
Betsy Garrett	Paul Maguffee	Nola Ruth	James & Bette Weiss
Nancy & David Hemenway	Robert E. McFall	Theodore R. Sadler, Jr.	Arvilla Wieland
	Judith Miles	Charles R. Samples	

The Missouri Review would like to recognize that major new marketing initiatives have been made possible by a grant from the Lila Wallace-Reader's Digest Literary Publishers Marketing Development Program, funded through the Council of Literary Magazines and Presses.